ALL QUIET

ON THE

HOME FRONT

ALL QUIET

ON THE

HOME FRONT

AN ORAL HISTORY OF LIFE IN BRITAIN
DURING THE FIRST WORLD WAR

RICHARD VAN EMDEN AND STEVE HUMPHRIES

headline

First published in 2003
by HEADLINE BOOK PUBLISHING

10 9 8 7 6 5 4 3 2 1

Cataloguing in Publication Data is available from the British Library

Typeset in Bembo by
Letterpart Limited, Reigate, Surrey

Printed and bound in Great Britain by
Mackays of Chatham plc, Chatham, Kent

ISBN 0 7553 1188 4

HEADLINE BOOK PUBLISHING
A division of Hodder Headline
338 Euston Road
London NW1 3BH

Contents

Acknowledgements

We would like to give particular thanks to Janice Hadlow, Channel 4 head of specialist factual programming, and Hamish Mykura, Channel 4 head of history, for their support for the programme, *Horror on the Home Front*, and this book, which is closely associated with the television project.

A special thank you to the staff at Headline, in particular to Emma Tait, the commissioning editor, for her faith in, and dedication to, this project. We are also indebted to the editor, Christine King, for the expertise and understanding she showed to the authors and their book. We are also grateful to Taff Gillingham, an acknowledged expert on the First World War, for reading and commenting on the text.

We are grateful to the Testimony Films team especially to assistant producer Mary Parsons, researcher Ellen Quinn, editor Daniel de Waal, production secretary Madge Reed, production manager Mike Humphries, and cameraman Mike Pharey. Thanks also to Jane Fish of the Imperial War Museum, Jan Faull of the BFI National Film and Television Archive and Larry McKenna of British Pathé for advice on archive material.

Thanks must also go to the family of Joyce Crow for their kindness in letting the authors quote from an unpublished family diary written by Letitia Sherington and to Jim Grundy for sending the story of Private Simpson, used in Chapter Eight. A big thank you too, must go to Brenda Field for permission to use the letters of Leila Champ, reproduced in Chapter Six. We are also indebted to David Empson for his kind permission to use the line illustrations that have been reproduced in the text on pages 13, 194, 283 and 314.

A heart-felt thanks to Joan van Emden for reading over the proofs, and her assiduous correction of small errors of grammar, before the final copy was sent to the editor. Thanks also to Anna Branch, Nick Fear, Jeremy Banning for their support and kindness throughout the project.

Unless otherwise stated the images used belong to the authors or to interviewees, who kindly gave photographs of loved ones for reproduction. However, the authors are particularly grateful to Irene Smith and Dr and Mrs Smallcombe.

Introduction

I N SEPTEMBER 2002, THE DOORBELL RANG IN A TERRACED house in Kelross Road, north London. On opening the door, the owner was surprised to find a very elderly gentleman outside, walking stick in hand to steady himself. He was with a younger man, who spoke first. 'Sorry to bother you, but my father lived here in 1917 when the house was hit by a bomb during a Zeppelin raid.' After a brief conversation, the two men were invited to come in but, rather than heading for the sitting room, the older man walked straight to the kitchen, and looked up. 'That's where it came through,' he said, pointing.

The owner of the house had been aware of the scars on the ceiling, but had never thought anything of them. The house, built in 1892, had been there long enough to have had all number of minor accidents, mostly leaks from the bathroom above, and they had all made an impression over time. Yet the elderly man was in no doubt about the veracity of his recall.

His name was Jack Burton, and he was making a final nostalgic trip back to the places of his childhood. Jack was born and raised in England but had moved to South Africa many years previously and now, aged almost ninety, he had flown with his son the 7,000 miles 'home' to see the places he once knew so well and to recall the events of late 1917.

Jack was just four years old at the time but what happened became ingrained on his memory. There had been an air-raid warning, and soon the anti-aircraft battery at Alexandra Palace had begun to pound away at an intruder. Jack remembered:

'We were all supposed to go down into the cellar. Well, we were having a family party – we didn't have much – but what we did have were chestnuts and we were roasting them in the fire. We children didn't want to stop the fun so, when we heard the guns, we just got under a big table in the kitchen; it seemed safe enough. Then there was an almighty bang, and a bomb, which must have come through the roof and through three floors, ended up in the kitchen and on the table. Two of the leaves had broken but it was a very heavy and sturdy table and it saved our lives.'

The current home owner, a friend of one of the authors of this book, knew that we were making a film about the home front as well as writing a book about it, so he took a contact number for Jack while he was staying in England, and passed it on to us. Sadly, Jack was going back to South Africa only days later and so we never met him, and only a telephone call was possible. During this, he told us:

'Gran came rushing in and grabbed us children out from underneath and we all ran out of the house. Grandfather told the police but when they started inspecting the bomb they found it wasn't from the Zeppelin, but a shell from the anti-aircraft battery that had failed to explode. The family was very nervous and upset after that. I'd already lost an elder brother in the fighting. Now they were terrified of something else happening and they evacuated my sisters and me to a little village near St Albans.'

Jack's story was a snapshot, an anecdote of a war now drifting from oral into written or recorded history. Jack is old, very old by almost anybody's standards, except perhaps by those few who served on the Western Front and survive still. Jack is over a decade too young to be one of those, for they are the oldest of the old. At the time of writing, almost all veterans of the war have died; the official records say that forty-two survive of the six million who fought. As for the soldiers' counterparts, the women who served, there are a few munitions workers left and one or two nurses or former members of the Land Army. Women tend to live longer than men, yet, as far fewer women served in those jobs than did men in the forces, their cumulative number today is perhaps no more than that of the veterans.

Those who have any memory of the Great War must have been born just before or very shortly after the conflict broke out in 1914. In researching and writing this book, we have sought out the rapidly dwindling generation who lived on the home front at the time. They are a generation that has almost gone: the oldest interviewee will be 110 this year, the youngest in her late eighties. Their stories of life in Britain have, in the main, never been recorded before. Yet they form an intimate portrait of a life that has been largely forgotten by historians concerned with the bigger picture of war on the Western Front, or government policy at home.

In the last ten or fifteen years, we have become accustomed to hearing the voices of First World War veterans in books, and in radio and television programmes. The terrifying world of the trenches that they survived – the mud, the petrified trees and the barbed wire – are now all unforgettably imprinted in our minds, and rightly so. For a long time, those who survived did not speak often of their experiences. The war was so catastrophic and traumatic in its loss of life that for some it had long been a taboo subject. Around a million servicemen from Britain and her Commonwealth and empire died. Two million more were injured or maimed. This was the first truly modern, industrial war and, understandably, most attention has been focused on the story of life and death at the front. However, the war also made a huge impact on the lives of people at home, profoundly touching almost every family in the land.

It is too easy to talk about casualty figures at the front, forgetting that the loss of each and every man meant devastation for a family back home. For all of them there would be four years of hardship, loss, occasional terror and, finally, bittersweet victory.

However, those on the home front were far from passive. Civilians played a vital role in the war effort. Yet, curiously, there has been no broad-ranging oral history of life on the home front during the First World War, such has been the preoccupation with trench life and the fighting soldier. The civilians, the last survivors from those years, also have important and deeply moving stories to tell, essential in helping to chronicle those momentous years. Indeed, only by hearing the stories of life on the home front can we ever gain an accurate perspective of life on the Western Front and the effect of the suffering at home on those who were fighting. Children or teenagers at the time, these are now the last witnesses to the war at home. They are now in their nineties and hundreds, and are a rapidly dwindling community. In writing this book, we have tried to preserve their memories.

In the ageing process, long-term memory is one of the last things to go. In our previous interviews with First World War veterans, we have often been amazed at the recall of detail stretching back over almost a hundred years. Memory is at its sharpest in youth when everything is surprising and new. There were so many questions we wanted to ask these last survivors who kept the home fires burning, in particular about the sacrifices war had forced upon them and their families. How did people at home cope and how far did morale hold up during the war? How did Britain as a nation keep going through four long years of privation and loss?

The challenge was to find the last survivors from the home front. We began tracking them down five or six years ago, when it was easier to find men and women born in the 1890s who had a clear memory of the war in Britain. Some of the stories recounted in this book are from filmed interviews or recordings we made then. One remarkable character we discovered, for example, was Florence Billington from Coventry. Born in 1898, she was a most vivacious and youthful woman with exceptional recall of her war. She had suffered more than most, losing her sweetheart in 1915. Sadly, Florence died suddenly in August 1998, shortly after we interviewed her and just before reaching the hundredth birthday she was so looking forward to. When very old men and women are talking about their childhood and youth, they can seem so young that it is easy to forget how close to death they are.

It was with this thought in our minds that, in the summer of 2001, we renewed our efforts and began a much more thorough campaign to find and record home front stories. But the people who, we hoped, would tell these stories proved very elusive. They were often more difficult to find than the veterans themselves, as the most active of these were relatively easy to meet through the First World War organisations. There is nothing similar for those who served on the home front. There are a few organisations like the Women's Land Army – but they told us that the last woman known to have served in the war died two years ago.

We resorted to a wide-ranging approach, putting letters in local newspapers right across Britain. We contacted many old people's homes, made appeals on local radio and spoke to libraries and museums. The Oral History Society has collected and recorded memories for the last thirty years and they and others gave us more contacts. In all, we discovered about 500 new people to talk to. About 100 were selected for interview on the basis of the vividness of their memories and the range of their stories. Our interviewees were drawn from all social classes, though we made a special effort to document the stories of those who came from a poor working-class background. Between 1914 and 1918, British society was rooted in manufacturing industry and marked by deep inequalities. Those who formed the bulk of the working class had to endure the toughest conditions, particularly a poor diet and bad housing, which frequently led to early death. Children born into this background are the least likely to live into their nineties and beyond. They are also unlikely to leave any written record of their lives, and their voices, we believe, give this book a unique flavour.

While conducting research for the book and the television programme, we received a large number of letters from those who had lived through the First World War as children. Their memories were, as one might expect, varied and vivid, and reading them gave us a wide range of anecdotes about the war, many of which have been incorporated into this book. One letter in particular caught our eye. It was from a lady, now in her mid-nineties, who was just six years old when the war began. She had written a lengthy letter but, unsure of what might or might not be of interest, she had slipped from one issue to another as each recollection caught her attention. The result was an interesting letter but one that did not particularly strike us. However, it was re-read by chance and, when all non-essential elements were removed, a terrible picture began to emerge. It is one that corresponds to the image that most people would associate with the First World War. It is one person's record of systematic and frequent loss, of family, friends and associates. The loss was not necessarily through death; some were 'only' irreparably injured physically and mentally by the war. The letter read:

On one occasion we were asked to take some pennies for
a collection for the family of one of the youngest
members of the Royal Navy to die, Jack Cornwall . . . At
Dr Triplett's school the Headmaster and Mistress lost both
of their young sons in France . . . We also had one or
more Zeppelins over and a bomb was dropped at
Brentford, killing 8 people, this was very frightening . . .
My father was shot through the neck, the bullet just
missing the jugular vein . . . a few days later my father got
double pneumonia and then his wound went septic . . . he
slowly recovered. An uncle was wounded and had
frostbitten feet, another uncle, a regular soldier in the
Royal Garrison Artillery, was wounded, later dying of
meningitis . . . Two aunts worked in munitions . . . one
getting T.B. from which she died aged 23 years, the other

lived on, but her sweetheart was killed in France and later in life she committed suicide. After the war I was working in Ealing Broadway and there was a home (St David's in Castle Bar Road) for shell-shocked soldiers and even then, some were shaking so much, they could not get their money out of their pockets, it was pitiful to see them . . . My father lived to be 77 but was crippled with arthritis, and had to use a wheelchair to be taken out, we think the poisoning was responsible for it, also the wet and muddy conditions.

We found that many of our interviewees had never spoken to their families in detail, or sometimes even at all, about the suffering endured on the home front. Undoubtedly, this was due in part to the fact that our oldest generation was not brought up to discuss emotions. Their way was the stiff upper lip, the stoic silence. At the time, there was little reason to stir up feelings that were painful, ambivalent and difficult to deal with. In a typically British way, they lay dormant for many years; possibly it was hoped that in time they would just go away. Talking was also inhibited, to an extent, by the belief that the greatest suffering had taken place on the battlefields of France and Flanders; it perhaps seemed self-indulgent to make a fuss about hardships at home. This attitude has remained deeply embedded to the present day, and the recent attention given to Western Front veterans has reinforced it. The soldiers were the only heroes, the men who still managed to rebuild their lives – and live to a ripe old age.

But the hurt and the pain and the repressed emotion of a nation that lost so many of its young men had not gone away. When the questions were asked, many elderly men and women found their voice. They told stories of how they coped with the death of a father or a brother killed in action. Or they recounted how their parents dealt with the loss of a beloved son. In a few families, coping meant never mentioning his name or looking at his photograph again. With little emotional vocabulary to deal with such a family catastrophe, many had tried to repress all feelings, and this had a traumatic and profound effect on the children.

This story of life on the home front has been led and shaped by the interviewees, as well as the subject. Some areas, such as the Zeppelin raids and the problem of food distribution, are so important in the war that they would automatically be covered. However, other subjects virtually forced their way on to the page owing to the quality of the oral history. Chapter 2, on the bombardment of Britain's east coast in December 1914, is a case in point. Five remarkable interviewees to this now little-known event ensured that a short chapter was devoted to the incident, even though only a few thousand people were affected and the entire attack lasted only a matter of hours.

While the personal testimony taken from our interviews is at the heart of what is new about this book, many other sources – diaries, letters, newspapers and official records – have also been consulted and used where they help to clarify or further illuminate the overall story. In particular, many letters are published here for the first time, while the books we found most useful have been listed in the select bibliography.

Of the hundred interviewees filmed for the programme, and who are quoted in this book, at least thirty have so far lived to reach their centenaries. There are perhaps two dozen more who have died just short of the mark, or others who are still alive and within two years of joining this elite club. The average age of our interviewees is around ninety-seven or ninety-eight. They are a generation we are about to lose, but those who survive have given us a final glimpse into an era most people must feel has long since disappeared into the historical ether.

It has been fascinating to meet and talk to so many of the nation's oldest citizens, who spoke with real emotional power and honesty. Their testimony shows the courage and insight we have become accustomed to hear from veterans on the Western Front. Their stories provide a new perception of what it felt like to live through the war, a war that destroyed so many families on

a hitherto unimaginable scale. We hope that we have done justice
to their memories.

Richard van Emden
Steve Humphries
January 2003

—CHAPTER ONE—

A Nation in Arms

Y EARS BEFORE A SHOT WAS EVER FIRED ON THE
Western Front, the British people were already fighting
the Germans – at least in their imagination. Since its
foundation in 1871, Germany as a nation had gone from
strength to strength; indeed, its rise economically and militarily
had been meteoric. By the turn of the new century, it could
compete with Britain on almost every level. Germany was
helped, in no small measure, by a dramatic increase in its
population from 41 million to 65.3 million in just forty years.
This rise ensured that by 1914 Germany was numerically the
largest nation west of Russia, and was more than a third as big
again as Great Britain.

For the British, still clinging to world pre-eminence, there was
no greater threat, and books and articles speculating about
German intentions flooded the market, picturing Teutonic inva-
sions and warning Britain against complacency. Books such as
Erskine Childers's *Riddle of the Sands* predicted an assault by
hordes of enemy soldiers, while spies abounded throughout the
island. Such fear was not restricted to the adult world but passed
down to the younger generation in magazines and comics,
including *Pearson's Weekly*, which ran a notably rip-roaring serial
that had Germans invading Kent only to be foiled by gallant Boy
Scouts.

Then there were the public shows for the whole family to
enjoy, such as the floodlit display performed in the grounds of
London's Crystal Palace. In 1907 Vic Cole, a ten-year-old

working-class boy from south London, accompanied his family to watch the spectacle. He noted later:

> ' "The Invasion", as it was called, featured a life-size English village complete with church and pub. Village folk walked slowly from the former and others drank beer outside the latter. Into this peaceful rural scene suddenly a German aeroplane swooped (it ran down a wire) and dropped some bombs which exploded with appropriate noise and a great deal of smoke. When the air cleared, it was seen that German soldiers occupied the village. All ended happily when the Territorials arrived and routed the enemy.'

Ruth Armstrong, the daughter of an agricultural labourer, was not even five when she began hearing about war. She grew up in Wiltshire, in the village of Tilshead, where some of her earliest recollections were of talk between her parents. 'My mother and father kept on about this Kaiser and I couldn't think what it was all about and they kept on, "Oh, we're going to war, we're going to war." I didn't know what war meant, but the memory has stuck in my mind as well as the question, "Who is this Kaiser?" '

Emily Galbraith, the daughter of a Methodist minister, was born in 1895 in Fenton, a small town in the Potteries. Now aged nearly 108, she recalls with remarkable clarity the pervading acceptance that war would come between Britain and Germany.

> 'In 1901, I was at a good fee-paying school in London. In class we had dual desks and I sat next to a German girl and she used to tell me that her king was coming over here to fight my king and her king was going to win. And we sat in these desks and I used to have a ruler and poke her and say my king would win and she used to poke me until we both got sore. Then, after school, on the way home, I took the train from Fenchurch Street Station. Now on this train you went into a cabin before stepping

into the main carriage. Boys used to congregate in these cabins and as the train went along, we would pass over fog signals. As the train passed each signal it made a very loud noise, a hefty bang, and the boys used to shout into the carriage, "The Germans are here! The Germans are here!" It was just a bit of fun. But you see, we knew that that war was coming, we knew long before it happened.'

Many boys found the prospect of war exciting, brought up as they were on ripping yarns of empire and the thin red line. Even military disasters and defeats could be 'spun' into heroic deeds, from the stand made by Gordon at Khartoum to the later crisis in South Africa during the Boer War. Adult patriotism, along with the threat of a potential enemy, was commonly passed down to children, who accepted the ideas automatically and largely without question. For boys especially, who would one day defend the empire, there were other weekly papers such as *The Magnet* and *The Boys' Herald*, which regaled hundreds of thousands of impressionable young lads with stories of derring-do; there was never any question of who would finally win.

Team spirit, personal sacrifice, dedication to the cause were extolled, teaching those who read such magazines that their country came first, over and above the self. It was a persuasive argument, fostered by the establishment not in a blatant desire to make soldiers of these boys but as a form of social control, to inculcate the notion of duty to a higher national cause.

To become a man entailed accepting a whole raft of ideals, in particular the teaching of what is often known as 'Muscular Christianity', which was vigorously taught in public schools. It was in essence a way of living suited to defending Britain and her empire. Boys were meant to be Christian, ready to enforce what was good and true, 'to fight the good fight' if necessary. Yet what was good and true was, almost invariably, synonymous with the country's self-interest. To this end, sports were advocated, as good health was seen as almost a religious and social duty. To achieve this, boys were taught that physical health and fitness were integral to mental strength and fortitude, from which would flow integrity and honesty; no surprise then that *The Boys' Herald* was subtitled 'A Healthy Paper For Manly Boys'.

Boxing, rugby, football and cricket would instil discipline, teamwork and duty, and would set boys on the right path for life. As a by-product, such training would be of immense help should the boys be needed to play the 'greater game' against an enemy. Sport, in and out of school hours, built character, as Richard Hawkins, born into an upper-middle-class family, recalls: 'My father and I used to do a lot of boxing when I was a boy. He used to kneel down so as to get to my level and then we would spar. On one occasion my parents had to call in the doctor because I was a bit swollen round the glands; they thought I'd got mumps. Well, I hadn't; my father had let fly perhaps a little bit too much.'

When war broke out ten years later, the then nineteen-year-old enlisted straight away, without question. 'It was our duty, nothing out of the ordinary, it was obvious, to protect our country. We were the best country in the world. Oh, I don't think we gave anyone else a thought, there was no need to. We had to go and defend the country against all invaders and to give, if necessary, our lives to do it.'

The ideals of Muscular Christianity percolated through to the lower-middle and working classes through youth organisations such as the Church Lads' Brigade, the Boys' Brigade, the Scouts and the Sea Scouts. Yet, before ever joining, the raw material, the boys themselves, had to be taught notions of obedience and conformity. This was first taught at home, then reinforced in school with cast-iron authority, as Londoner Vic Cole recalled.

'The discipline at school was to be marvelled at. At the first few strokes of the assembly bell, kids would drop all games and snap into their class formation like guardsmen. There were several teachers who could rap out words of command like sergeant majors. The children would spring smartly to attention at the order, right or left turn as one man and march into their respective classrooms.'

A respect for discipline was maintained even out of school:

'Although somewhat given to violent combat as a means
of settling disputes, they were on the whole a pretty good
lot of youngsters at school. Fights, though frequent, were
kept clean and proper by mutual observance of the
so-called "fair-play" code of those days, which laid down
the various conditions under which blows could or could
not be exchanged. To strike a boy smaller than oneself was
definitely not done. This would bring forth cries of
"coward" and "bully" or "hit one yer own size!" '

While Vic's schooling was rough and tumble, there were many
other children in the poorest areas whose education was far more
confrontational. In many schools, notions of obedience and
discipline were frequently contested by older, increasingly mar-
ginalised pupils, who had little interest or belief in such codes of
conduct.

It has been estimated that approximately 40 per cent of boys
joined one or other of the formal youth organisations, drawn
into a world in which patriotism, teamwork and mutual help
were extolled as manly virtues. It is self-evident that there was
another 60 per cent who were not attracted to such organisations. These were children primarily from the poorest families,
boys who frequently felt little connection to the nation's prevailing hopes and objectives. These children were suspicious of the
Scouts and the Boys' Brigade, seeing them as an attempt to
exercise authoritarian control over their lives. The fact that 'subs'
were charged to take part hardly improved matters, for it was
money that the poorest families could ill afford. It is not
surprising that many continued their disorganised lives, prefer-
ring unfettered fun in the back street to controlled games in the
Scout hut.

The boys who did join, while attracted from many walks of
life, were generally those who were 'better behaved'. Boys'
organisations were in action everywhere. There were exhibitions

at Earls Court and the Crystal Palace, where Boys' Cavalry Brigades drilled and paraded, sponsored by some of the big daily newspapers, particularly those that led the way in reporting the 'German threat', such as the *Daily Mail*. It did not require a great leap of imagination to see these Boy Scouts, with their badges, bands and banners, making the transition to the army when the time required. These organisations had been designed to give boys experience of the adventurous life most craved. Nevertheless, when war broke out, when thousands of young men flocked to join up, those who had learnt some semblance of drill or musketry in the Scouts or Boys' Brigades were at a distinct advantage, as one officer commissioned into Kitchener's volunteer army saw. 'You had four platoon sergeants which you had to choose from your men,' recalled Richard Hawkins, 'and by Jove if one had been in the Boy Scouts, well, he was a corporal straight away. Otherwise we had no previous experience of soldiering.'

In the days before war broke out, it would appear that only the politicians were undecided as to whether Britain should be plunged into a general European conflict. The Prime Minister, Asquith, noted in his diary for 31 July:

> We had cabinet at 11 and a very interesting discussion, especially about the neutrality of Belgium . . . are we to go in or stand aside? Of course everybody longs to stand aside, but I need not say that France is pressing strongly for a reassuring declaration. We are under no obligation [to France so] that we could give no pledges and that our actions must depend upon the course of events . . . and the direction of public opinion here.

If Asquith was worried about public opinion, then he only had to look out of his window or drive around in his car for reassurance. Of course there were dissenting voices. The veteran politician and former Labour Party leader, Keir Hardie, made an impassioned speech against the war on 2 August, and later a small anti-war rally took place in Trafalgar Square. But these demonstrations quickly fell away once war was a reality. The pretext for going to war, according to a vocal and vociferous press, was an invasion of Belgian soil by Germany, and the public was seemingly in almost full support. When Germany did indeed invade Belgium, on 3 August, the country at large was hardly surprised when Britain declared war the next day. That afternoon, as Asquith's car left Parliament, the Prime Minister noted, 'It is curious how going to and from the House we are now always escorted and surrounded by cheering crowds of loafers and holidaymakers.'

That weekend there had been a bank holiday, which meant that at the precise moment Britain plunged into war, an unusually large number of people were in the capital. *The Times* had reported the excited mood:

> A great majority of these holidaymakers had been attracted
> to London by a desire to be present in the capital in this
> moment of grave crisis. They were eager for news and
> impatient to learn what part England was to play.
> Miniature Union Jacks and tricolors were sold in the
> streets, and quickly bought . . . In the evening thousands
> of people gathered in Trafalgar Square and the Mall and
> outside Buckingham Palace. Up and down the Mall,
> processions, carrying Union Jacks and the French tricolor,
> marched continually, cheering and singing . . . The
> demonstration of patriotism and loyalty became almost
> ecstatic until at last the enormous crowd eventually
> dispersed in processions which flooded the streets of the
> West End.

Vic Cole was just one of the many thousands of people who witnessed events that day.

> 'The evening newspapers were all pretty certain that
> before many hours Britain would be at war with

Germany. In the afternoon I went up town and wandered about in front of Buckingham Palace and down the Mall. There was a great crowd of people outside the Palace and other crowds were congregating in Whitehall and towards Westminster. Later on that night, just before midnight, the word went around that, the ultimatum having expired, we were now at war with Germany. I was terribly excited; the thing that people had been talking about for years had at last come about and at any moment (I thought) the invasion of England would begin. I conjured up brave visions of myself lying behind a hedge, rifle in hand, firing round after round at hordes of Germans advancing through the fields of Kent on their way to besiege London. I wanted to be in the army with a gun in hand like the boys I had so often read about in books and magazines. Little did I realise in those days how well I had been brainwashed.'

Broadly speaking, the British public had little doubt that the Germans were responsible for the war, that Britain's hand had been forced. As one patriot, a young girl who was to work in nursing, munitions and the Land Army, wrote, 'I believe we're fighting for an ethical truth, and that the war is a struggle between civilisation, and all it stands for, on one side, against Germany's barbarism, which seems the result of their extraordinary rapid and material progress of the last forty years, which isn't based on a solid civilisation.' Her words were determined and sure, a mood reflected by most who associated themselves with the views of 'middle England'. Yet behind such words of courage there was anxiety and fear, particularly among those old enough to know better.

Florence Nield, a working-class girl from Swansea, was at home when war broke out.

'The newsboy was outside calling out that England had declared war on Germany. I was not quite fifteen years old at the time and I was quite pleased, being a youngster, I thought it was like two people sparring up to each other. My mother and father were on the doorstep and I said, "Oh lovely, we're going to have a fight, you know," and I was surprised when my mother gave me a quick slap.'

No one wanted to contemplate a war lasting beyond Christmas time, and there was a deep-seated desire to see it won convincingly and quickly. There was an inherent public belief in the capabilities of the British army when called to action; although in truth most military commanders, Lord Kitchener among them, saw that the war would be anything but short. Britain's small, highly trained regular army was no match in terms of numbers for the huge German forces which, within a week of mobilisation, had 3.8 million men under arms. Kitchener foresaw that a new citizens' army would be required, made up of volunteers.

In times of war, the government had envisaged that the regular and Territorial armies would simply grow organically, taking on new recruits and expanding as required. Lord Kitchener, who had little enough faith in the prowess of the new Territorial Force (formed in 1908 with part-time soldiers, originally meant for home defence), decided to discard the idea and, as the new Secretary of State for War, create an entirely New Army of 100,000 men. However, such was the apparent enthusiasm to fight that some 300,000 civilians enlisted in August, before word ever got out that this New Amy was needed. Then, when Kitchener launched his famous appeal, epitomised by the poster 'Your Country Needs You', there came a second, spontaneous response, hundreds of thousands of men besieging recruiting stations set up right across the country.

One of the first to enlist, even before the appeal, was farmer's son George Whitehead, the eldest brother of seven-year-old Len, who recalls:

'Everybody was terribly excited, and there was nobody more excited than my elder brother George. He was going, he said, "first thing tomorrow morning". We were having a bit of leg pulling and we sang him the song:

No more will I work in the harvest to reap the
   golden corn
But I'm going to join the army and I'm off
   tomorrow morn.
Hurrah for the scarlet and blue
See the helmets glitter in the sun
See the bayonets flash like lightning
To the beating of the old militia drum.

'Dad didn't want him to enlist, he tried to persuade him against going so soon – stop to see the harvest in. But George was keen to go and here was his chance, and he went into my mother's bedroom – she was not very well at the time – and he picked up a stick which she used to rap on the floor if she wanted anything. "This is how I shall strut about the London parks," he said, jokingly of course. It was the glamour of it all, nobody sort of gave it a second thought that they might never come back.

'In the early part of the war, small squads of soldiers used to march through the villages – it was part of the recruiting drive, you see, and they sang a song, "You ought to join Kitchener's Army. Seven bob a week, plenty of grub to eat, great big boots make blisters on your feet, you ought to join." Of course we used to run alongside these soldiers; they had a drum and a fife band, or a bugle. I think we used to poke fun at them. It wasn't military music but enough perhaps to stir some young men to want to join up.'

One of those eager to go was Jack Davis, then nineteen years old and working at the National Liberal Club in London's Whitehall Place. He had not seen the popular hysteria on the streets as he had been working, but that did not matter and he went along to enlist on 3 September, during the first week of Kitchener's appeal. Of all those men who enlisted, Jack, now aged 108, is possibly the very last surviving volunteer.

'I was in the Boys' Brigade and was a member of an athletics club too, so I both accepted discipline and had an organised life. It meant the call of the army quite naturally attracted me. I enlisted at New Scotland Yard with thirty of my colleagues, en masse, because our manager at the Liberal Club was a patriotic Frenchman and so we had no difficulty joining up and letting the women take over our jobs. Then we had a night out, the group of us, for once you had accepted the traditional king's shilling, you're in. So, it being our last night of freedom, we made the best of it with the boys. We were told to assemble at St Martin in the Fields, on the forecourt, the next morning, and there we were, 750 of us, all young civilians all eager for what we thought was excitement. Once the roll call was taken and all other details completed, we were marched to Paddington Station where a special train took us all to Falmouth. It was only then that we knew that we were going to join the Duke of Cornwall's Light Infantry.'

Two nights later, it was Vic Cole's turn to enlist.

'September 5th 1914, George Pulley (son of our local butcher) and I attended our first and last recruiting meeting. A leather-lunged gentleman was urging the crowd to throw up their jobs and fight. The way he spoke, it was just a matter of coming up, drawing a rifle and ammunition and proceeding straight away to France. The sergeant already had his eagle eye upon George and I and he was most pleased to greet us, possibly because out of all that crowd we were the only ones to join up that night. When I got home, my poor aunt and gran could scarcely believe their ears. Hardly waiting to close the door, I called out, "I've joined the army!" "Oh dear! Oh dear!" said Gran. "My poor boy." Neither of them were at all demonstrative but when I sat down, Gran put her old arm about me for a moment. My aunt shed a tear and then said, "Well, I suppose you'd like a cup of tea now." '

Across the length and breadth of the country, thousands of recruitment rallies were held. Posters were placed on every available hoarding to announce that a 'Public War Meeting' would occur at a certain place and time. On such occasions, a recruiting officer would 'attend to give information and speak' – although why anyone should need persuading to join the army was something of an enigma, for, as one poster noted, pointedly, 'ALL MEN who have already made up their minds to act for their Country's good and their own, can be attested after the meeting.' In the exuberance of the moment, Vic had enlisted, a decision made by thousands of others tempted by recruiting sergeants who often let it be known that every girl liked a boy in uniform.

Over-enthusiasm to play a part explains why many young men were enlisted, but by no means all. Some men simply spoiled for a fight, or felt the war gave them a chance for redemption. One interesting case is that of Arthur Borton, an upper-middle-class boy educated at Eton. He had proved to be nothing other than a failure in civilian life, losing money hand-over-fist in misguided business ventures. His family despaired. The outbreak of war offered him a final chance to prove his worth. Over the following four years, he turned out to be a consummate soldier, winning the Victoria Cross and the Distinguished Service Order for bravery, only to lose his way again once the war was over and he was demobbed. Arthur's case was clearly exceptional in terms of the awards he won, although many civilians who were turned into soldiers probably identified with his story.

In reality, there were a myriad reasons for enlisting. Everyone had their own: many were tempted by friends, others just followed the works crowd down to the recruiting office. Some were bored, sick of repetitive jobs, others were 'encouraged' out

PUBLIC

WAR MEETING

A Meeting will take place

at __THE DOCKS.__

on __SAT. 21ˢᵗ Novᵉ__

A RECRUITING OFFICER

OF THIS DISTRICT

will attend to give information and speak.

In the Chair __LIEUT PHILIPPS.__

"God Save the King."

NOTICE.

ALL MEN who have already made up their minds to act for their Country's good and their own, can be attested after the meeting.

A notice inviting people to attend a public meeting, which was nothing more than a recruitment rally.

of their employment and into the army. And then there were the 500,000 men made redundant in the weeks after war broke out as industries shed employees in the face of economic uncertainty. For these men, many of whom would soon be hungry, the army at least guaranteed the bare essentials of food, clothing and accommodation.

In Jack Davis's case, as perhaps with most volunteers, there was not one defining motive but rather an assortment of reasons for enlisting.

'I don't think people realised the seriousness of it then. We understood that we were in danger from the Kaiser and that we had to defend our territory by all means. It came as no surprise that war was declared. For me it was a bit of excitement and I thought, "Well, might as well enlist" – "fresh fields" and all that. I never realised then what it meant, we had no idea what we were going into. My first six months at the front were characterised by part depression and part disbelief that this could be war.'

The Butler family from Canning Town in London were to prove themselves one of the more patriotic families in the war. As soon as war broke out, Harold, the eldest son, enlisted into the cavalry before later being transferred to the infantry. He was followed not only by his two brothers but by his father, who was in his late forties and technically over-age for service. Harold had enlisted so quickly that by early September he was not only thinking about leave, but had already learnt a cunning way of getting it.

11/9/14

My dear Sister

I am getting along nicely thank you, I wish I were nearer so as to see you more often, still if ever I can get leave I will be over like a shot. I have played my fiddle here, they are all mad on it, one corporal with tears in his eyes handed me some money after I played 'Cavalleria

Rusticana' but of course I refused it. Well Elsie look after
dear old Ma, and give her a few, or at least give her heaps
of kisses for me and remember me to Dad and Walter.

I remain your affectionate brother, Harold

PS If a letter was sent to me telling me that Ma was
very ill etc, I could show it to the Major and he may let
me have a couple of days leave, so please send one to that
effect, stating this: 'Mother is ill, etc etc try and get home
to see her etc . . .'

Not all jumped straight into the fray. Emily Galbraith's family
agonised over whether her brother Peter should enlist. Before the
war, the family very firmly believed that killing was wrong in all
circumstances.

'Peter and I were great pals and he was very clever and
ambitious. He had studied at Palmer's School at Greys in
Barking, and wanted to be a missionary. My brother,
indeed the whole family, were conscientious objectors.
Shortly after the war broke out, we sat in the house
discussing the matter, as my brother was wondering
whether he, in fact, ought to volunteer. We were talking,
whether it would be right or wrong to join, to go and kill
people, and of course we said no, it was wrong, "Thou
shalt not kill". We were in mid-discussion when my
brother suddenly stood up and said, "You know, Mother,
supposing people were to come into this room," and he
pointed, "come in that door and attack you and Emily."
He said, "I shouldn't sit here and let them do it." So he
said, "I've got to go, the Germans are coming here, we all
know the stories they are telling. I've got to protect you
from them. I'm not a conscientious objector; I'm here as a
defender and I've a right to defend you." That was my
brother's attitude. We didn't want to go and fight anybody,
we wanted to live in peace. However, we weren't allowed
to because of Germany, it wasn't our fault.'

The defeat of Germany was expected by Christmas, but in the meantime certain people on the home front took precautions, just in case. At the start of hostilities there had been a rush to stock up on food, with those who could afford it buying large quantities of non-perishables, in particular sugar and tinned foods. Although the bank holiday had been extended to prevent a run on the banks, retail shops had reopened as normal on the Tuesday, 4 August, and were besieged by women, shelves being cleared of food in many towns. On 9 August, the *Tottenham and Edmonton Herald* reported the case of a lady who walked into a grocer's store in Palmers Green and spent the huge sum of £17. So effectively did she empty the shelves that it was forced to close for three days until new supplies could be obtained.

As a result of such panic buying, wholesale prices rose quickly. The *Hull Daily Mail* reported that in Grimsby the price of wholesale flour had risen from 27 to 40 shillings per 20-stone sack. Invariably such rises hit the shops, and prices of staple foodstuffs briefly spiralled, the price of bread nearly doubling. 'The stories of food-hoarders are already beginning to be numerous and amusing,' wrote Edward Heron-Allen in his *Journal of the Great War*. 'One hears of dowager duchesses raiding country towns in their Rolls-Royce cars and Daimler limousines, and returning to their baronial halls buried under heaps of ham, bushels of artichokes and pyramids of tinned meat and sardines.' Such self-serving behaviour was hardly patriotic, although those who could afford the food, like Heron-Allen, sought to justify their expenditure as almost altruistic. 'I am patriarch of a tribe of twenty-five – it behoves me to make some small provision of food as well as of money, however wildly the people who are not in a position to do so will rave about the unpatriotism of "hoarding".' His logic was simple. If the war ended quickly, then his hoarding would be irrelevant, while in a long conflict he would ensure that he could rely on his private supply, removing him from the queue for future foodstuffs.

The panic abated within days, although the problem of severe food shortages was to recur later in the war. On 8 August the government passed the Defence of the Realm Act, giving it almost arbitrary power to act to protect national security. This Act was extended and amended later in the month and at various times throughout the war, and an ever-lengthening list of orders was sent from ministries, controlling any aspect of life deemed important, from lighting restrictions to trading hours, from food prices and control to press reporting of the war. To guarantee a steady supply of food, a Cabinet Committee on Food Supplies was set up, while Parliament passed the Unreasonable Withholding of Foodstuffs Act, an anti-profiteering measure designed to ensure that no one hoarded food beyond what was personally consumable, while the state's assertion of control over the railway network appeared to make sure that supplies would not be interrupted.

The initial shock of actually being at war passed and thousands of holidaymakers poured down in mid-August to the beaches of Eastbourne, to take in the seasonal sun. 'That a Great War was in progress seemed inconceivable,' wrote one onlooker; 'the sands were thick with chairs.' Those who went to the beach were not necessarily inactive. While there were over 5 million women in employment, more than twice as many, 12.9 million, did not work. Many of these women turned to knitting, with apparently unbounded zeal. They knitted scarves, gloves, waistcoats and socks, on the beach, on trains, on trams, in theatres and in parks. Emily Galbraith was touring in Scotland with her minister father soon after war was declared. 'Everyone started knitting for the war effort. I remember we were staying on the shores of Loch Fyne and the women were knitting and they appealed to my father if it was right or wrong to knit socks on Sundays for the soldiers, and my father said it was quite right and they were all very pleased.'

In the world of paid work, many jobs that traditionally employed women were axed, such as in the garment industry, the fishing industry (where women were employed as fish gutters), and among confectionery makers. In all, some one in seven women lost their jobs, and charities were set up to find them employment. Those industries that had shaken out almost half a million male workers during the first days of the war were traditionally male-dominated; when they later looked to refill the vacancies they would consider only other men, not women. As the unions had yet to agree to giving jobs to women, they gravitated towards the secretarial and clerical posts vacated by men enlisting; indeed, 50 per cent more women were to work in white-collar jobs during the war than in industry and agriculture.

The vast majority of these 'new' workers were married women tempted back into work, or girls who joined the workforce earlier than normal, and they were often consummately exploited. Relatively few middle- and upper-class women had worked before the war, but some were now coaxed into the labour force – though in the main, gravitating towards those jobs most associated with ladies of social standing, in purely supervisory roles or in professions such as nursing.

There was a numerically small, elite group of women who wanted to be directly involved in the war. One observer, Elsie Knocker, wrote: 'Committees proliferated, all intent on beating each other in the race to get to "the Front", and most of them, especially those involving women, rejected by the War Office and the British Red Cross. Many ideas burned out in a blaze of talk or died in a welter of vagueness. Others crumbled at the first touch of reality.' This writer later proved to be one of the more determined and remarkable women of the war, when, with a friend, she set up and privately financed an emergency post, close to the front line at Pervyse, to treat wounded soldiers.

It was a similar spirit of adventure that encouraged many young girls to join the Voluntary Aid Detachments, or other groups such as the Women's Emergency Corps that encouraged women to train as doctors, nurses and motorcycle messengers. Later in the year, the Women's Defence Relief Corps was formed, as well as the Women's Hospital Corps and the Women's Police Volunteers. War was exciting, and the same sort of infectious desire that had made men become 'involved' also effected a similar response among young women who came mostly from financially stable backgrounds – or, in other words, women who could afford to be excited about this new challenge in their lives.

Many remarkable women came from this social grouping but they were the exception, for the numbers involved, as a proportion of the total female workforce, were relatively small. Emily Galbraith's was typical of the spirit shown by young, well-to-do girls at the time, anxious to capitalise on their new-found freedoms.

> 'I wrote to Lord Kitchener while I was at a girls' college training to be a teacher in Derby and said we were able-bodied young women and I didn't see why we shouldn't be a Home Guard and fight at home so as to let the boys go and do the job of fighting the Germans. I asked whether he would allow us, because we were capable and could protect our country, to learn to fire a rifle. Shortly after, I received a very nice handwritten letter back from Kitchener and he said he didn't approve of women fighting; it was the men's job to look after the women, but he thanked me very much.'

There were thousands of women employed in jobs of great drudgery, to whom the excitement of war was distant. They were poor, inarticulate, and would never have dreamed of writing to the local vicar, never mind the Secretary of State for War. One sixteen-year-old girl recalled being in domestic service on a farm in Yorkshire, and being unaware that Britain was even involved in an international conflict. The farm was isolated, and the owners never spoke to her unless it was to point her in the direction of the next job. There were no newspapers to read, and so she was unaware of the fighting until, in November 1914, a chance conversation enlightened her. This case was unusual but not unique, and many women working on farms could live through the war with relatively little or no contact with the consequences.

Living on an isolated Scottish farm near Balerno, Maria Pettigrew was nearly twenty-one years old and heavily pregnant with her first child when war broke out. Now aged 109, she recalls that the war had little effect on her husband's and her daily life.

'My husband was a ploughman, and was in a reserved occupation. We worked very hard, getting up at 4.50 a.m. with my husband not finishing until 6 p.m. Even then he had to go and look after the horses at night, in his own time. We had enough food and, as the war went on, we were required to put any surplus out, such as eggs or milk, to be picked up by the authorities for distribution elsewhere, which we did, of course, though we made sure we had enough first. I was soon a young wife with a young family, and my life was centred on the house, and I had plenty to do there.'

Only towards the end of the year did it become apparent that the rapid enlistment of skilled and semi-skilled men into the army was causing a great shortage in the labour market and in the industries essential to the prosecution, even the continuation, of the war. This was the unforeseen downside to all the wild enthusiasm for war. Skilled workers, vital to the war effort, were presenting themselves in large groups to enlist and serve together. Some 160,000 miners joined up in the first six months of the war, as did 10,000 engineers, while agriculture and transport were also badly hit. The army had traditionally relied upon vagrants, the temporarily unemployed and the hungry to fill the ranks; now, under Kitchener's free-for-all, the technically able and highly educated were enlisting too. The effect was to seriously undermine the economy, causing a serious dislocation within essential industries. Only in time would the government act to help manage the problem, ordering the discharge of a number of men, including miners, who were vital to the war economy. The politician's predicament of discouraging the enlistment of highly skilled men, when they were keen to fight, was never entirely resolved.

The reality was that women were desperately needed to fill the gap in the labour market, but the approval of the trade unions to 'dilution', the employment of unskilled women in jobs previously restricted to craftsmen, was required. Such approval was not taken for granted, and there was much horse-trading before large numbers of women entered the market. Even then, it was not until April 1915 that the number of employed was equal to that before the war. The big difference came with pay in war-related industries where, in time, women were to earn wages undreamt of elsewhere.

For those whose husbands had gone to war, there were separation allowances to offset the loss of income. The rates had not increased since the Boer War ended in 1902, but rose to 12s 6d (62p) a week with an extra 2s (10p) for each child, even though the actual dispersal of the money was anything but quick or free from confusion. The amounts rarely compensated the family for the financial loss, and while soldiers at the front could allocate part of their wages to families at home, any allowance from a private's income of 7s (35p) a week was likely to be meagre.

In the first weeks and months of the war, both the government and commerce strove to give the impression that it was 'business as usual', and notices saying as much were displayed in shop windows. The first war budget in November maintained the perception that things were all right, with an increase in income tax paid for by the middle classes and a small increase in tax, most notably on beer. Once the economic gloom in the first days of war had subsided, there was, as in most war economies, a boom, as government spending rose dramatically and this money was filtered through the economy. In many cities, restaurants appeared full, and theatres were packed, but the consequent rise in the price of basic foodstuffs hit many of the poorest in society with disproportionate effect. Within months, it was found that the price of flour had risen by 75 per cent, and meat by an average of 9 per cent. Sugar was increasingly hard to find and the spectre of a shortage across the UK saw even restaurant-goers secreting sugar in their pockets, for later use.

According to the men of the original British Expeditionary Force (the regular army sent to France), the only restaurants worth considering were those in the German capital. Within two weeks of war breaking out, the force was pouring towards the Channel ports in trains, along the sides of which was commonly chalked 'Next Stop Berlin'. As they left England and crossed the Channel to France, they left their barracks empty for thousands of Territorial soldiers and, in time, the new recruits who were busily signing up. As the regulars fought the Battles of the Marne, Aisne and later the First Battle of Ypres, the new Kitchener units began their training in parks, on commons and on barrack squares.

As with most children whose fathers were in uniform, six-year-old Ellen Elston was very proud of her dad. He was a company sergeant major in the East Surrey Regiment, a regular who, in the first instance, remained in England to train some of the new recruits.

'I remember going with my mother and brother on a visit to see my dad at Dover Castle. Dad had to drill the men and it was exciting to see all the soldiers lined up and our own dad taking them through their paces. We thought that was marvellous, watching through the arrow slits in the wall. Afterwards all the men clustered round him and us; these were the sergeant major's kids, and we were carried around the square on the men's shoulders. One or two of the men put their new stiff hats on our heads, and others gave us a few coppers in change, so that we had lots to talk about when we went back to school.'

In Liverpool Florence Billington witnessed the transformation of these civilians into soldiers.

'I and my friend Alice would be out shopping, getting something for tea, and all these young men were coming past, all like in a regiment, but in their ordinary everyday

civilian clothes. And they were calling out to us as they
walked past, about five or six abreast, "Hello, Flo, hello,
Alice," and "Throw us an apple, mam," to the grandmas
and that, and they did, they threw them an apple. The
next day we went to the park with the children and we
saw these same boys and they were all sticking bayonets
into sacks of straw attached to the trees where the children
used to play. They were taking two or three men at a time
and they were running towards the sacks and were told
just whereabouts in the straw that bayonet had to go.
Nobody stopped us looking, and we realised that those
sacks were supposed to represent Germans.'

Areas like parks and lawns were often commandeered to provide
training grounds. With the huge influx of volunteers, there was a
desperate shortage of facilities to turn the new recruits into
soldiers, so intensive training was undertaken in any available
space. Liverpudlian Sydney Bond watched as his beloved playground was taken over by the army.

'Opposite to where we lived was the Wavertree
Playground, a huge place bequeathed to the children of
the district and marvellous for football, and then it was
suddenly taken from us. I only had to go into this
playground to see men practising throwing a bomb. They
made a few slit trenches and put blokes in there and the
sergeant would try to teach them to lob a bomb over, and
that went on continually.'

Such were the numbers of volunteers that the army could afford
to be selective, and rejected large numbers of men almost out of
hand: they were too short, too short-sighted, flat-footed; they
had previously undiagnosed heart murmurs, they had bad teeth.
In the last week of August and the first week of September, the
most successful weeks for recruitment, the army was so overwhelmed with the numbers attempting to join that something

radical had to be done. On 11 September, the army raised the minimum height stipulation from 5 feet 3 inches to 5 feet 6 inches to stem the numbers waiting outside the recruitment offices. The new restriction dissuaded a few from joining up, but men who were desperate to enlist could always try to cheat, standing on tip-toes to gain height, just as the short-sighted could memorise the letters on the optician's card in order to 'see' better. One man who sought to enlist in the Bristol's Own Battalion popped down to his dentist to have all his teeth removed, after they were diagnosed by the army as being too poor to allow his enlistment.

Arthur Burge was one of those rejected in 1914. He had been studying in the German city of Metz just as the war broke out. His narrow escape from internment was a piece of luck, and now he was back in England.

'I was going to London one day when, by chance, I saw my aunt at the railway station. We met on the platform, but instead of walking together she shouted at me in a high voice from the other side of the station, "Arthur, not in khaki yet?" I thought, "That's a nasty one for me because she had said to the whole of Shiplake that I was a coward and I was very well known in the town as a very good amateur punter.

'I couldn't bear the insult so the next day I decided that I would go to the recruiting office in Reading. I couldn't stand being spoken to like that and said to my father, "Look here, Father, I must enlist at once." He said, "Don't be silly, boy, you are not fit to be a soldier." I replied, "Don't forget, Father, I went to Malvern College where they were very keen on the army." We were in the Officer Training Corps and if I didn't join up my name would be mud, they were very patriotic indeed. He said, "I can't stop you but I think you're silly," so I said, "Well, I'm going to be silly then."

'I went to enlist and the doctor examined me and said,

"Your heart is all right, your blood pressure is all right, but your lungs are in a poor state." I was given a certificate which read, "A young man wished to join HM Forces for the rest of the war. A. J. Burge unfit, poor physique." I thought, at least no one can call me a coward now I have a certificate.'

The keenness that many men showed in enlisting only highlighted the tardiness of others in making their way down to the recruiting office. Some needed a push. To help enlistment, some local government authorities withheld relief payments to able-bodied men, leading to a commensurate increase in the numbers seen down at the recruitment office. Other less subtle pressures were exerted too, including the launching of bloodstained bandages, brought from military hospitals, into the gardens of un-enlisted men. Yet by far and away the best-known weapon used against 'shirkers' was the white feather, the hard-hitting public sign of cowardice that was vigorously awarded by women to men 'not yet in khaki'.

The Order of the White Feather was formed in 1914 by a former admiral, Charles Fitzgerald. He recruited a group of thirty over-zealous women to publicly humiliate recalcitrant men who were not yet in khaki and award them the white feather. It was an organisation that grew quickly across the country, supported by some of the leading female writers of the day as well as well-known suffragettes, such as the Pankhursts, Emmeline and daughter Christabel. Male civilians were harangued everywhere, with boys as young as fifteen and sixteen being given feathers, as well as married men over forty, neither of which group was sought for enlistment.

Joe Yarwood was the right age and willing to serve, but he had been rejected.

'The only thing wrong with me was I was a bit skinny. I went to the town hall and I went in and I was shocked unimaginably, to think they'd turned me down. I went in

25

a shop in Soho and a lady behind the counter said, "Why aren't you in the army?" In those days they would give you a white feather, implying that you were a poltroon or coward. I was very indignant because I went and they'd stamped my form "totally rejected" and I felt angry, I don't mind telling you, I felt like slapping her face but I wouldn't do that of course.'

For Joe, there was no other choice but to try and enlist somewhere else.

'The women didn't have to make the decision to go but they were very good at slinging out the dirty insults. Of course a great many men, I fancy, who didn't want to go would have been very glad to have got that news, but not in my case. I wasn't having any woman doubting my manhood, so I went back straight away to Trafalgar Square and I found to my astonishment that I got through quite easily.

'My mother was furious but I told her, "We've got to have at least five or six months' training in England." She was happy with that, she said, "Oh that's all right, the outing will do you good and you'll be home for Christmas." '

In time, men who had been discharged as medically unfit were given feathers and it is said that at least one former prisoner of war, after donning civilian clothes to aid his escape, was similarly insulted as he arrived at Victoria Station. Even men who had enlisted were targets, for the dire shortage of uniforms forced many to drill in civilian clothes for weeks before wearing khaki. Later, in 1915, it was found that they who had registered for the Derby Scheme (whereby they assented to serve but were not called until needed) were frequently embarrassed, so khaki armbands with a red crown were issued to prevent mistakes. Similar protection had had to be given to other groups, state employees for example, who had often been accosted, forcing the government to act in their defence. In 1914, circular lapel badges had been struck in brass with the distinctive words 'On War Service' and these were handed to civilians who were, for the time being at least, on other essential work. It saved many from attack, while exposing those whose lapels were made more conspicuous by the absence of the small blue and gold insignia.

For those who still avoided the recruitment sergeant, there were posters to back up the white feathers. Campaigns directed at young girls asked them to look closely at their boyfriends if they were not in uniform. 'To The Young Women Of London', read one poster, 'Is your "Best Boy" wearing khaki? If not, don't YOU THINK he should be? If he does not think that you and your country are worth fighting for – do you think he is WORTHY of you?' The poster goes on to ask pointedly whether, if the boyfriend is happy to neglect his country, there may come a time when he will neglect his girlfriend too.

Harold Butler's girlfriend Maude had no question marks on that point. Her boyfriend had been among the very first to enlist, and she knew with certainty that Harold was the only boy for her. Maude had received regular letters from her 'best boy' ever since he had joined up and she was proud of his progress in His Majesty's forces. In early December, Harold received a promotion, and a flurry of letters to his family followed, letting them all know of his first rise up the ranks.

6th December 1914

Dear Ma and Pa

I would have written before, only I have heaps to think about here now. My name has been sent in to the Major for a stripe for smartness, so when I get it I will be Lance Corporal. I hope to be wearing it when I come home Xmas time. Xmas is almost here so I hope to see you all then have some Xmas pudding. I hope father is doing plenty of work, and Ma is not worrying over nothing as she always is. I am enjoying myself here in fact having a ripping time with the boys, plenty of sport etc.

With best wishes to all, Harold

In many cases, it took a full year for the new civilian soldiers to be fully trained, and although some volunteers like Harold Butler would leave for France in 1915, most Kitchener men would not see action until the following year, 1916. But whether leaving for camp or for France after a week's embarkation leave, the departure from home was a poignant moment. Len Whitehead witnessed his brother leaving.

'The next day we watched him set out with a sort of parcel tucked under his arm, with his towel and shaving gear. He went up the farm chase which was about half a mile long and he was gone, to the nearest village railway station at Rayne. The village was so empty, it seemed so, you see there were so many young men although they didn't all go together, they went in sort of dribs and drabs – they would meet perhaps in an evening – there was a reading room, a sort of place where they would meet and say, "Right, we're off," perhaps five or six of them. "Meet at the village pump tomorrow morning and we'll go," and they did, of course. We were very proud to say he'd gone. "You know my brother, he's in the 9th Battalion of the Essex Regiment," you see. Other children had got people in more glamorous regiments but we didn't care, we'd got a brother soldiering.'

Florence Billington had watched with pride the civilians march-ing off to their training camps and the boyish enthusiasm they all seemed to carry with them. Much as she admired them, they were still amateurs compared to her boyfriend, Ted Felton. Ted had joined the army before the war, in the King's Liverpool Regiment. Private 11066 had cut a dashing figure in his khaki uniform when she met him.

'He seemed to take a fancy to me straight away and I liked him. We talked and when it was time to leave he wanted to see me again, which was quite all right. We met often,

and quickly became very fond of each other. We decided
that when the war was over, which would be around
Christmas, we would get engaged; it was like a promise. I
thought the world of him. Each time I saw him I used to
put my arms round his neck and tell him that I'd always,
always wait for him and that I wouldn't bother with
anyone else, our future would be together. We were very
entranced with each other and I kept thinking of him all
the time.'

Ted's battalion left for the Western Front early the following year,
but now he was about to leave the love of his short life, and the
anxiety and the fear were terrible.

'I didn't know what to say – I knew nothing about war
and all I could tell him to do was look on the bright side,
that there were better days in store. He was quite
convinced that he was going to be killed so that I spent all
my time comforting him. The breach became too bad by
the time he had to go. He wouldn't have felt it nearly so
much if he'd gone before he met me, but I think meeting
me made him wish that he didn't have to pay the sacrifice,
you see. I told him when he did go that I would write to
him regularly, which I did.
    'On the morning they were sailing, I went all haywire
and hysterical – I had to do something. I knew I couldn't
go down to Dover, nobody did, because they'd been
rushed, being pushed out, quickly, so I went to see a girl
friend and we danced and danced and tried to clear the
depression away. There was a street organ in the road and
it was playing the latest songs and one of them was "Baby
Doll" and it began:

> Listen, my honey love to my tale of woe
> Listen, my honey love I just love you so
> I've been looking around

Ho, ho, guess what I've found
I found a honey bee buzzing round my hat
It's been a-stinging me from the very start,
Stinging with love that is almost a pain
Come, honey, let me explain
You're my baby doll
You're my baby doll.

'And we were dancing in the road and letting ourselves
go, and having a lovely time, but then when that had
gone, the gloom came down again because the boys had
gone that day, they'd embarked for France. In time I
discovered he was fighting at Ypres and you could hear
them, you could hear the guns firing, and if you were out
in the dark you could see the flashes over in France, of the
actual war going on, and he was there.'

The pain of departure could be masked by frivolity, but as the
war dragged on there was no getting away from the reality that
no one was sure of coming home. Leaving could become so
intense that even children could become indelibly marked by the
occasion, remembering every moment. Ten-year-old Lucy Walter
(née Neale) never forgot a detail of her father's departure.

'In the evening, my father called me in and said he'd got
to go back to Kidderminster, back to barracks. "Will you
walk with me a little way, just up the hill, will you come
with me?" Of course I would. He said goodbye to my
mother, who was crying, and we went off down the road
and then up this long hill. It was a ten-minute walk, I
suppose, but we didn't hurry, we just walked slowly up the
hill and I really can't remember what we talked about, we
must have talked, I think. I held on to his hand so tight,
and when we got to the top, he said, "I won't take you
any further, you must go back now and I'll stand here and
watch you until you're out of sight," and he put his arms

round me and held me so close to him I remember feeling how rough that khaki uniform was, and he said, "Now I want you to promise me three things. You'll look after your mother, and I want you to go to church because I bought you that nice new prayer book and I would like to think you were going to use it and go to church, and then the last thing I want you to promise me is that you'll grow up to be a good girl."

'He picked me up against him and put his arms round me and held me tight to him and he kissed my cheeks and put me down and he said, "You must go now, wave to me at the bottom, won't you?" And I went, I left him standing there and I went down the hill and I kept looking back and waving and he was still there, just standing there. I got to the bottom and then I'd got to turn off to go to where we lived, so I stopped and waved to him and he gestured as much as to say, "Go on, you must go home now", sort of thing, ever so gently gestured, and then he waved and he was still waving when I went, and that was the last I ever saw of him.'

Lucy's father, Sergeant Harry Neale, died of dysentery with the British army in Africa.

As a married man, Ruth Armstrong's father was not called up to fight straight away but eventually the letter came.

'My father said to my mother, "I've got to go tomorrow, my group is called up," and of course she was very, very upset and us two children, oh well, the end of the world had come for us with Daddy going, and next day he went off to Salisbury and we never saw him again until the end of the war, excepting one short leave, that was all. Dad saw to all the little things, fastening the windows at night, locking the door, chopping the wood, bringing in the bucket of coal every evening, and Mum had to do all these jobs and Dad was greatly missed for that. I missed my Dad so much – I used to cry every night for him and I used to say a little prayer and ask God to send him back.'

The sense of loss was not always understood by the soldiers who went overseas, especially if they were keen to go. Vic Cole's battalion was due to embark for France in mid-1915. However, final training was still required before his unit would be ready to leave.

'We marched from Essex into Suffolk along the gritty dusty roads in blazing sunshine and at the day's end down a long hill into Ipswich town. We probably looked very romantic in our dusty khaki with sunshields on our caps and full packs upon our backs! As the band struck up the "Hundred Pipers", our regimental march, thousands of citizens who lined the sidewalks began to cheer and wave like mad, but strangely, it seemed to me then, not fully understanding, many women had tears on their cheeks.'

CHAPTER TWO

East Coast Bombardment

BRITAIN'S ISLAND STATUS WAS BOTH A HELP AND A hindrance to the nation's security on the outbreak of war: a help, because the sea provided a natural barrier to invasion and had preserved Britain's territorial integrity for close on nine hundred years, since the Norman Conquest; a hindrance, because its long, convoluted coastline was vulnerable to raids. The east coast, facing as it does continental Europe, offered an enemy the best target for an assault and the easiest means of escape homewards.

The Royal Navy had long ensured British supremacy at sea, but in recent years the Germans had built a large fleet including cruisers capable of 28 knots; with such speeds, they could cross the North Sea in one night. Leaving ports such as Wilhelmshaven on Germany's northern coast, the Kaiser's newest ships, such as the *Blücher* and the *Seydlitz*, could launch lightning attacks, aided perhaps by an autumnal fog or a long-drawn-out winter night. Even in good weather, Britain's navy, the largest in the world, lacked the capacity to defend some 600 miles of eastern coastline, when anything beyond the horizon was, without prior intelligence, all but invisible. An answer might have been to station ships in the North Sea warding off attacks by their presence, but their effective immobility would have made them vulnerable to a new form of attack, the submarine, in particular the German U-boat.

Britain's coastline was not totally unprotected. Important coastal towns such as Dover and Sheerness in Kent were defended with guns and forts, but militarily unimportant towns, such as Scarborough and Whitby in Yorkshire, were by their nature not deemed targets. Others, like Hartlepool in the North-East, well known for its shipbuilding, had minor gun emplacements, effectively pea-shooters ranged against the modern calibre of 11- and 12-inch guns mounted on the latest generation of battleships and cruisers.

For the populations of such towns, the threat of enemy attack became a genuine concern, sitting as they did in Britain's new home front line. Rumours abounded in towns such as Scarborough that an attack was possible. In a notice signed by the Mayor, C. C. Graham, and dated 10 August, an 'Official Denial of Mischievous Rumours' scotched 'alarming' thoughts as 'foolish' and 'groundless'. Sadly, the notice is not explicit, other than to say that the Spa, Floral Hall, theatres and all other amusements would continue in full swing. Certainly the Liberal MP for Scarborough, Walter Rea, is on record as telling local civilians that an attack on Scarborough by the Germans was sheer 'bogey'.

The first demonstration that the east coast was vulnerable to raids came on 3 November 1914, when eight German cruisers crossed the sea at night to bombard Yarmouth in East Anglia. Firing at a distance of nearly ten miles, for fear of encountering mines closer to shore, the ships hammered away for fifteen minutes before leaving. Their shellfire was largely ineffective, many shots falling short into the water, others ploughing into the beach. So ineffectual was the gunnery that many residents of Yarmouth and nearby Lowestoft walked down to the water's edge to see flash after flash on the horizon followed by a column of water rising from the sea. The ships themselves could be seen only with the most powerful of binoculars. The town survived practically undamaged, and the inept nature of the raid undermined any resolve to undertake further defensive precautions in Yarmouth or elsewhere. The Germans had been unwilling to venture close to the coast and had turned tail and fled after just a few minutes. The authorities felt it would be inadvisable to attach too much significance to the attack or to offer civilians advice as to what to do in a future raid, for fear of scaremongering. There was, apparently, little to fear.

Five weeks later, at 7.30 on the morning of 16 December 1914, fourteen-year-old William Roberts arrived for work in the printing department of the *Northern Daily Mail* in Hartlepool. This was William's first job after leaving school the previous August. Being an apprentice, he arrived earlier than most of the staff in order to get the room ready.

> 'I had a little slow combustion stove for warmth and I
> used to sit in a small room in the back with an old
> gentleman, who was a cripple, and we used to read copy
> due to appear in the newspaper that day. I was in the toilet
> washing my hands when one of the line of typists came
> in, a chap called Fraser Engels. He started washing his
> hands next to me. This would be about three minutes to
> eight when, suddenly, I heard a deep zoom followed by a
> boom, boom in the distance. Fraser jumped up on the
> toilets and peeped through a small window and looked
> seawards over Lynn Street, where he could clearly see
> three German ships pounding away at the shore. He
> quickly turned to me and told me what he could see and
> said, "Scatter, young 'un," and without another word I ran
> out of the toilet into the main typing room, grabbing my
> overcoat as I went, before running down the steps and out
> of the building.'

A couple of miles away, six-year-old Emma Cussons was still fast asleep in bed when the first shells landed close to her home.

> 'My mam was doing the washing when she heard what
> she thought was someone beating a carpet. She went to
> the door with my baby sister and met a lady who lived
> opposite, who had come out into the street looking for
> her sister. She cried to my mam, "Oh my God, the

Germans are here." My mam told the lady, "My three bairns are still in bed." Well, this lady said, "Go into my house and see to my mother, and I'll get your children up." My mam went to see her but the old lady was ill and was apparently going berserk with the shelling. Mam told me later there was nothing she could do for her. Every minute seemed like an hour for mam, as she left the house to cross the road home again, but when she got to the front door she saw a flash. It was a shell exploding, shrapnel hitting her just below the knee and in the shoulder, my mam said it seemed as though her arm just rolled up into a ball.

'I had heard what I thought was thunder, after which this neighbour came into my bedroom to get us all out of bed. We were half asleep, but I remember this lady saying, "Come on, come on, you've got to come downstairs with me." We were literally dragged out of bed, no slippers or anything. I was very confused, I mean, a six-year-old, you can't think what it's all about. We were coming downstairs when I heard a terrible bang, well, that was the shell that got my mam. She was sat downstairs when I saw her. I remember that she wanted a drink and tried to lift the kettle but her arm just flopped and then she looked down at a pool of blood on the floor. She was losing so much blood; I could see it trickling down her face. Mam must have felt herself getting faint because she said, "I can't stay in here or I'll bleed to death. Come on." '

The attack on Hartlepool coincided with attacks on Scarborough and, an hour later, Whitby. There were eight enemy ships, which had split up as they neared the English coast, apparently without fear of encountering any mines. The German bombardment caused devastation, particularly in Hartlepool, where the assault lasted considerably longer than at the other two towns combined. The decision to attack was possibly in retaliation for the destruction of the German Pacific fleet near the Falklands on 8 December, when the British navy had chased and sunk four enemy ships that had been threatening Allied trade routes.

War had previously been good to Hartlepool, with orders for ships filling the books of builders such as Messrs William Grey & Co. and Messrs Richardson, Westgrath & Co. The books were full for the next eighteen months, providing employment for an ever increasing population. Hartlepool was in fact two towns, for Hartlepool and West Hartlepool were separate boroughs of 25,000 and 75,000 people respectively. Scarborough and Whitby were smaller, far more sedate towns, appealing to tourists who enjoyed the parkland, cliff walks and picturesque streets. Scarborough in particular had become a home for retired and wealthy people drawn to the town's evident charms and sophistication. Whitby maintained its quaint fishing-town atmosphere, while boasting the ruins of a beautiful abbey on the cliff top. Unlike Hartlepool, neither town seemed to provide any logistical targets for enemy gunners, and, also unlike Hartlepool, neither town had any defences whatsoever.

Hartlepool was defended by three ageing 6-inch guns and manned by men of the Durham Royal Garrison Artillery, a Territorial unit. Two guns were positioned in a small fort, the other sited 150 yards away near the lighthouse; all three were on what was known as the Heugh Headland. Just yards away from the headland, living in a small terrace house, was seventeen-year-old Norman Collins. He was having breakfast in his house at around 8 a.m. before leaving for work at Messrs William Grey & Co. where he was serving an apprenticeship.

'I was still eating when a terrific explosion rocked the house. We had two shore batteries sited nearby and during normal firing practice we received prior warning to open our windows to avoid the glass being shattered by the guns' blast. This was no normal firing practice, for following the inferno of noise there came a reek of high explosive. I didn't know what had happened so I rushed outside. Clouds of brick dust and smoke eddied around me before I ran towards the promenade, which was only fifty yards away. On the seafront, half left, were three huge grey German ships, blazing away, and in the dull light of a winter's morning it was like looking into a furnace. At first I didn't understand the screeching noise that passed over my head like huge pencils on slate, and then I realised they were shells. The ships were firing at the shore batteries, each of which had small 6-inch guns. I was fifty yards from the lighthouse battery. This battery had a small naval gun and I could see that it was hammering away at one ship in particular, although I could not hear it above the blast of the German guns as they belched clouds of flame and smoke. Each ship had about eight large guns, so that there were about twenty-four large shells being fired on the town at any one time.

'I stood there watching them, and, you know, it was an amazing sight to watch broadsides from battlecruisers as close as that. There would be a broadside, then they turned about and fired another broadside, and this went on for at least half an hour.'

William Roberts had left his place of work only minutes before the building took two direct hits, one on the mailroom, the other close to where William would have been.

'My one thought was to make my way home. I was running parallel to the sea and the first street that I came to I saw a scantily dressed woman sat on the pavement with her feet in the roadway, rocking to and fro, nursing a baby in her arms. I stopped for a moment as a man came along and whipped off his overcoat and put it over her, and I went on my way. Shortly after I saw another lady running about naked as if she had just got out of the bath, she was making a funny screeching sound. I ran on with my head down, inclined away from the source of the noise and shells, it was all a bit of nonsense but it was just natural to protect one's face. At one point I passed a big enamelled advertising board for Fry's Chocolates and I remember I could hear the tinkle of shrapnel as bits hit the plate.

'I lived on the outskirts of West Hartlepool, Calinso Street, so I ran along Avenue Road, and past the school where afterwards I found out a shell had dropped. As I ran I have a distinct recollection of these dark objects out at sea, but I didn't stop to look, I was too scared to know what fear was!'

The German ships were pumping shell after shell into the place, primarily around the docks and the old part of town, nearest the seashore. When the shells burst, they sent lethal lumps of red-hot shrapnel in every direction, from tiny slivers of metal right up to 40-pound chunks of steel. The two batteries were also engaged, one ship being seen to swing round before firing three shells directly at the small fort, one shell killing several men. The gunners returned fire, aiming not for the heavily armoured sides but for the gun turrets and the upper decks, at least one shell landing a direct hit. At the lighthouse battery two gunners and two infantrymen were killed; seven men were wounded.

Norman Collins was standing at the base of the breakwater where it joined the promenade.

'I wondered if the Germans were going to land, so I turned away and retraced my steps to my home in Rowell Street and turned left towards the Baptist chapel. A great hole appeared in its stone façade as I approached it, yet I had no feeling of panic whatsoever. Just as I turned the corner into Lumley Street, I saw the body of Sammy Woods, aged nineteen, a school and Sunday school friend of mine; he was lying half in and half out of his doorway, dead of course. He had been caught by a shell that had fallen to my left, into the rectory that belonged to St Hilda's Church. A shell had burst just as he stepped out and a second before I turned the corner.

'I continued walking. I looked at St Hilda's. Shells were dropping close but I didn't see any hit, so I kept on going. I walked down towards the docks and I saw the town gasometer receive a hit and, of course, with the gas escaping, it went down and collapsed. The shells were dropping too along the dockside, among the pit props on the quayside. These props were all going up in the air just like boxes of matches, only of course they weighed over a hundredweight each.'

Little Millicent Gilfoyle was just three and a half years old and lived at 51 Elliot Street, one of the many terraces directly under the shelling. Almost directly opposite lived Millicent's grandparents, the Drings, at Number 30. Her grandfather, George Dring, worked as a dock pilot and was already at work when the shelling began.

'I have the faintest recollections of him before the war, he used to put me on his knee and talk to me; I was very fond of him. Anyway this attack started and the first thing we knew about it was my aunt, who was on her way to work as a bookbinder, met a man at the top of the street who told her to get out. Everybody was told to leave the town and go into the country. I remember my aunt wrapping the Christmas cake up and then I remember walking up with my uncle and seeing places being knocked down as we went. I recall the terrible noise of the shells but I wasn't quite aware of what it was all about. Everybody was running, we made our way to the park. I remember someone wondering "where your da is", my grandfather, but of course we didn't know and then the next thing we knew he had been blown to bits at his place of work, they said he was just in pieces.'

While people ran in terror or cowered in their homes, Norman

Collins continued his walk around town as if watching the most dramatic of dramatic theatre productions, laid on especially for him. Having exhausted his view of the pit props, he walked on into the town, under the railway bridge and round to the other side of the docks to where William Grey & Co. had its marine works.

'I can't remember being frightened. I wouldn't have been human if I wasn't, but the whole thing was too much of a shock really, so out of the ordinary, and that suppresses fear. I wondered what was going on there because nobody had turned up for duty or, if they had, they'd gone. I was looking at the docks from the opposite side but there was nothing new, so I decided then I'd better go back and see what had happened to my parents. I don't know why I hadn't thought of that before. As I made my way back I saw plenty of women running around, screaming, with babies in their arms, trying to get rid of them, to give them to somebody who could help, but there was nobody. I saw two women rush up to a soldier who was obviously trying to make his way to the garrison, and try and push a baby into his arms. Of course he couldn't take it, he was on duty in any case, so he refused.'

Emma Cussons's house had been hit during the latter stages of the assault, and the injury to her mother was very serious. After resolving that they must get help, Emma's mother led her brood out on to the street, fearful that at any moment German soldiers might appear around the corner. In great pain, she held her arm out protectively, ushering her children behind her. The firing had just ended as they advanced up the road. Emma remembers:

'We walked down the street, well, it was just a little cul-de-sac, and you could smell that smell when things have been hit like cement, powdered cement. I can remember it was so quiet, not a sound of any kind, everything was dead quiet. I could see that one house was completely demolished, a man and woman were killed in there and there was dust and smoke everywhere. Everybody had gone; they'd left the houses, leaving all the doors wide open as they went. Mam told us to keep behind her, and she looked around to see if there were any Germans. We followed her to my aunt's house where Mam told me, "Get all the drawers open, and get some shawls out to cover you up," because we kids were still in our night things. We wrapped the shawls around us and went outside again just in time for Mam to see a man go back into a house, so we followed him in to get help.

'I think there was a young lad there who was in bed getting over pneumonia. Anyway, he was turfed out of bed and my mother was put in, and the bed was pushed nearer the fire.

'We were there for some while because there was more or less a crowd outside the house; I guess they'd heard what had happened. I knew Mam had been hurt, but we were being fussed over, so I don't think I realised the danger we had all been in. At one point I had to push my way through to get to her, and people were saying, "Hey, hey," as if to say don't push, and I said, "It's my mam!"

'We kids were put in front of the fire with her, because it was bitterly cold and we were freezing, being in our bare feet. We crowded round Mam and began crying because she had lost an awful lot of blood and had bits of shrapnel all over her body. We were also covered in her blood, because I remember these people looking at us to see if we'd been hurt. A long time afterwards, Mam told me that as she lay there, she kept going into a faint, and each one was a bit longer than the last, and that was when she was given brandy and hot tea. She said she could feel the glow going right through her body, and Mam said that saved her life.

'There were no ambulances around, so a man who used

to sell fish door to door brought his cart round to take my mother to hospital. She was just wrapped in blankets and taken away, and we were taken to my grandmother's until my dad managed to get home from work.'

The mass exodus from town had begun straight after the shelling began, people carrying anything of value in bags, some precious possessions tucked underneath their arms. Not everything was a family heirloom. Norman Collins recalled seeing 'one realist' carrying a mattress on his head as he staggered up Hart Lane, presumably for protection against flying shrapnel. In the absence of official information on what to do, the decision simply to leave was the most common response.

Young Cora Tucker lived on the other side of town, in West Hartlepool, and was away from the worst shelling. Her back garden afforded her family a clear sight of the thousands of people now making their way in the country, and out of harm's way.

'My mother was ill in bed when we heard the bangs in the distance, and we thought, "Oh, it's our ships practising." We didn't realise the war had started. We were looking over the garden wall, and across the Byrne Valley and we saw all these people going up the road in droves and out into the country, taking their possessions with them, bags and parcels. We didn't know why it was, until it got to nearly teatime, and we were told the place had been shelled and people had been killed. Of course we were horrified, although we couldn't go anywhere, with my mother ill in bed. We lived away from the main destruction, in Colwyn Road, and right opposite us was Thirlmere Street. A lady who lived there was cooking breakfast and a piece of shrapnel came through the window into the scullery and killed her. That was fairly close to us. But the main damage was in the old town, nearer to where the shipyards and the aerodrome were. I was only ten years old and I couldn't understand why the

Germans were killing civilians, it didn't make any sense.'

Norman Collins was making his way home when the noise of the shells began to lessen at about 8.50 a.m., with only the occasional explosion and then silence.

'A proclamation was made by the mayor and delivered through the town crier. He appeared and started shouting for everyone to keep calm, letting people know that the shelling had stopped and that there was no immediate danger, and no landing had taken place. He informed us that the situation was now secure, whatever that meant! I got back to the promenade and asked someone if they had seen my father. They replied that he had last been seen pushing a wheelchair towards the open country with an invalid in it.'

The bombardment had lasted approximately fifty minutes, during which time around 1,500 shells had landed in and around the town. Many failed to explode and were salvaged later; some went into the sea, a few further inland beyond the town. Most landed in and around the docks and the gas and water works, others in the old town, wrecking dozens of the narrow streets, fewer in the residential areas of West Hartlepool where Cora Tucker lived. So indiscriminate was the shelling that it was impossible to believe that such an attack was the result of poor marksmanship, rather that it was a deliberate attempt to spread fear across the entire town.

In the aftermath of the attack, families sought out loved ones to check that they were all right and to hear their stories of survival.

William Roberts had relatives in an area called Greenland, between what was known as the Central Estate and West Hartlepool.

'My aunt Sarah, children in tow, had left her house to get away from the guns and was passing a part of the town where the tram sheds and a steel bridge were. Well, as they passed, a shell came through the bridge and exploded. One of the children, my cousin Ralph, got a piece of shrapnel in the arm and a friend was also struck in the left foot. With them was Ralph's brother Charlie. He whipped off his coat, tore his shirt off and made a tourniquet for his brother's arm, got him on his back and carried him to Cameron Hospital, in West Hartlepool, a long way. That took some doing; he was only seventeen. His action saved Ralph's life but didn't save his arm, which was partially amputated before a second operation shortened it some more, so it went completely.'

Norman Collins finally got back home where he found his mother in the kitchen stoically making strong cups of tea for anyone who wanted one.

'I thought, "Well, that's just like Mother." I went in and there she was, as calm as could be, so I began calling on relatives near at hand, and apart from a connection by marriage who had lost a limb in Victoria Place, we had suffered no serious injuries. Later that morning I went and collected pieces of shell. There was debris every-where. Shell fragments, some weighing several pounds, were being collected as souvenirs and I still have several which came through the roof of our house. They bristle with jagged edges and the mortar is still lodged in the steel. Elsewhere I found a dead donkey that had been grazing in the Friarage Field, the home ground of the Hartlepool Rovers Rugby Football Club, and I have the piece of shell that killed it.'

Emma Cussons's mother had been taken to hospital where she remained for about six months, recovering from multiple injuries including one to her leg, which at one time doctors thought they might have to amputate.

'Even when she came home, she still had a bad scab on her head, but the doctor did not seem worried about it and told her it would drop off. Well, it did drop off, but it would fester again and that went on for nine months. She went to my granny's and my gran said, "Don't you think it should be better by now? Do you think there is anything in it?" Mam didn't think so but my gran said she'd put a bread poultice on. This was made by laying strips of bread in linen after which boiling water was poured into the bread and then the linen twisted and slapped on to the wound. It was very painful but it worked. She put the poultice on my mother's head and when she took it off, she looked, and there was a piece of shell. It was the size of a sixpence and it was as shiny as anything.

'There was an awful lot of damage to our street and our house. My mother had a picture and there was a piece of shell embedded in it, and there was a chest of drawers, a bookshelf, and a chair and pieces of shell had gone through them all. The explosion had taken out all the windows, and the chimneys were down, and there were bits of shrapnel in the walls. One piece of glass in the bookcase had a hole through it but the glass hadn't shattered. Dad didn't want to have it mended, you know, to keep it as a souvenir, but Mam said no. She received eight pounds' compensation for the trauma and the damage they'd gone through.

'The effect of the bombardment was terrible on the town. There was one woman in particular who lived close to us, and she had lost three of her children, and lost a leg herself, it was blown off. Her name was Dixon, and I saw her after the war walking around on crutches with her one leg. She had another three children after, and she named them all the same as the three she had lost.'

Cora Tucker was one of many who visited the old part of town to see the damage. 'On the Sunday my father took me over to see all the houses and the destruction was terrific. One old man did very well. He sat in front of his open fire with all the walls down and he made quite a lot out of people. He just sat there telling what had happened, and they gave him shilling after shilling.'

The decision not to issue public instructions as to what to do in a raid had proved costly. People did not know whether to leave home or take shelter inside. Many fled to the railway station, a potential target, and had to be ushered away by policemen who knew that one direct hit could kill dozens. Those who sought help were directed out of the town, leaving by roads that took them past the home of Cora Tucker. Many people had been buried in their homes, unwilling to go or incapable of leaving. Two sisters were killed just behind the lighthouse battery, one having been blown literally to pieces. Others, such as Norman Collins's friend Sammy Woods, were killed as they stepped outside their homes; some as they ran through the narrow streets, killed by the blast of shells exploding in confined spaces. Of those who were found injured, more than twenty were to die later in hospital as doctors fought to operate on the critically ill. Wounds varied greatly in severity and included those not caused directly by flying steel but by splintered wood or lumps of stone smashed by the explosions. The hospital was soon surrounded by worried relatives, demanding to know if loved ones had survived, a few being directed to the mortuary instead.

One girl had a miraculous escape. Having been certified dead, she was taken to the mortuary slab where she lay under a sheet. Later that day her family came to see her body, whereupon her brother saw his sister's finger twitch under the sheet. She was rescued and despite serious head injuries survived. Owing to the severity of her wounds she had to wear a soft hat all her life. She is still alive today.

In all, nine soldiers, ninety-seven civilian men and women and thirty-seven children were killed; a further 466 were wounded. The youngest to die was a six-month-old baby, the oldest an eighty-six-year-old lady. Twenty-four of the victims were aged ten years or younger.

The clear-up began almost straight away, with glaziers repairing windows within an hour of the attack ending. A proclamation was issued, asking people to stay in their homes as far as possible while unexploded shells were cleared, and a 7 p.m. curfew was enforced. Committees were formed for the care of the distressed and wounded, while a civilian force was organised to work with the special police to clear debris. As many as 600 dwellings were destroyed or damaged, leaving many families homeless. Temporary accommodation was made available, although others decided to leave the town and stay with relatives, inland.

William Roberts's father had already joined the army and was in training 250 miles away in Reading. As a result, William's mother took the decision to leave and move in with relatives in Birmingham, and by teatime on the day of the attack trunks had already been packed, the house locked and the family gone. Emma Cussons's father had come home from work in a frantic state, not knowing what had happened to his family. On discovering his wife was in hospital, he quickly bundled up some clothes and sent the children into relative safety, Emma and her sister staying with relations in Middlesbrough while his house was repaired.

Most people decided to stay in the belief that the worst was over. However, that Friday, panic set in when reports were received that the Germans had returned. Cora Tucker recalls the ensuing chaos.

'We were on our way to school when we were stopped. "Go back again, the Germans are coming." Who put that about I don't know, but it was a false alarm, but I didn't know that then. I had some little pet bantam hens, I was so scared, I said to my father, "If we go away and I leave my pet bantams, the Germans will come and eat them." I was so upset. During the scare, my aunt decided she would come round to our house. She had her baby in one hand and the Christmas cake in the other. She met a woman on the way over, and she was carrying candles in one hand and her Christmas cake in the other, and they looked at one another and laughed. The women had all made their lovely Christmas cakes and were saving them from the Germans, if nothing else.'

It was a moment of light relief in what had been a serious incident. A report had been placed in the Post Office that a message had been received 'to look out for hostile airship. Warn all constables to warn all residents . . . Rumours may be false, but everyone to be prepared.' Inevitably, with nerves already taut, the rumours quickly escalated into certainties, and people ran from their homes to escape from a now anticipated invasion. The effect of such a warning was a last straw for many families, who fled the town, some not returning for the rest of the war.

For unknown reasons, the authorities tried to minimise the death toll, but in a tight-knit community it was soon apparent that the acknowledged toll of twenty-two dead and fifty injured was woefully low. The same attitude, which had withheld information in case of a raid, appeared to reassert itself briefly, although it was soon realised that the public was more alarmed by not knowing what to do in a raid than by being given advice that might cause mild consternation.

The decision to tone down the information had been driven by two desires: first, to minimise the fear factor among civilian populations living on the east coast of Britain and, second, to divert criticism away from the navy which was conspicuous by its absence during each bombardment. The layman wanted to know how the Germans were able to launch such an audacious raid and escape apparently unchallenged, a question never properly confronted by the Admiralty, which preferred to state that such attacks could not divert 'general naval policy'. In fact the navy had had prior knowledge that an attack was imminent on the east coast, having broken German codes months earlier. The Admiralty had preferred to set a trap in order to have a decisive battle out at sea; however, poor weather and ill luck after the raid conspired to let the raiders go. Nothing was known of this secret intelligence for many years afterwards.

News of the attack would later be used as something of a propaganda coup for the government, eager to seize on examples of German 'atrociousness'. In the immediate aftermath of the attack, such news was slow to leak out and was haphazardly reported. In Essex, news of the bombardment reached the village of Great Leighs by four in the afternoon. Yet, when Cora Tucker's family visited relatives in Cardiff, they were amazed at how local people lived their lives utterly oblivious to the effects of war being felt by those living within range of enemy bombs. 'They didn't know there was a war on. They couldn't believe we had been bombarded, to which my mother got very annoyed particularly when someone asked us if it really happened or did we just imagine it.' Such ignorance was common at first. When Norman Collins joined the army in June 1915 he found that most of the recruits had never heard of the attack and were very interested to see some photographs he held.

The raids on Scarborough and Whitby, being less prolonged than that on Hartlepool, had created less destruction, with a combined toll of some twenty-one killed and around a hundred wounded. In Scarborough, where rumours of a possible raid had been dismissed, there was considerable damage to the town's more prominent buildings, including the castle, the lighthouse and the Grand Hotel. One private residence of particular note that received a direct hit was, ironically, the home of the Liberal MP, Walter Rea. The front of his house now bore a gaping hole where a shell had smashed through his living-room window. His assertion that any idea of a raid was pure 'bogey' was recalled by at least one correspondent, who wryly noted the MP's scepticism on the rear of a picture showing the damage wrought.

Yet there was scant cause for any amusement at what had happened. The anger felt by many people led to an immediate upsurge in enlistment in those areas directly affected. Further afield, the news that so many civilians had been killed or wounded brought others into the army's fold, including one twenty-year-old man from as far away as Torquay in Devon. His given reason for enlisting was the attack hundreds of miles away, and the realisation that if such an attack could happen there, it could just as well happen in his own coastal town. But the greatest bitterness and anger was felt in the North-East, as Cora Tucker remembers.

'It was a terrible thing to do, we were angry, not afraid, more angry. Why had little children been killed going to school? Why had babies been killed? Why had that lady in Thirlmere Street, so close to my own home, been killed? The poor soul was only cooking her breakfast. I think that put a hatred of the Germans into us.'

CHAPTER THREE

The Enemy Within

O N CHRISTMAS DAY 1914, ARCHIE STANLEY, A private in the East Kent Regiment, advanced with his comrades into No Man's Land to meet German soldiers in temporary friendship. It was a fleeting few hours' respite from a war that had already inflicted tens of thousands of casualties on both sides. The informal truce has become a classic moment in history, fêted as a unique occasion in military records.

'We met the Germans in mid No Man's Land,' recalled Archie, 'and they offered us cigars and we traded bully beef. A little while later I heard somebody talking English so I looked around and I said, "Do you speak English?" And this man said, "Cor blimey, mate, I was in a London hotel when the war broke out." '

At about the same time, a little further along the line, Frank Sumpter, a nineteen-year-old private in the Rifle Brigade, was busily striking up a conversation with another German who spoke perfect English. Surprised by the man's accent, Frank quickly discovered that not only did they come from the same part of London, but that the German had worked in a shop familiar to Frank and that they both knew a local pub, The Jolly Farmer. 'So I asked him, "Do you know the hairdresser's just near there?" Not only did this German know it but he had his hair cut there. "Well, it's my uncle that cuts your hair!" '

On the outbreak of war, there were around 53,000 Germans living in Britain, with many more born of German parents but who classed themselves as thoroughly British, living, in almost every way, wholly British lives with the exception of their

German names. Surprisingly, Germans amounted to the third largest immigrant group in Britain, behind the Irish and the Jews. They were well-known and often well-respected members of the local community: they were pork butchers, waiters, barbers, hoteliers, governesses and teachers, and were resident in almost every part of the country, although most were found in London, the Midlands and the North-East.

Many of Britain's leading lights in the political and literary world had German blood and, of course, there was the King himself, the grandson of a German who had married the Queen of England. The royal family had the most German of German surnames, Saxe-Coburg-Gotha, a misfortune when it came to war, although they were never to suffer any of the indignities or cruelties heaped upon so many British subjects with German ancestry in the First World War.

By the end of the war, there were only 22,000 Germans left. Tens of thousands had been rounded up into internment camps, many being deported at the end of the war irrespective of their ties in Britain. Even those married to English-born women, who had given birth to thoroughly English children, were sent packing. It was, and remains, an ugly chapter in British history, akin to the treatment of the Japanese Americans in the United States during the Second World War. It was far worse than anything meted out in the second war in Britain. Then, a more rational and understanding approach was taken to those of German heritage or birth, to the extent that German Jews were offered a chance to leave internment to serve in the British army, while one German, who had served the Kaiser in the first war, received a commission in the British army because of his proclaimed opposition to the Nazis. Other immigrants of German origin, though in apparent danger of internment, were eventually required to hand over nothing more than their cameras in fair exchange for preserving their liberty.

So why was the First World War such an exception? The answer lies in a confluence of influences and attitudes peculiar to an island race, which before the war was largely ignorant of other races and cultures. Britain might rule a third of the globe, but the vast majority of Britons had never set foot, nor were ever likely to set foot, in another country. Part of the incentive to enlist for so many young boys in 1914 was their idea of going abroad, visiting other nations, almost as if the war was the ultimate back-packers' jaunt. For a huge majority, the army offered the only opportunity to see the world; otherwise, it was a life spent at home, with bank holidays by the sea. It is still quite possible to meet older Britons who have never crossed the water.

Before 1914, Britain had difficulty in adjusting to the idea that being the world's supreme power was not a God-given right. Under apparent threat from a strident Germany asserting its demand for a place in the sun, the British people became increasingly concerned about the new continental upstart threatening Britain's pre-eminence. Stories were rife about the threats posed by Germany, threats that were real enough but often exaggerated to ridiculous lengths. Every German aspiration was viewed with suspicion; every move had to have an ulterior motive. The knowledge that war would come was widespread: as seen in Chapter One, it was not a question of if, but when.

Thousands of Germans had settled in Britain in the nineteenth century and for the most part had become individually liked and respected. In every town, Germans had got on and done well, contributing to local society, culture and commerce. It was only collectively that they were feared. One family that had built up a well-respected business was the Hohenreins in Hull. George Hohenrein had come to England by choice in 1848, and had begun work as a pork butcher, quickly building a business that stocked the very best produce from Germany and Britain. When he died, he left a considerable fortune that passed to his two sons, George and Charles. While they had been born to German parents, they had lived all their lives in Britain. Fortunate enough to be bilingual, they often visited Germany to see family and friends as well as to further the business interests of the company.

The elder son, George, eventually and very reluctantly, moved to Germany with his family, while Charles took over the company and married a local girl, Lillian Westwood, in 1911. Both sons considered themselves nothing other than British, taking an active part in the local community and both, at one time or other, serving in the East Riding of Yorkshire Imperial Yeomanry. So British were they that, when the war broke out, George was interned in Germany, while Charles immediately offered his fleet of vans for the British war effort, an act for which he was commended for his 'most patriotic gesture'. Charles soon volunteered for military service but was exempted until 1917, when he was rejected on medical grounds. In every respect he had, in modern parlance, passed the cricket test. Such assimilation would not guarantee his immunity.

Another German family living in England was the Druhms of north London. Elfie Druhm, now ninety-two, was the only daughter of a German who had come to Britain when he was just seventeen. He had arrived in London straight after leaving school and had subsequently fallen in love with the country. Elfie recalls:

'He had arrived at the turn of the century and had set up a hairdressing salon, which had done extremely well. He had never gone back to Germany, because he liked it here. Then he met my mother and they were married; both my parents worked in the ladies' hairdressing shop. I know that my grandmother didn't approve of the match. She, as well as my aunts, strongly frowned upon the engagement, and in revenge they didn't go to the wedding. Well, there wasn't a wedding really, it all had to be hush-hush because nobody wanted her to marry a German.'

Such widespread disapproval was to have serious long-term ramifications for the family when war broke out.

Anti-German attitudes had been driven largely by the newspapers of the day, aided implicitly by burgeoning public literacy, which towards the end of the nineteenth century had given the press a new, exalted role in British public life. Millions of people could now digest daily events, sent by telegraph to the offices of national and regional newspapers and then consigned to print in hours rather than days or weeks. News could be disseminated by the press to a ready audience, willing to believe that the written word was always true. With the national newspapers controlled by three principal barons, Northcliffe, Rothermere and Beaverbrook, such men had enormous power to influence the debate on any issue that came to hand. With effectively no source for contrary views, the power vested in the newspapers to mould public opinion was overwhelming. The *Daily Mail's* circulation rose by 15 per cent in the first days of the war to over 1.1 million, a figure that remained steady for the following two years, while the less influential *Daily Express* saw its sales rise 30 per cent in a year to 370,000. Public cynicism would slowly come, but much later in the war. In the meantime, the press went to work reporting war news, rarely letting the facts get in the way of a good story.

Newspapers were essential to the government's policy. Propaganda might be heavy-handed or sophisticated but it was essential because Britain had no large standing army and men would be needed for the front. One of the most notorious was hardly a newspaper at all. *John Bull* was owned by Horatio Bottomley, a bombastic former Liberal MP, whose colourful past included two bankruptcies, neither of which appeared to hinder his progress in life. His rabble-rousing paper, which regularly sold between 1 and 2 million copies an issue, warned the public against the enemy within, namely the 'Hun'. Never short of a cause, his paper campaigned against men such as Sir Edgar Speyer and Sir Ernest Cassel, both members of the Privy Council, and both saddled with German names. Such public figures would always be deemed dangerous to the state, although Bottomley was at least egalitarian in his regular call for 'a vendetta against every German in Britain'. In this aim he was supported by organisations railing against Germans in Britain, such as the transparently named Anti-German Union, which was driven by the well-connected Scotsman, Sir George Makgill. Sir George and the Union were vociferous in their distaste for anything German, calling on every patriotic Briton to join in a campaign that was simple in its aims and rhetoric: 'NO German Goods, NO German Labour, NO German Influence', adding, just for good measure, 'Britain for the British'.

Such frankness was popular among large sections of the population preoccupied by uncertainty and fear. Horatio Bottomley was the most articulate of the 'plain-speakers' and the public loved his simplicity and bluntness. 'If by chance you should discover one day in a restaurant that you are being served by a German waiter, you will throw the soup on his foul face,' he unashamedly directed. Bottomley's ability to affect public attitudes to the Germans and to the war had a significant effect on recruitment, regularly pulling crowds of thousands to hear him speak at venues such as Trafalgar Square. Indeed, at his first recruitment rally in September 1914, he was unabashed when he told the audience, 'I'm going to be the unofficial recruiting agent for the British Empire,' and indeed he was directly responsible for the enlistment of many thousands into the army.

Owing to a well-cultivated notoriety, Bottomley's profile loomed large in the public's consciousness during the war. If it wasn't the man himself, it was his newspaper and the image of John Bull, the pot-bellied, Union Jack-waistcoated character, appealing for recruits. His was one poster among many that were published either to demonise the Germans or to aid recruitment, or preferably both. It was artful and it was art, the government employing several leading illustrators and writers to design some 110 different posters that were published in the first twelve months of war, with 2.5 million copies being distributed to every corner of the country.

War propaganda was vociferous, and helped fundamentally to influence the public's attitude to Germans living in Britain. As Liverpudlian Sydney Bond recalls:

'The fact was that every national paper, and every provincial paper, had really two centre pages entirely devoted to propaganda belittling the German and his behaviour in the war. This had an enormous effect on us all. These broadsheets began to contain deliberate propaganda, blackening the German and his attitude, brought on by the sinking of ships and the attacks on the east coast. These broadsheets had lurid details, and they hurriedly got every artist they could to draw a vivid picture. And then they sank the *Lusitania*, and that caused such a stink that it was then all full-blast propaganda, to turn the German into an absolute swine.'

These papers had talked freely about the mendacity of the Germans in the days leading up to the war, but still *The Times* honourably placed front-page advertisements from the German and Austrian Embassies calling for all nationals eligible for service to return home immediately. A day later, on 5 August, the first full day of war, the government introduced the Aliens Registration Act, emergency legislation preventing all those of enemy nationality from travelling without a permit and requiring them to register at local police stations. The clampdown had begun, although not before several hundred young Germans and Austrians had left the country to join up, two of whom were later to meet Archie Stanley and Frank Sumpter in No Man's Land.

The advance by the German army through Belgium and France was devastating. The British Expeditionary Force started to land in France barely ten days after the declaration of war, and had begun to advance, ready to engage an enemy whose size and strength could only be speculated on. After the opening shots were fired at Mons, there began a famous retreat, with the British army, on the left flank of the French, being driven almost to the gates of Paris. This was not war as it had been predicted, and the press, starved of information, resorted to publishing lurid stories of German atrocities. The kernel of many was true. Germany had sacked various towns; they had burnt the famous library at Louvain. Civilians had been used as human shields, and some had been summarily executed, such as in the Belgian town of Dinant. Yet half-truths were outweighed

---

by wholesale fabrications, in which the Hun was characterised as a wicked, maniacal beast capable of bayoneting babies onto church doors, cutting off the breasts or hands of young girls, and the wholesale ransacking of homes.

Atrocities by Germans against civilians were inevitable in war-time, when huge numbers of mainly conscript soldiers were engaged on foreign soil. The public believed that British soldiers were unlikely to commit such acts of barbarity and to an extent this was true, for the British army was a highly trained professional army, and it was fighting on Allied soil.

War atrocities were a recurring theme throughout the conflict and indeed, at its conclusion, over 3,000 Germans were cited for war crimes. Detailed dossiers were kept and reports made from 'reliable' sources. Books such as J. H. Morgan's *German Atrocities: An Official Investigation* were popular, in this case being reprinted eight times between March and June 1916. Belgian refugees, who had escaped to England, were full of tales, as were returning soldiers wounded at the front. Children had been found by the roadside decapitated, noted an Essex clergyman, the Reverend Andrew Clark, in his diary, adding it had been ascertained that 'at a convent at Bocking there really *is* a young Belgian girl with both hands hacked off'. The italics, while stressing the report's 'validity', also underlined the fact that the public had, up to that point, not actually found a victim with such injuries, though the story was often repeated.

Similarly, after meeting a wounded British soldier who had returned from the front, the Reverend Clark wrote that the man had 'met the parents of two teenage girls who had had their breasts hacked off and bled to death'. The same man then went on to show the vicar some bullets. 'The British bullet, which is clean and makes a merciful wound . . . and the German bullet, which has a disc at the back end. When the point penetrates a body the disc causes the bullet to expand, so causing a terrible wound in the flesh.' Such first-hand histories from wounded Tommies were unlikely to be challenged – rather they were taken as gospel, coming as they did from the mouths of heroes.

Not all British subjects needed evidence before launching attacks on German homes and shops. In Hull, attacks began straight away, as the local newspaper recorded. Two men, Victor Parker and Joseph Connell, had broken a plate-glass window in the Hohenreins' shop the day after war was declared. The men were tried at Hull Police Court and, although found guilty, their actions were noted by the judge as being no doubt due to over-excitement and over-eager patriotism. On hearing that the men were on the way to enlist when the incident happened, the judge added that he did not wish to stand in the way of two young men wishing to join up, and imposed a fine. The press reported the incident as 'a regrettable instance of rowdyism in Hull'. It was not quite open season on Germans in Hull, but things were about to change.

In London, Elfie Druhm's parents had become a target for a mob assault on their salon at 72 Haverstock Hill. The incident, which happened before a shot had been fired on the Western Front, was terrifying for the family.

'The anti-German feeling before the first war was terrific. The government and the press stirred up the hatred. Our shop was smashed within a couple of weeks of the war breaking out and we had to leave because there was so much hostility there. I was there but I can't say I remember it happening as a proper memory as I was in bed, but I do know that we cleared out of that house very suddenly. Father was taken away, and Mother left at the same time. We had nowhere to go and we had to find furnished rooms very quickly. Mother never said much about that night as it was a very painful part of her life. She had to leave everything behind and there was one relative who tried to help, a husband of my aunt, and he helped dispose of certain things, the furniture and the lease on the shop. He sold the furniture but she got very little for that, Mother had very little. My grandmother lived nearby as did one aunt, but they did little to help, which caused a lot of bad feeling for years.'

Elfie's father was interned in a large building in Holloway, where he was to spend the next four years. A relative, who was visiting the family at the time, was also taken away. At first, internees were collected and housed in temporary accommodation. The exhibition hall at Olympia was used, as was Alexandra Palace which held 3,000 'enemy' subjects. Most were moved on eventually to the Isle of Man and a camp at Knockaloe which held 30,000 people in all, doubling the local population of the island. Elfie's visiting cousin was one of those to go and he never returned, dying there of tuberculosis. Elfie's father was lucky: being a married man, he was held at Holloway, enabling his family to visit.

Without her husband, Elfie's mother eventually took a room in the West End of London.

'My mother tried to find work telling the truth, saying who she was, why she was looking for a job and where her husband was. Nobody would help because she was married to a German, even though she was totally English and had only once stepped out of the country. So she changed her name to Miss Norris, her maiden name, and as soon as she went as Miss Norris she was employed at a salon in Oxford Street. The owner was a Swiss man. He liked the Germans, and in fact he got to know our secret. My mother wanted to know what she could do with me during the day while she worked and this man advised her to put me in the convent. I was aged four, and he said the Sisters would have me, so my mother tried and yes, they were proper nuns and they took me at once into their school.

'Mother didn't get away from her place of work until six, by which time all the other children were picked up; I was always the last one. And she used to say to me, "If we meet anyone in the street don't call me Mummy," because she was meant to be Miss Norris and not have any children. "And don't ever tell anybody where your daddy is." I obeyed, I wasn't to know who I could speak to and who not, and I was really very secretive about it, and to grow up with the secret of your whole life at that age is quite something for a child psychologically, it's difficult to grow up like that. As a little girl, I lived a lie, I always had something to hide.'

'German phobia' quickly became a national obsession. 'A German barber in Church Road on Sunday was reported to have said that if an Englishman came into his shop to be shaved he would cut his throat,' reported one north London newspaper. No one seemed to ponder why a barber might wish to kill his paying clients, thereby cutting his own proverbial throat. 'Soon afterwards,' noted the paper, 'he had to put up with a bombardment of his house by neighbours, and it was considerably damaged, especially the glass, while he was assaulted. The shop is now closed.'

All Germans in Britain were enemy agents of one type or another: German watch-makers were closet constructors of bombs; German waiters poisoned food. In this atmosphere, it is little wonder that by October 1914, all German waiters in London had been sacked from their jobs, inherently detrimental, as they inevitably became, to trade. Increasing numbers of attacks across the country, from Tunbridge Wells to Liverpool, from Crewe to north London, ensured that more Germans were interned, as much for their own protection as for national security.

Not every German was systematically attacked. In Sussex, near the town of Lewes, a German doctor by the name of Steinhauser continued to work freely with no apparent animosity, practising and visiting patients at times when, nationally, anti-German feeling had reached boiling point. Similarly, in south London, one old German lady who, with her husband, ran a well-known bakery, was protected by the community. The baker's wife was known to have given long lines of credit and even free bread to many of the poorest in the neighbourhood. Now she was supported herself by a group of women who vowed to protect the old lady from internment.

In fact only around a fifth of all Germans were interned in the first two months of the war, for accommodation was in short supply and all available space was required for Kitchener's new recruits. The Alien Restrictions Act of early August had required all foreigners to register where they lived with the police and, indeed, around 93 per cent of Germans living in Britain had done so within a month. There were stiff punishments for those who transgressed, even if they were not from an enemy country. The *Hull Daily Mail* recorded how one foreigner, a Dane, was given two months in prison for failing to notify the police of his change of address. The man, a sailor, had been away at sea, and returned to find that his landlady, who had moved, had not also registered her tenant's change at the same time.

After the initial round-up, the government felt that most Germans could continue to stay at home and would only be arrested and interned if they were felt to pose a threat. Many German civilians, even young men, were allowed to apply for permits either to return home or, if they were of military age, to leave for a third, neutral country. In January 1915, the writer Edward Heron-Allen noted that it was still possible to leave Britain for Germany with 'comparative ease'. He accompanied his children's German governess to the permit office in London, where he procured for her a permit to leave for home 'without any difficulty'. While there he saw a corridor 'lined with careworn Germans trying to get their papers', including one young German, a former manager of the Criterion restaurant, who was attempting to leave for America.

Those German subjects whose children were born in Britain and had chosen to serve in the British army were also likely to escape imprisonment. Thousands of British men with German ancestry served in the army. A quick check at the Public Record Office shows that 132 men under the name of Muller served in the army, 94 under Schneider and 33 under Kohler. For some, the name was the only link to another country, while others were first-generation children of German immigrants, and were more likely to be those with German Christian names, such as

Fritz Muller and Ludwig Schneider. Their families and others who were naturalised British were generally left alone by the state to continue their lives, even if they did not necessarily escape a brick through their window or paint daubed on their walls.

How far any of these people were ever watched by British Intelligence is unclear, although as Heron-Allen left the permit office he was followed and stopped. Heron-Allen had incurred suspicion by talking with some of the Germans waiting in the corridor. '[A British agent] asked me all about myself, and I found that I could not get out of the building until he had been back to the head of the department and verified my account.'

There were certainly a number of German spies in Britain, many of whom were known to British Intelligence. On the outbreak of war, twenty-two were arrested immediately and imprisoned, followed quickly by a further fourteen. One of those caught early included a forty-three-year-old man, Karl Ernst, a British-born subject of German parents. Since 1899 he had owned a barber's shop at 405A Caledonian Road, London, which had for many years been an effective 'letter box' for German spies in Britain. In effect, spies left their reports at the shop knowing that they would be forwarded to Germany. Ernst was caught, tried and found guilty, and was remarkably lucky to be sentenced to just seven years in prison. Others were less fortunate, a total of eleven spies were shot in the Tower of London during the war.

Those who were arrested were generally not those reported for police investigation by the over-anxious, over-zealous public. Spy-hunting, or 'spymania' as some called it, was a national sport, picking on foreigners – they did not have to be German – who were overwhelmingly law-abiding citizens. As the Home Secretary admitted to Parliament in September 1914, of the first 9,000 'spy cases' that had been investigated by the Metropolitan Police in the first weeks of the war, not one had been proven. In one classic incident, a special policeman was required to stand and watch a house from which signalling had been reported. It was later discovered that a member of the family had merely switched a light on, before pulling down a blind. On his leaving the room the light had been extinguished, whereupon the blind had suddenly rolled back up again. The room light was switched on once more and the blind immediately pulled down. Those two brief blazes of light emanating from the house had been enough to start an investigation outside.

Despite the many false accusations, the desire to catch an enemy spy remained undiminished. Anybody with a foreign name, however un-German it sounded (and occasionally even those that were French), was a potential suspect. If books were not inciting the public with tales of atrocities, they speculated about spies. Books such as *German Spies in England* were snapped up by the general public, 40,000 copies being sold in one week in 1915. Maud Cox, who was eight at the time and lived in Methil, Fifeshire, recalls the general excitement.

'There was some ship detained at the mouth of the River Forth and they said it was German, and contained German spies. Everybody was always seeing German spies; somebody had seen one German family, the Fiennes, and they had been seen showing a light. So the next night, in the very early hours, all their windows were smashed. They lived in a flat above the shop and both the shop windows and the windows upstairs had all been smashed and fire crackers thrown in. By the time we got up there they had gone. Whether they ran for it or whether the police took them away we never knew, they just disappeared, but my mother said they were not spies, they had lived there all their lives.

'It was just people panicking. Mr Schiffler, the pork butcher, he was taken away and his shop was all boarded up too. I think he was interned. I was vexed about them because I liked Mrs Schiffler, she was a nice old lady but typically German, she'd lived there for years but she couldn't speak very good English. Mr Schiffler had the German band, they played oompah music – on a Saturday

night outside the railway station – and they used to sit
with Mr Schiffler with his Tyrolean hat on and play. It was
such a happy town at the time, before the war started.
Then it all changed and there was a very great
anti-German feeling, the Germans were the bogeymen
and anybody the least bit different was a spy.'

Both Austrian and German bands had been a feature of many
towns, and had been enjoyed, particularly by children amused by
their dress and music. But with war, the bands had been
reassessed. In Hartlepool, where a German band had been a
prominent feature for years, its presence was now seen as
evidence of spying. The bandsmen had marched around town
playing their music for the 'simple reason' that it gave them the
perfect cover for covert operations, reporting back precise dispo-
sitions of troops and coastal installations to their paymasters in
Germany. Rumours abounded. Weather vanes on house roofs
were being used to point the way for Zeppelins, some claimed.
Elsewhere, the British had broken the German codes and had
sailed up the east coast flashing signals to shore and had received
more than half a dozen replies, indicating spies at work all along
the east coast. How ordinary civilians came by this confidential
information was never made clear, but it was part and parcel of
popular tittle-tattle.

The Reverend Andrew Clark recorded some of the hysteria
around the village of Great Leighs in Essex. His diary entries
reach comical proportions. There are the potentially serious
reports of attempts to poison the reservoir at Chingford in Essex,
in which five people were supposedly seized, and reports of an
elderly lady with a German accent being arrested as a possible spy
while she sold lace at Little Waltham. Even when she was able to
prove her innocence, she continued to be watched. And then
there are notes of simply farcical incidents.

Miss Madge Gold says that in Little Waltham the populace
have discovered another 'German fort': Cranhams' was

owned by Herr Wagner, who is said now to be an
Austrian . . . The villagers say that at [the shop] (a) there is
a concrete floor for the emplacement of heavy guns of a
fort which would command Chelmsford and the Marconi
works there; and (b) there is a store of arms and
ammunition.

Within tight-knit communities, everyone's face was known, and
outsiders – indeed anyone who looked strange or out of place –
was viewed with suspicion either as a potential spy or an escaped
prisoner of war. Pity the poor tramp who knocked on a door
asking for food, for he ran the risk of being turned in rather than
just turned away. A stranger did not have to be unkempt to be
arrested. The Reverend Clark records the trials and tribulations
of one man working for the Ordnance Survey, who, while
attempting to revise maps, was arrested in each village he passed
through, first by soldiers of the Bedfordshire Yeomanry, then by a
local farmer, then by a sub-postmaster, and on six occasions by
special constables alerted by worried civilians. The man eventually had to ask for military protection in order to carry on his
work unmolested.

Everything associated with Germany was attacked or rejected.
Dachshunds were kicked or abused in the street, and in one or
two cases even burnt alive. German shepherd dogs were redesig-
nated Alsatians, and German measles was renamed 'Belgian flush'.
There were elaborate explanations in Boots the Chemist that eau
de Cologne had nothing to do with the city but was entirely
British, as were traditional German sausages and sauerkraut which
were suddenly anglicised. Perrier, which advertised itself as 'The
Table Water of the Allies', asked in adverts if 'You Are Drinking
German Waters?' Apollinaris water came from Germany, whereas
Perrier 'Comes from France'. German music was no longer
played, nor were many Steinway pianos, the lids of which were
shut for the duration of the war. Then people began changing
their names: Prince Louis of Battenberg resigned as First Lord of
the Admiralty and changed his name to Mountbatten, and, most

famously of all, the royal family was renamed in July 1917, losing Saxe-Coburg-Gotha and gaining Windsor.

Anyone judged to have German blood or even sympathies was both slandered and libelled, particularly those who served in the government, which, as time passed, took on a very British hue. Lord Haldane was attacked because his dog was named Kaiser, and he was believed to like Germans. In Asquith's diary, the Prime Minister noted as early as November 1914 that 'Poor old H[aldane] has been violently attacked, apropos of spies and such nonsense, by the *Morning Post*, as a thinly veiled friend of Germany'. Such claims and others of their ilk were, Asquith said, 'fanatical and malignant outcries which from time to time disgrace our national character'.

Leading the campaign to oust Haldane was the *Daily Mail*, owned by Lord Northcliffe, the paper magnate who also owned *The Times*. His high-profile attacks led to much of the anti-German hysteria and, ironically, his own rise to government office, when later in the war he was awarded the position of Director of Propaganda against enemy states. It was true that Lord Haldane had been educated in Germany, and had been instrumental in attempting to iron out Anglo–German naval rivalries two years before war, but this was proof of nothing. Yet such 'sympathies' were cause enough to have his genuine and very real achievements reinterpreted, including his much needed pre-war reform of the British army which was now seen as an attempt to weaken it. As Haldane said himself, he was in the end accused of everything under the sun, the most preposterous being that he was the illegitimate brother of the Kaiser. The attacks were too frequent and vociferous for Lord Haldane's good, and it was the end of the line for him politically. When Asquith formed his new coalition government in May 1915, there was no longer room for his colleague and friend.

In many ways, May 1915 was the nadir for anyone living in Britain who had associations with Germany. The idea of Germans committing atrocities as a matter of course was well established in the public mind, and would increase with the shooting of the nurse turned international heroine, Edith Cavell, in October 1915, and later the execution of Charles Fryatt, the captain of an unarmed steamer that had tried to ram a U-boat. The British used both shootings to whip up worldwide protest against German barbarism, despite the fact that Cavell – the more celebrated of the two killings – had used her position as a nurse to help secure the escape of some 200 British soldiers caught behind enemy lines. This fact was suitably lost. It was far more pertinent to record for the public the 'fact' that the execution party's first volley had failed to kill the nurse, leaving the *coup de grâce* to a German officer's pistol. One lesser known but nevertheless publicised detail was the reported shooting of one of the firing squad, a certain Private Rammler, who refused to execute the nurse. If there had ever been one 'good Hun' in the war then he had, in any case, been mercilessly shot by his own side.

The ability of the Allies to win the propaganda war was due, in part, to the Germans' inability to master the art, or indeed to develop an inclination even to take part. Instead of turning the tables on the Allies by highlighting some of their enemy's atrocities, the German attitude was largely defensive, justifying actions that the world had already condemned. The fact that the French had shot two German nurses for offences not dissimilar to those of Edith Cavell was not pointed out by the Germans at all, for the simple reason that the executions were seen as legally and therefore morally legitimate.

Cavell's martyrdom was yet to come when, in April and May 1915, the Germans committed a string of injudicious attacks that appeared to confirm reports of their outrageous behaviour. On 22 April 1915, they launched the world's first gas attack, using chlorine gas and causing panic in Allied lines. At the same time, news broke that a Canadian soldier had been found crucified in a German trench, a story which, although probably apocryphal, was very widely believed. By far the worst assault was the sinking of the great liner *Lusitania* and the death of 1,198 passengers, 128 of whom were American citizens. The sinking was condemned across the world, not least in America, where both Germany and

Britain were attempting to curry favour. Then, as if matters could not get any worse, a Report of the Committee on Alleged German Atrocities was published in mid-May, a week after the sinking. The report, aimed primarily at swaying overseas opinion, was nevertheless such an astonishing read that its 360 pages were sold for home consumption as well, priced 1d, the average cost of a daily twenty-page newspaper. The accusations made in the report were given automatic credence, owing to the other atrocities committed during that month.

The sinking of the *Lusitania* just off the coast of Ireland was devastating. Torpedoed by a German submarine as it finished its voyage from New York to Liverpool, the ship sank rapidly. The German Embassy in Washington had placed advertisements in American newspapers warning of the dangers of sailing into a war zone, but no one had ever believed they would sink an unarmed cruise liner. For the Germans, their warning had exonerated them of any culpability, but the rest of the world failed to see it in the same way.

Alice Drury was a trained nurse and professional nanny. Aged eighteen, she had taken her first job with a wealthy American family looking after two of their four children, Audrey, a three-month-old baby, and Stuart, a four-year-old boy. A Danish girl had recently been employed to look after the other two children, Amy and Susan.

'It was May 7th and it was a lovely, lovely day, the sun was shining, and we could see the coast of Ireland in the distance, the passengers were looking landwards. It was just after lunchtime between one and two – I couldn't say precisely – when we were torpedoed. The baby, Audrey, had just had her bottle and I was with the boy, Stuart. I had taken him down below to have a rest after lunch when there was a terrific bang. I grabbed the baby and climbed the three flights of stairs from my cabin to the top where the lifeboats were kept. It is surprising what you can do when you don't have time to think, because water was flooding into the ship and had started coming into the cabin straight away. The baby was on a bunk lying on a shawl so I picked the shawl up and tied the two ends around my neck because I wanted both my hands to get up the stairs. I had the boy, Stuart, with me. He was yelling and screaming, "I don't want to be drowned," because he was old enough to know what was happening. We made our way down the corridor but he was still screaming so I hit him in the end, the only way I could stop him screaming. I hurt him, no doubt, because I gave him a real good slap, he was so frightened. He stopped straight away and I've never hit a child before or since.

'I don't remember any great panic, but a lot of people rushed for the lift, which of course was a mistake because they would become trapped. I didn't, I made for the stairs and I managed to get into a lifeboat and watched the ship go down. We were lucky not to be drawn down with it, the suction was so great, the terror was in the suction, you could feel it drawing the lifeboat back in. I saw that ship go under right to the very end, to the last bit of funnel. I know the boat I was in was number seven. Having the baby in my arms I was occupied and as there were no men on board, the stewardesses and some of the female passengers took turns in rowing. We were twelve hours on the open sea.

'It was about two in the morning before we arrived in Queenstown. People were marvellous, in the way we were treated. Eventually, I was taken to a guest house where one of the guests went to a chemist's and woke them up to get food for the baby. Later I discovered that the children's mother had hung on to a deck chair and was picked up after several hours floating, and that their father had survived too.'

However, the Danish nanny and the two other children were drowned. The ship had sunk in just eighteen minutes.

Most of the *Lusitania*'s crew had come from Liverpool, including the captain, so that when news filtered through that the ship had been sunk, the reaction in the city was immediate and violent. Seven years old at the time, Sydney Bond was a Liverpudlian born and bred. Within hours of the sinking, he witnessed an attack on a German-owned shop.

'This was different to anything that had gone on before. Of course in Liverpool the main employment was the docks, and the Germans were sinking lots of ships, but this was the *Lusitania*, a Liverpool-registered ship, and of course there's nothing worse than some of the lads down at the docks for suddenly creating a bloody great riot. A mob had gathered down where the docks are and it grew and grew in number and then marched through the town and the police couldn't do very much, they were understaffed because so many had joined up. They were gathering in Ullett Road off the main road to town and they were meeting and they were screaming, shouting, singing, until they reached Smithdown Road, a very beautiful area, and did an enormous amount of damage.
    'Now in those days the Germans were pork butchers in every city, well known, with beautifully decorated windows, works of art, yet they'd smashed the front window and were pinching all the meats. Then they smashed all the fittings in the shop and then went up into the house which was very well furnished. These Germans were very well-to-do, very well liked, they got into the house and up the stairs and this mob had three floors to go up. They'd got weapons from somewhere, hammers and chisels, and they chiselled the window out, the complete frame of the window. I went and stood on the corner to look on, sensibly I didn't go any further, and I watched them throw this grand piano out of the window. They got a hammer and smashed all the window surround to get it out and I can remember to this day what excitement it

was for a kid to see this whacking great grand piano slowly, it didn't come out straight, it came out part way but once the aperture was bigger, through came the grand piano.

'By this time the crowd was enormous, they were cheering and waiting, and eventually these louts tipped the piano and tipped it until out it came. It was an object that came down big and flat, and there was an enormous yell, fear, I suppose it was. Down it came and the noise when it landed on the flat pavement was incredible, an enormous bash, in fact it reverberated for what felt like minutes afterwards, everything in the piano continued to move. I was thrilled to bits, I didn't care it was a beautiful grand piano.

'Not only did they smash the pork butcher's up but they went a little further to a gentlemen's outfitters, so that was bashed up too. In fact, the better part of a block, containing eight or nine good-class shops, were destroyed. In the end they didn't bother with just German shops, when no one was looking they had a bash at all the others. These people were so pathetically poor they just went mad, looting. My father owned a shop nearby and one or two customers had gone to watch what was happening and I was spotted, looking on. I had been missing for so long that my parents began to worry themselves daft, so that when I got home I was given the belt. But I didn't bother, there was something fantastic happening, you don't often see grand pianos thrown out of a window.'

The riots in Liverpool had caused £40,000-worth of damage (the equivalent of £2.5 million today). In the end, some 200 buildings were left damaged and in some cases gutted. Across the country, anti-German riots left at least seven Germans dead and many more injured, ensuring that many more would be interned. In London alone there was reported disorder in nineteen of the twenty-one districts. It wasn't just young men who indulged in the orgy of violence, as Florence Billington recalled.

> 'There wasn't much sympathy for them and their shops were looted and broken into. I had known some nice Germans before the war but I didn't blame the people that did it because I knew the bitterness was there and I knew that the Germans had really asked for it this time. I had a friend, Alice Malone, and when I came back from working in Buxton my parents said, "Did you know that Alice was one of them that looted Emmett's?" "Oh," I said, "did Alice do that?" They said, "Yes, she did, and she was as bad as anybody." '

In Hull, the Hohenreins were now targeted by the mob. The family had suffered sporadic insults and aggression since the German naval attacks at nearby Scarborough the year before. Now they were without doubt the enemy. In a warning sent to the family, the Hohenreins were warned of an imminent attack on their shop as a direct retaliation for the sinking of the *Lusitania*:

> Dear Sir
> I belong to a secret gang but want to be your friend. I wish to warn you that your shop's in danger and perhaps life for God's sake take this as a warning from one who wishes you no harm (Don't treat this as an idel [sic] joke) – Friendship.
> I have signed Friendship but I don't know you and you don't know me.

Then on a separate sheet the writer added:

> TAKE A GOOD TIP, DON'T BE ON PREMISES MAY 13–15 OR MAY 20–15 [sic]

As if to underline the danger, the author wrote again, later that day.

Dear Sir
  I hope you got my last letter and I hope you have taken notice of it as your shop is going to be broken up . . . I dare not let you know too much as I would be found and I would have to suffer. The reason I have taken such an interest in warning you is because when I was a boy your parents and those who kept your shop were very good to me and many a time when I was hungry and needed bread so you see I wish you no harm in any way. Your shop is not the only shop but there are others and I am warning you and I shall have to carry out my work when I am ordered by my chief the captain. Sir, if you will put a letter in the Daily Mail I will know you have got my letter. I do not mean a bold one but one of a mild kind.
  The reason of it is to avenge
  LUSITANIA
  Friendship – 2nd

The attack took place, with a gang consisting of youths and young men. After midnight, two youths threw a large stone through the window but were identified and arrested, the crowd making no attempt at rescue. It was pointed out that Mr Hohenrein was a member of the East Riding Yeomanry and that his father was naturalised British. Yet attacks on Yorkshire by Zeppelins only made the Hohenreins' situation worse. On 4 June, Driffield earned the dubious distinction of being the first town in Yorkshire to be raided, and shortly afterwards a more serious raid on Hull took place. The Old Town was particularly hit, with thirteen high-explosive and forty incendiary bombs being dropped, killing twenty-five and injuring a further forty, including children. That night a number of unspecified but serious 'incidents' occurred at the Hohenreins' premises, resulting in Charles Hohenrein appealing to the Chief

Constable's office for confirmation of his nationality. The response was:

> The bearer, Mr C. H. Hohenrein, is a British-born subject whom I have known since his youth. He is a man of the highest integrity and honour, and I have the most implicit confidence and reliance in him. He is well known to most of the leading citizens in this district.

In addition, Charles Hohenrein offered the huge sum of £500 (equivalent to £30,000 today) to any charity to anyone who could prove his family was not English. The counter-offensive failed to work and in the end he decided to close the sixty-five-year-old business until a time when they could reopen without being 'subjected to unjust threats, insults and much inconvenience'. In a letter he referred to 'base insinuations . . . by people whose character and morals do not bear investigation'.

In the aftermath of the sinking of the *Lusitania*, a metal worker from Munich, Karl Goetz, produced a medal commemorating the event. The medal was an attempt to highlight the Germans' assertion that the British had been illegally carrying arms from the USA on board the civilian passenger ship, in contravention of international law. The medal also underlined the culpability of the Cunard Line in ignoring the warnings made in the press that ships entering enemy waters were likely to be attacked. The German belief that the ship was carrying armaments, including shell cases and bullets, was correct, yet the medal, unofficial as it was, was seized on by the British as proof that the Germans were in fact congratulating the U-boat on its 'kill'.

In no time at all, the British had seized the medal and produced 300,000 copies, which were sold for one shilling each. Each medal came in its own commemorative box and accompanying leaflet of explanation that encouraged owners to distribute the evidence. 'Please do not destroy this when you have read it carefully, though kindly pass it on to a friend,' read the leaflet. Inside the box there was a label stating that the medal was an 'exact replica' of the original. 'This indicates the true feeling the War Lords endeavour to stimulate, and is proof positive that such crimes are not merely regarded favourably, but are given every encouragement in the land of Kultur,' the label affirmed. Once again, the British had been able to score another propaganda victory over the Germans.

Charles Hohenrein did not suffer the final indignity of being interned, unlike the father of Elfie Druhm. At least his young family could visit him in Holloway throughout the war, as Elfie recalls.

'We used to visit him on Saturday afternoon for a few hours and I can still actually remember going through big gates with policemen on either side. In front of the building there was a flight of steps, at the top of which were long lines of German men, standing there looking out for their wives. And we went in and sat down and talked for two hours. We weren't supposed to take any foodstuffs with us, a policeman there was supposed to search us, but I don't think he ever did. My mother had a muff, in those days that was the fashion, and she could have hidden things in there but she thought that would be the first place they would look, so she stuffed food into the elastic of my bloomers, packets of chocolate, oranges even. All the men were receiving the same sort of smuggled food. We weren't being watched, or guarded. When we were in there, we were free to move around in what looked like a doctor's waiting room so it was quite easy to hand the food over.

'In Internment they were not badly treated. There was a little room where Father used to make little boxes, marquetry, decorated with tiny pieces of wood, to pass the time. The building was a grey, cold stone kind of place, it wasn't comfortable. The windows weren't barred as I recall, but the place was secure. I remember a big fence round the building and in the summers we used to sit outside in the garden along with the other men and their

Cheering Britain's entry into war on 4 August 1914. The public expected the war to be 'over by Christmas'. (*Hulton Getty*)

October 1914, new recruit Vic Cole (centre, with pipe) stands with other volunteers of the 7th Royal West Kent Regiment. He is wearing 'Kitchener Blues'. The uniforms were blue because prior to the war khaki dye had come from Germany and it took many weeks before a replacement could be made in Britain.

Left: New recruits being led in training by their sergeant. The training was seen as fun, and war as exciting. The enthusiasm of the young soldiers is well captured in this photograph. Although civilians expected the war would soon be over, the senior army officers knew better.

Below: Turning men into soldiers. The recruits are measured for their uniforms.
(*Imperial War Museum*)

Then and now. Pictures of the west end of Whitby Abbey, before and after the bombardment of 16 December 1914. In three consecutively timed raids, the towns of Hartlepool, Scarborough and Whitby were shelled from the sea by German cruisers, resulting in over 700 civilian casualties.

Top: Children congregate outside two homes destroyed during the bombardment of Hartlepool. Remarkably, no one was killed here.

Right and inset: A shell entered the front of this Baptist chapel in Hartlepool, went straight through the building, and left it through the back.

Right: Public humiliation of a German in a British street. Anti-German feeling intensified during the war against the 53,000-strong German community living in Britain. After the sinking of the *Lusitania* in May 1915, hatred exploded into violence and several Germans were killed. (*Topham Picturepoint*)

Below: A German shop is looted in Poplar, east London. German shops were targets for mob violence, with hundreds being attacked. In one incident, a grand piano was pushed from the upper floor of a German-owned flat, smashing on the street below. (*Hulton Getty*)

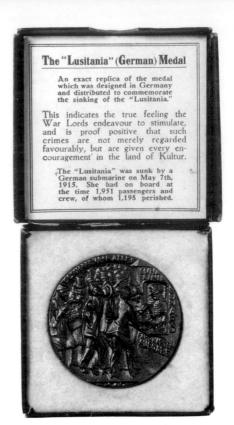

The *Lusitania* medal, widely reproduced in England as a sign of Germany's 'frightfulness'. This medal was made after the Germans sank the civilian liner with the loss of 1,198 lives, including 128 American passengers.

Edith Cavell's funeral procession in London after the war. The celebrated nurse was executed by the Germans in October 1915, after she helped British soldiers caught behind enemy lines to escape. Her shooting, while technically legitimate, proved a propaganda coup for the British, who reported her death as evidence of German war crimes. Edith Cavell's body lies in Norwich Cathedral.

Kathleen Barron was a part-time cinema pianist during the war, and accompanied the silent feature film of the Battle of the Somme.

Len Whitehead's elder brother George, shown here in his uniform, was killed at the Battle of Loos in September 1915. His body was never found.

Florence Billington, photographed two years after the death of her fiancé Ted Felton. Her love letters to Ted were found on his body and returned to England. For the following year Florence's life was plagued by depression and anxiety.

Lance Corporal Harold Butler was one of the missing of the 1916 Battle of the Somme. Tragically, optimistic letters sent from home by his mother and sister reveal that he had been misreported as lightly wounded.

The poignant grave of Ernest Fry of the 12th Gloucestershire Regiment, killed in an attack during September 1916. His grave is marked by a cross, made of shell cases. His body was subsequently lost, a fate that befell many hastily buried soldiers. Not knowing what had happened to loved ones fuelled a mass of correspondence between the Red Cross and families desperate to find out the truth.

1917. An elderly post woman, recruited to release men for the front, hands a letter to a waiting housewife. Wives and mothers lived in fear of the dreaded knock on the door. (*Hulton Getty*)

wives and I remember looking at that fence, but not really understanding what it meant.'

Living in London was hard on Mrs Druhm without help from her family. Rented rooms were exchanged on several occasions when they were found to be unsuitable. However, the family was not entirely alone. At the salon, Mrs Druhm had made friends with a lady, Miss Hope, the only one who worked there (apart from the owner) to be let in on the family secret.

'Miss Hope was very left wing, although we didn't realise that until later on, but her uncle was a conscientious objector and her father owned a pub called the Wat Tyler. [Tyler was the original trade unionist, a rebel leader during the time of Richard II, who sought the abolition of serfdom back in the fourteenth century.] Miss Hope was that way inclined, and had an international mind, and often travelled abroad. My mother could tell that she was the sort of person she could speak to, and, with Miss Hope, we would all drop in at her parents' every Sunday for lunch at the pub.'

George Hohenrein, who had moved to Germany before the war, had been interned with his son William, a medical student. Both had spent months in Ruhleben camp, and had corresponded frequently with home. In letters sent to Hull in 1915, George wrote:

There seem to be quite a number of prisoners interned here who complain that, on account of their possessing German names, their wives and children in England have been subject to violence and outrages. This I cannot believe, this is entirely un-English and until I have more definite news upon the subject shall very much doubt its accuracy. Besides what is a name? Merely a legacy inherited from our ancestors and in our case one of which we may be justly proud. But at any rate this would be impossible to happen to us. Our services in the interests of the British public will not be easily forgotten and our loyal sentiments no one can doubt.

George was sadly mistaken; perhaps he was not quite as English in every attitude as he had once believed.

The British public was apt to believe any story they were fed about 'German frightfulness', owing in part to a natural inclination to believe the worst of the enemy. They were helped inadvertently by the German tendency to provide raw material, as a result of a more advanced concept of total war, an idea foreign to the British mentality at that time. The Germans bombarded and bombed British civilians in 1914, and they intensified submarine warfare in 1915. They introduced poison gas to the battlefield, as well as flamethrowers: both weapons were employed before the end of 1915. The British, in time, would use all these weapons, to a greater or lesser extent, as the country geared up for total war, and by 1918 they too would bomb cities in Germany, killing civilians. But the damage in terms of international credibility had been done to Germany, not Britain.

When stories were circulated in April 1917 that the Germans were boiling down the bodies of dead soldiers for their fat, it could well be believed; after all, Germany had been the subject of a blockade since 1914 and was now short of many raw materials. The story was totally untrue, and was a deliberate misinterpretation of the German word *Kadaver*, meaning the body of an animal, yet in terms of propaganda it helped keep the pot boiling for the rest of the war.

While George Hohenrein languished in an internment camp near Berlin, his brother Charles had finally decided enough was enough. Charles had resolved to rid himself of the 'legacy inherited'. Soon after the sinking of the *Lusitania*, the Hohenreins were no more. Charles 'Ross' now owned the shop, and under this new guise he began to trade again in November 1915, successfully.

—CHAPTER FOUR—

'It is my painful duty . . .'

BY NOVEMBER 1915, HAROLD BUTLER, THE ENTHUSI-
astic volunteer from Canning Town, was already safely
back in England and in a hospital bed. He was recovering
from gunshot wounds to his shoulder and left leg. They were
serious injuries, ones that would keep him out of the war for a
few months, but not much longer. Harold did not seem to mind;
his letters home appear to show that he was not too worried at
the prospect of going back to France if he had to. Nevertheless,
in the meantime he intended to enjoy the respite while it lasted.

Although a Kitchener recruit, Harold had been drafted into a
regular battalion of the East Kent Regiment and had gone to
France in the summer of 1915. Within three months of arrival he
had taken part in the Battle of Loos, his first action. The battle,
launched on 25 September, had been an initial success but strong
counterattacks later drove the British troops back. It was the first
action in which three Kitchener divisions had also played a part,
proving their determination to fight, and fight well, but at a
terrible cost in life. Harold's involvement in the fighting came on
28 September, when his battalion had assaulted the German
trenches at bayonet point. He had been hit within a dozen yards
of his own line, but staggered on until hit again, taking refuge in
a shell hole. He later made his own way back down the line to a
first-aid post, before being sent back to a hospital in France, then
to England.

Despite his injuries, Harold had seemingly lost little of his
boyish sense of adventure, although, as he himself acknowledged

in one letter home, the war had not been quite what he had expected.

Oct 31st 1915
Red Cross Hospital, Barnstaple

My dearest Sisters

I have just got your sweet charming letter. I am so pleased to hear father has joined and I feel <u>proud</u> of him, now I want Roland [his brother] to hurry up and we shall all be in the fight, good old <u>Butlers</u> – who said England is beaten? Well I hope Father is still going strong. I'd like to see him in khaki. I feel as proud as a dog with nine tails. So Walter [his brother] thinks of joining. I knew he would, oh well good luck to him. I wish I was a civilian again I'd join right away. I don't mind going out again and having another smack at them after their cruelty to that good nurse [Edith Cavell] . . .

I remain your ever loving brother, Harold

The chance to have another 'smack' came early the following year. While at an embarkation camp in Dover, Harold wrote, 'I am warned for the draft and have been medically inspected so we expect to go any day now. I think we go to the 6th Battalion. Well my darlings you must keep a good heart, and I hope to be lucky again, anyway I will trust to God for that, so don't forget, <u>don't worry</u>.' Harold was sent back in mid-March 1916, first to Belgium, then later making his way south by stages and to a district that had so far seen little action in the war, the Somme. The battlefield, north of the River Somme, had been held by the British since the summer of 1915, but for almost a full year few actions of any note had taken place. It was a 'quiet sector' in as far as any sector was ever quiet.

Then, in February 1916, the Germans launched a huge offensive in front of the French-held garrison town of Verdun. The intention had been to 'bleed the French army white', to the extent that France might be forced to capitulate. For months, both sides poured men in their tens of thousands into the maelstrom. To take the pressure off her own increasingly belea-guered forces, France made a desperate appeal to her ally, Britain, to make an attack further north. The British agreed and, after discussion, the Somme region was chosen for the assault. It was to be an Anglo–French affair and a date was set by the Allies for early summer but, as the time grew closer, French participation was reduced owing to continued fighting at Verdun. The battle would now have to be a primarily British affair, with some 120,000 men deployed in action on the opening day. As luck would have it, Harold's battalion would not take part in the very first assault, although his time would come soon enough.

Three months later and the whole country was alive with expectation that a 'Great Push' on the Somme was imminent. It was to be preceded by the greatest bombardment in history, one that would shatter the German trenches before an infantry assault was delivered of truly epic proportions. For most of the popula-tion there was little news, nothing tangible, nothing concrete, other than wild rumours that the preparatory bombardment was already under way. The speculation, for once, was right, for when the wind was in the right direction, Londoners as far north as Hampstead Heath could hear the distant thunder of shellfire. To those living closest of all, in parts of Essex and Kent, and in the villages near the coast, the sound of the guns was not only clear but enough to shake the sash-cords in the windows; even houses appeared to quiver, according to one observer. To nine-year-old Len Whitehead, the farmer's boy from Braintree in Essex, the shelling was quite discernible. 'The noise was continuous and it used to rattle the old iron-framed windows with the lead lights. My mother used to listen and say in a resigned voice, "Oh, those poor boys out there."'

There seemed no obvious reason to pity the young men out in France as they began final preparations for the attack. The soldiers had only marvelled at the demonstration of firepower. Surely no German could survive such a whirlwind of steel exploding over the German lines – for the shelling had gone on around the clock, averaging some 9,000 shells an hour. The bombardment was due to last a full five days, then, owing to bad weather, it was extended a further forty-eight hours, delaying the infantry assault until the morning of 1 July. One of those who could hear the noise was the Reverend Andrew Clark in Great Leighs. In his daily diary of events during the war, he noted the positive news emanating from France. On the morning of the second day of the offensive he wrote enthusiastically, 'All the village was talking of the good news.' Later that day, he took note of an Official Bulletin put up at the local post office confirming what he had heard; it read: 'Attack launched 7.30 a.m. north of Somme combined with French. British broken into German forward system on 16-mile front. French attack equally satisfactory.'

The general public needed good news: 1916 had not, so far, been a year of success. In January, the British had finally evacuated the Gallipoli Peninsula after a costly and ultimately futile eight-month campaign. In April, they had been forced to surrender at the town of Kut in Mesopotamia (now Iraq), after a wholly inadequate display of leadership, and this a week after the Easter Uprising in Ireland. Then, at the end of May, there had been the inconclusive naval battle at Jutland. Losses in terms of ships and men had been considerably higher for the Royal Navy than for the German Grand Fleet, even if historians later judged the battle a strategic success for Britain. Then Lord Kitchener, the great architect of the New Army, was drowned when his ship, HMS *Hampshire*, was sunk by a mine. His death stunned the nation.

Kitchener might be dead but his legacy would live on if, as expected, his New Army spearheaded the assault on the Somme and decisively broke the German defences in the west. The success would be captured on film and shown at cinemas at home, while the press would be encouraged to participate too, reporting events as they unfurled, although correspondents would remain well behind the firing line. The press would be fed stories, but in an apparently new, open and more mutually beneficial relationship; the army and the government had for too long seen the press as at best mischievous and at worst downright dangerous and unpatriotic. The Northcliffe Press, which owned *The Times* and the *Daily Mail*, had been heavily criticised by Douglas Haig in 1915 for publishing 'much which had helped the enemy'. Yet, by the time of the Battle of the Somme, Haig's view had radically altered. In the name of patriotism, the publisher of *The Times*, and the majority of the British press, was willing to be suborned by the commander-in-chief.

The improved atmosphere between the two was gratefully acknowledged by the editor of *The Times*: 'We must express both to General Haig and to the War Office the thanks of the public for the steady stream of news which has been permitted to flow since the battle began. For the first time since the outbreak of war our people are able to watch in spirit the exploits of their countrymen.' 'In spirit' was right. This was a headquarters view of the war. 'I must say that the correspondents have played up splendidly,' confirmed Haig in his diary. 'We never once had to complain of them since I took over command.'

Invariably, press stories of advances were based on official reports which, in the fog of war, often proved speculative in the extreme but which were released to feed a public hungry for any scrap of news. 'What at present is certain is that we have gained ground all along the line, in some places having pushed even beyond the high water-mark of our expectation . . . So far the day goes well for England,' one newspaper pontificated. Yet such excited headlines masked, temporarily, the extent of British casualties. The Allied dead were not referred to in early reports, and the first images of wounded were accompanied by optimistic captions – 'Telling the story of victory', as a lightly injured soldier is seen to sit nonchalantly on the bed of another convalescent comrade.

Tucked away in the deluge of war news in *The Times* of 3 July is a 'semi-official' report sent from Paris. It read: 'The success is not a thunderbolt as has happened earlier in similar operations, but it is important because it is rich in promise. It is no longer a question here of attempts to pierce as with a knife; it is rather a slow, continuous, and methodical push, sparing in lives until the day when the enemy's resistance, incessantly hammered at, will crumble.' Pushing Germany out of France was dependent on defeating the enemy, and this could only be done through prolonged attrition, a lesson that the British public would come to learn. The Great Push was being redefined, expectations subtly managed.

If ever a year brought home to the country at large the effects of death on a mass scale, it was 1916. The number of casualties at the front was such that they could neither be ignored nor hidden and, as reports filtered through that battalions had been destroyed, so worried families besieged local newspapers, desperate to find out more. In the end the blooding of Kitchener's New Army on 1 July 1916 was just that, a disaster in which as many men died on one day as had perished in the full four and a half months of fighting in France and Flanders in 1914.

Only then did it become apparent that the great strength and the tragedy of so many of the Kitchener units was born out of its method of recruitment. For, up and down the land, boroughs had raised their own battalions and offered them to the War Office for service. Great pride was born in towns across the country that they had formed not just one but often two, three and even four battalions of 1,000 men each, all local men, lads who had worked together in foundries and factories, played in the same football teams and had attended the same Sunday schools together. The camaraderie within these units was wonderful, but fearful losses in a few hours could paralyse the communities from which they came, for everyone knew everyone else, and not a few were interrelated by marriage. Tight-knit communities such as Blackburn, Chorley and Bradford were paralysed by sorrow when the lists of dead and wounded were published.

Edith Storey, now 104 years old, was born and raised in Sheffield.

'When the news came through it was terrible. Several of the boys I went to Sunday School with had joined the Sheffield Pals. We'd grown up together and they'd all joined together as a crowd. They were lovely boys. I remember I was working in the window of my father's shop and Dad came in and said he had something very sad to tell me. They'd all been killed on the Somme. I was devastated.'

Within a week, the tone of the papers changed, from early reports that claimed 'Kitchener's Boys: New Armies Make Good' to 'Heavy Toll of the City Units'.

The shock waves extended to the small mining village of Methil in Fife on the east coast of Scotland. Here, the news of fresh casualties was marked with a frenzy of interest around the grocer's shop where a list of new names was regularly pasted up in the window. Maud Cox was six at the time, the daughter of the shop owner, and she vividly recalls the impending drama as the crowds awaited the news.

'When the villagers heard the train come in, I mean the train was practically in the high street as it was just a little village, well, then they'd know that news was arriving and they'd start to gather. Then the lorry came from the station and dumped the bills and my mother went out with a bucket full of paste and a big white wash brush, and by that time there was a crowd waiting for her. The lists were always in alphabetical order and as people read them they shouted out to friends, who were too far away to see, "You're all right, your lad's not on it." Then you'd hear somebody start to cry. I remember one time going outside and there was a woman and she was rolling on the pavement and screaming her head off and my mother just grabbed me and brought me in. She said, "What are you doing out there?" And Jessie, a girl who worked for Mum in the shop, said, "I'm so sorry for Mrs Greer. She's lost her man and she's left with six steps and stairs." I couldna think why anybody was getting excited about steps and stairs, I didn't realise at the time that it meant six .children with only about a year between them all.'

Such were the numbers killed on 1 July 1916 that the casualty lists for that one day alone throw up tragedies of almost incomprehensible proportions. In his book, *Soldiers Killed on the First Day of the Somme*, Ernest Bell identified one Lydia Ayre, living in London after the death of her husband in Newfoundland. Now she lost her only two sons, as well as two nephews. 'By their death Mrs Ayre has lost every member of her family,' a newspaper reported. The elder son, Bernard, had been studying at Cambridge University before enlisting in the 8th Battalion of the Norfolk Regiment. Sadly, hers was not the only multiple death to hit the unit that day. Louisa Bailey from West Rudham, near King's Lynn, was about to discover the full horror of war, for her three sons who had enlisted so enthusiastically in the Kitchener Battalion back in September 1914 had all been killed: Ernest, George and Robert.

Multiple deaths within one family were not peculiar to what had become the worst day for the British army in history. A week later, Lieutenants Arthur and Leonard Tregaskis, brothers serving in the same battalion, were killed in the same attack, while in September 1916, Frances Lee, waiting at home in east London, received two telegrams informing her of the death of her forty-four-year-old husband George and her nineteen-year-old son Robert, both killed in the same explosion at their gun battery. And then there was William and Julia Souls of Great Rissington. Before the offensive began they lost their first son in action, to be followed in July and August 1916 by two more of their boys, Frederick and Walter. Two years later they lost two more sons, while a sixth died of meningitis.

Despite the carnage, the Battle of the Somme was not the worst battle in terms of casualties per day. The fighting at Arras in April and May 1917 was considerably more lethal, as too were the battles of 1918. However, the Somme, which cost the British army some 415,000 casualties, dwarfed in number anything that had happened in 1914 or 1915. The fighting on the Somme had also sucked in every New Army division serving on the Western Front, ensuring that terrific casualties were suffered in every community across Great Britain.

By 1916 the machinery of informing people of deaths was well established. However, the vast majority were notified by letter not by telegram, contrary to popular belief today that recalls well-known wires sent to the writer Vera Brittain on the death of her brother, and to the family home of the poet Wilfred Owen just as the church bells pealed in celebration of the Armistice. Telegrams notifying that a soldier was killed or wounded were sent almost exclusively to officers during the war, not to Other Ranks, and Edward Brittain and Wilfred Owen were officers. The popular conception of thousands of telegram boys delivering the terrible news to street upon street is therefore largely a myth. These children were employed in large numbers by the Post Office and had for many years delivered telegrams concerning matters merely of day-to-day importance. Yet with the advent of war they were often seen as the harbingers of terrible news, and the sight of a telegram boy made many a heart miss a beat. Sydney Bond recalls them sitting cherub-like in his aunt's post office in Wavertree Road in Liverpool.

'At the back of one of the counters there was a crude seating arrangement and there sat four or five little boys in uniform, with tall hats and shining buttons, waiting for the telegram, ready to rush out with the dreaded news. No one wanted to see them come up their street, but of course they did, with notification that a son or a husband had been killed. It was such a common sight that we got to the point that, as children, we weren't really moved by their appearance, but to adults, they were dreaded.'

However, the vast majority heard the fate of a loved one on receipt not of a telegram but of a buff-coloured envelope with

OHMS (On His Majesty's Service) printed on the outside. These letters were delivered by the postman as part and parcel of his daily round, and were sent in their thousands on a daily basis by military record offices dotted across the country. The envelope gave no clue as to the fate of the soldier whose details it carried, and it was no doubt with a pounding heart and shaking hands that each and every one was opened. The envelope would contain one of several possible enclosures depending on the nature of the casualty: army form B.104–80 and later 81 dealt with wounds; B.104–83 dealt with those who were missing. However, most feared was the envelope containing the army form B.104–82B. This document issued by the War Office began without prevarication: 'It is my painful duty to inform you that a report has been received from the War Office notifying the death of: —'

As the war progressed, each form was honed slightly, perhaps to make it easier to read, perhaps in order to add more information, perhaps to soften the blow. Army form B.104–82B indicated a slight modification to the original army form B.104–82, which had followed the perfunctory report with two paragraphs outlining how the deceased's property would be forwarded and the restrictions imposed on the next of kin as to its disposal. Now, midway through the war, and perhaps in view of the sensitivity of the moment, a new single paragraph was issued instead, expressing the 'sympathy' of 'Their Gracious Majesties the King and Queen' as well as the 'regret' of the Army Council.

No one could prepare themselves for the arrival of bad news, whether brought by telegram boy or the postman, for the daily knock on the front door sounded much like any other.

'In those days all the postmen knocked on the door to let you know that the post had arrived,' recalled Kathleen Barron at the age of ninety-nine. Thirteen years old in 1915, she was at home when the postman came.

'My mother would always ask me to go and fetch the letters, only this time I picked up an official-looking envelope. I knew straight away what it was and that it must relate to my brother Dick who was fighting at Gallipoli. I handed the letter to Mother but when she saw it she couldn't open it and it became my business to read what it said. I looked at Mother and saw her face absolutely ashen white. I opened the letter and read out loud that Dick was ill in hospital with dysentery. I think in a way Mother was a little relieved, because he wasn't killed, but it was a horrible moment nevertheless.'

Dick Barron eventually recovered, but there was no such reprieve for the family of eight-year-old Dennis Gilfeather. He recalls the moment when the letter arrived at his house informing the family of the death of his father; it has been a moment etched on his mind ever since.

'It was on a Saturday morning and my mum was feeding us. The kid was in the high chair, and she's serving out, when there was a hammering at the door. I remember her slight annoyance at the disruption as she went to answer it. And then I saw her opening the door and taking the letter. She tore it open, she was nervous, her hands started shaking, then she read it and collapsed to the floor. John, the eldest boy, told me to go to Mrs Lawson's, a neighbour of ours. So I went and knocked at her door and said, "Would you come please, my mum doesn't seem well."'

Apart from the army's official notification there would often be, as a matter of courtesy, a letter written to the deceased soldier's family by his platoon officer. This was written at the first opportunity and, given the general excellence of the military post, often arrived before the army's own telegram. A personal letter written by an officer would perhaps help soften the blow. However, unless the man was particularly known to the officer such letters expressed standard sentiments: sadness at the loss, that the soldier was one of the 'best in the company' and would be 'greatly missed' by all. William Roberts, the clerk from Hartle-pool who lived through the German bombardment there, was fifteen when his father was killed in December 1915 while serving with the Royal Engineers. He died during a relatively quiet time in the line and the officer was able to write to his widow the next day. Mrs Roberts would probably have heard within a week to ten days that her husband was dead, well before official word was received.

11/12/15

Dear Mrs Roberts

   It is with deepest regret that I write concerning the unfortunate death of your husband . . . He was I think the oldest man in our section but at the same time one of the most trustworthy and respected and was held in affection by all of the section. He and his brother Robert, who recently left us [with trench fever], were two of the best workers I have known . . . We were engaged as usual on dangerous work repairing trenches and some of the sappers including your husband were carrying stores up to the front trench. The firing was rather brisk and Sapper Roberts was hit on the chest by a bullet which passed through his heart. He did not speak a word as death was instantaneous and could have felt no pain . . .

   Yours truly

   W. A. Leckie 2nd Lieutenant Royal Engineers

These letters might be formulaic but they were not uncaring. In this example, Lieutenant Walter Leckie was able to give not only a description of the circumstances of Roberts's death but also where the body was buried 'The remains were interred in a small cemetery, the resting place of many brave soldiers, about three-quarters of a mile east of Zillebeke near the road which runs east through that village in the place we know as Armagh Wood.' As in many cases where the fighting was intense, the grave was subsequently lost. Lieutenant Leckie was himself killed in action just ten weeks later.

In infantry units, the turnover in personnel was often rapid during offensives, and writing quick-fire platitudes, as we might see them today, was nevertheless necessary. There were only so many possible permutations when sending condolences and it was perfectly conceivable that an officer would write about a man he barely knew, and could not picture in his mind's eye. If the deceased had only just arrived at the front, there was no point in pretending that the officer knew the man well. However, while acknowledging that 'your husband/son had only been with us a short time' it was a kindness to say that he had 'impressed all who met him . . .' Any communication was of inestimable comfort to the family, for they were penned by a subaltern whose duties included one of care to the men under him and who, therefore, would probably have been in close proximity to the man when he died. That closeness, physically and even spiritually, may help explain the large number of replies sent to junior officers by grief-stricken families requesting 'any further news' while fervently hoping for the future safe return of the officer. 'Sir, I pray that you may get through all right and that your nearest and dearest may be spared the terrible blow,' wrote one bereaved mother on news that her own son was dead.

Invariably the most heartfelt information came from the soldier's own friends. These men were under no obligation to write, but most did. A close friend of Sapper Roberts sent the following. Nearly ninety years on, both letters remain in immaculate condition, the personal possessions of Sapper Roberts's son, William.

Saturday 11th December 1915

Dear Madam

I very much regret to inform you that your husband was killed on the 10th and I, dear friend, I will call you friend as your husband and I have been the best of friends since the company was formed. It breaks my heart to have to break the sad news to you. He was like a father to me

[and] I will never forget my dear old pal. We buried him behind the firing line along with his comrades. The officer said the Lord's Prayer over him and I have got a photo of him which I will keep, if you don't mind and I hope that God will watch over you and your family. May God bless you and yours in this your darkest hour and let me know what you would like done to the grave. We will make him a nice cross [and] all his personal goods will be sent to you. I cannot write anymore as I am full to write, so I will close. Believe me your sincere friend and God bless you and your family.
Sapper Kelly

Not all official communiqués from the military were as definite as to whether a man had been killed, wounded or taken prisoner. Well over 40 per cent of casualties who died in the Great War have no known grave. For those who 'disappeared', there was the army form B.104-83: 'I regret to have to inform you that a report has been received from the War Office to the effect that — was posted as missing on —' As the form went on to stipulate, this did not mean the soldier was dead, although in most cases he was. Joyce Crow was eight years old when her family received word that her brother Arthur, who had been serving with the London Rifle Brigade, was 'missing, presumed killed'.

'My brother had only been in France fighting on the Somme for a matter of a few weeks when we heard he was missing. And that was the awfulness, not knowing. Father, because he was a journalist, pulled every string to try and find out whether he might still be alive. We were in limbo. You felt you were letting your brother down if you doubted he was alive, because there was always hope, however small. Equally you didn't pretend that he was alive either, you carried on as usual because there was that feeling that everyone must be brave about this until we knew more.'

Knowing more might never happen, and it was often a year or two before final confirmation was received on army form 82A that: 'It is my painful duty to inform you that no further news having been received relative to — the Army Council have been regretfully constrained to conclude that he is dead.'

So many men were missing, so many more who had died in circumstances the precise nature of which was unknown. Families desperate for news posted adverts in the papers: 'Lieut Clarke, reported "missing" after action at Ypres, June 2 or 3. Will anyone having seen or spoken to him just before or during the action or having any knowledge of him since kindly WRITE with particulars.' Miracles did happen, and a man would turn up, offering a sliver of hope to others that they too might yet find their soldier alive. Similarly, simple administrative errors were occasionally to blame. 'Killed in Action' was retained for those who were supposed to be verified dead, and should have closed the door on any expectations to the contrary. Yet, in the confusion of large-scale fighting, names became mixed up, units confused and a man reported as dead had survived.

When Private Richards of the 15th Battalion Tank Corps was reported killed in action, he had in fact been confused with Private Richards of the 25th Battalion, who had actually been killed taking part in the same assault. Only when the survivor was told of the error by his officer was he able to write home quickly rectifying the position. His was a rare but no means unique case, although the difference in their respective Christian names, Archibald and Sydney, should have ensured no mistake in the first place. Such misinformation, as well as the odd miracle, was inevitable in war and gave undoubted hope to many. Sadly, in Lieutenant Clarke's case, despite the newspaper pleas, his whereabouts were never discovered. He was twenty-two years old when he died.

In August 1916, the Butler family was to receive news that their son had been wounded again, though not seriously. Harold had been acting as a stretcher bearer in an attack launched by his battalion in early August and was, according to the news,

injured in the face. Harold's sister and mother quickly wrote off
to France.

Monday 14.8.16

My dearest Harold

Just a few lines dear trusting they will find you much
better. We had a report from the War Office last Saturday
telling us you had been wounded again, you little darling
and you never let us know dear, I suppose you thought it
would worry us brave thoughtful Boy, I admire you for
it . . . Walter went to France last Friday, I do hope you
will meet out there, and let's hope this awful war will soon
end and then, please God, we will have our dear ones
with us once again, won't it be glorious.

Fondest love and kisses from your most loving and
devoted sister, Elsie.

Harold my dearest son just a few lines to you and to
let you know that I heard from the War Office that you
had been wounded again. Dear Harold by what I have
heard from dear Maude you are out of danger. I do
hope and trust you are, oh this awful war, what a trying
time it is for everyone, but still Harold dear we can only
hope for the best. Dear Harold don't you worry about
me I wish you were as safe as I was, never mind God is
good, he still spares you and I still hope and trust you
will, also your father, be spared to come safe home to
me again . . .

With fondest love Ma xxxxxx

The letters were never to reach Harold. Whatever news the
Butler family had been given regarding their son had been
misleading. Harold had in fact been killed during a night attack
early on 4 August, a full ten days before his family wrote to him.
In all, four officers were wounded and a further 114 other ranks,
including Harold, were killed or wounded, or reported missing.

It is possible that Harold was not badly wounded, although an injury to the face (the wound reported) was often difficult to bandage, and many soldiers quickly died through an inexorable loss of blood. If Harold was buried and his position marked, then his grave did not survive the war and, as with so many others, he is now commemorated on the Thiepval Memorial to the Missing on the Somme. Walter, Harold's brother, received the news soon after arriving in France.

My dear Elsie

I received your letter containing the horrible news, and I feel absolutely choked, to think that our dear Harold is killed. He was the dearest boy that I have ever known, it has hit us very hard. I feel absolutely done over it, there is not interest in anything for me now. I will never forget him, and may God bless him. Can you imagine my feelings about Germans, fancy the blasted damn rotters shooting a stretcher bearer, as you know they wear a white armlet. I think my darling that you must take the news as being correct, I wish to God it wasn't, but in your letter dear you put the date as December 2nd but I expect you mean August. I am deeply sorry for Maude, I am afraid that he was the only boy for her, I too think she will never get over it, what a terrible war. Darling, we have been hit badly but the only sympathy you get from strangers is that their trouble is worse.

Try to look forward to the end of this war, it cannot last much longer and then we shall meet again, and for good. Does Dad know the awful truth yet? Do you think it would be best to tell him? I must carry on, Harold's dear life as much as it means to us counts nothing with anybody out here, all I can do is get on with my own and be content with my own thoughts, I have broken down more than once, but I am glad you did not keep the news from me . . .

Walter

In searching for the 'awful truth', requests for former comrades to get in touch or to be put in contact with families were common. Arthur Barraclough, lying wounded in hospital in Wigan, heard a familiar name when a list of 'missing' men was read out on his ward. Arthur had served in the same machine-gun team with the missing man and was able to confirm that the man was in fact dead. Assuming that was the end of the matter, Arthur was surprised when he was invited to visit the man's parents in a mining village near Chesterfield. Now aged 105, Arthur recalls the day when, as a nineteen-year-old, he took the train to Chesterfield. 'I went and told them they wouldn't have to expect him coming home. They had been hoping he was a prisoner. They were heartbroken really, but they thanked me for going to tell them.'

Requests for information crossed all social boundaries. Herbert Cripps, a private in the Rifle Brigade, was on leave when he was 'asked' to visit Lord Desborough at his home at Taplow Court in Buckinghamshire. His son, the Honorable Gerald William 'Billy' Grenfell, had been killed in action right next to the young private during a counter-attack at Hooge in July 1915. Billy's death was not in doubt; rather it was the precise details about the moment he had died that were important to the family. 'I told his father that I was just laying the side of him when somebody blew a whistle and he jumped up and shouted, "Come on, if you know you're Englishmen." He was a big man and went down with such a thud, as he was shot straight through the chest.'

In the chest, or 'in the head' as another witness asserted in a letter to Lord Desborough – either way, the words were meant to comfort a family looking for reassurance that their son did not suffer. 'He must have been killed instantaneously,' affirmed letters encouragingly. In head injuries some disfigurement was implied, and in a preponderance of cases an effort was made to imply that not only had the soldier died straight away but that the injuries were, in essence, internal, leaving the body 'serene' prior to burial. Shot through the heart was by far the most common cause of death for, as one soldier put it, 'What else could you tell

Sir,

It is my painful duty to inform you that a report has this day been received from the War Office notifying the death of

(No.) *6547.* (Rank) *L/Cpl*

(Name) *H. H. Butler* (Regiment) *The Buffs*

East Kent which occurred at *The British*

Expeditionary Force France. on the *4th*

of *August 1916* , and I am to express to you the sympathy and regret of the Army Council at your loss. The cause of death was

Killed in Action

If any articles of private property left by the deceased are found, they will be forwarded to this Office, but some time will probably elapse before their receipt, and when received they cannot be disposed of until authority is received from the War Office.

Application regarding the disposal of any such personal effects, or of any amount that may eventually be found to be due to the late soldier's estate, should be addressed to " The Secretary, War Office, London, S.W.," and marked outside " Effects."

I am,
Sir,
Your obedient Servant,

[signature]

Major for Colonel.
I/C Infantry Records. Hounslow
Officer in charge of Records.

The official letter confirming the death of a loved one, in this case Harold Butler.

them? That he'd been blown to bits!'

Wherever possible, the dead man's belongings were sent back to his family. William Roberts's mother received, among other things, the wallet she had bought for her husband's birthday. A keepsake such as this was of great sentimental importance and an absence of such personal belongings was of deep concern to relatives: rings, photographs, a diary, anything that gave the bereaved a link to their dead was sought both as a comfort and as tangible evidence that a loved one was not coming home. It was considered neither ghoulish nor unusual for a bloodstained wallet or handkerchief to make its way back from France to be treasured by the dead man's family.

With the exponential growth in casualty rates during the war, more and more children became affected by family loss, although in a world in which children were seen and not heard, their own sense of bereavement and confusion was often ignored or played down. Their story has often been forgotten, leaving many children to harbour feelings of guilt and insecurity for their entire lives. Statistics have been garnered by historians to highlight improvements or otherwise in health care, or to underline the numbers sent prematurely to work in aid of the war effort. Yet understanding the feelings of over 340,000 children who lost one or both parents in the war, with perhaps a greater number losing a brother or close relative, has been overlooked. The war swirled around children's everyday exist-ence, on one level fearful of Zeppelin raids, curious or bemused by the sight of wounded soldiers, on another level made anxious by the obvious fears and concerns of their elders. Children too played an integral part in the war, fund raising or knitting comforts for the soldiers abroad. There was little escape from the conflict at home or even in school where the war touched their lives on a frequent basis when old boys or former masters were killed.

The extent of such loss was profound and can be seen in the Rolls of Honour published by many schools. Eton produced a book listing all those who had served in the war and those who had fallen, a book of some 281 pages. Repton commemorated in print the 347 old boys it lost; Harrow recorded its 516 old boys who died in the war, an average of one every three days. It was not just the grand public schools that produced such rolls: Birkenhead High School produced a 212-page book with portraits of over 100 former pupils who died in the war, as did Portsmouth Boys' Secondary School, with biographical details of sixty-nine dead. Little wonder that morning assembly in schools right across Great Britain could frequently be akin to attending a wake.

The pain of such loss sticks in the memory of Kathleen Barron who recalls the trauma, as a thirteen-year-old, of seeing her headmaster Mr Garside announce the death of an old boy.

'And do you know he actually cried; the tears rolled down his face. The sight amazed me really, yet it made me like him more, because of how he felt about the old boys. We would have a hymn then there would be silence, and that would affect us all. My brother Dick was an old boy of the school and of course I was always afraid that he might one day read out his name.'

School life was bound up with the war and was frequently interrupted. Former pupils regularly returned on leave to visit, to be fêted by the headmaster and the pupils. Many younger soldiers had only recently left school, and went ostensibly to pick up a younger brother but also to enjoy the acclaim heaped on returning heroes, especially if they brought a gas mask or enemy helmet with which to enthral the children. Fathers too, returning from leave, often popped in to see a child, to the delight and pride of the boy or girl concerned. These visits, while welcomed, also increased the intensity of loss when a former pupil, or a father, was killed.

Young Lucy Walter (née Neale), born near Kidderminster, was in the middle of lessons when her father turned up unexpectedly at her school.

'I suppose it was about ten o'clock in the morning and there was a knock at the door. We couldn't see who was on the other side, as the teacher, Mrs Beeston, went to answer it. I heard her say, "Oh Mr Neale, how lovely to see you, you're on leave then?" And then she closed the door, much to my annoyance, and I couldn't hear a thing. Then she opened the door and beckoned me and she said, "Come along, Lucy, you can go home now, you don't want to be in school any longer today." It was my tenth birthday and I was so proud, and he looked lovely in his khaki uniform.'

Lucy did not attend school the day she heard her father had died at the front, but returned the next day, quietly explaining why she had been absent to Mrs Bywater, the headmistress. When school started, the three classes were brought together for the usual prayers, only this time Mrs Bywater spoke to the children. 'I just want to tell you that Lucy has lost her father, so I think we ought to pray this morning for Lucy and her mother.' Lucy, now aged ninety-six, recalls that assembly.

'I couldn't take it in, I was in a dream. The Lord's Prayer was said, and the usual prayers and a little hymn we used to sing, but I just couldn't, or I wouldn't, perhaps, face the fact that I would never see him again. That day was the worst day, and then a day or two later another girl, she lost her father, and we said prayers again for her.'

'At school the war was with you all the time,' recalls Liverpool-born Sydney Bond, who was an eight-year-old schoolboy in 1916.

'It was a common sight to see the headmaster or mistress. They would suddenly appear, cross over to the teacher's desk talking very quietly, almost in the teacher's ear, and we all knew what had happened. We would watch the teacher nodding his head then, once the headmaster had gone, he would settle the class, and the next thing he would say was, "Oh, Willie Robinson, you're to go home." We all knew what that meant, the home of Willie Robinson had just received a letter saying his brother or dad had been killed in action, and at that time, God, they were ten a penny.'

Sydney Bond's half-brother was serving in the Merchant Navy and had already been plucked once from the sea after his first ship was torpedoed; now he was back out on another ship. One day at school Sydney was working in class when the headmaster made his solemn entrance.

'You always expected the news to be about somebody else, but this time as they whispered I could hear that they were discussing me. To this day I can still see the faces of these people carrying out this scene, anyway I was to go home and I really thought it was to face up to the fact that my brother had gone, that he was dead.'

Sydney raced home to find his luck was in again. His brother had survived his second immersion in the Irish Sea, although in this case the length of time he had had to swim before being picked up meant that his health suffered for the rest of his life.

Death did not just take its toll among old boys but among their masters too. Just six in 1915, Maud Cox was devoted to her teacher at school, Mr Brown, a handsome Scotsman from Killin, in Perthshire.

'We'd never had a male teacher before, so we were thrilled to bits. The first day he went through the register he was going through the names and he said, "Oh we have a Maud, stand up, Maud." So I stood up and he crooked his little finger and said "Come here." He told us he was a singer and that his favourite song was "Come into the

Garden, Maud", so he says, "That'll be our song, won't it?" And oh, of course I was thrilled.'

In due course Mr Brown was called up and went to France, from where he regularly sent postcards to the school to let the children know how he was getting on. Then one day the headmaster, Mr Christie, called the children into assembly with some news. Maud recalls:

' "Now Mr Brown and the fiancés of Miss Jessie and Miss McCloud have all been killed at a place called the Somme in France," and he pointed it out on a map and put a cross on it. "Now I want you all to say a prayer for the dead and then we'll sing the first verse of 'Oh God our Help in Ages Past' and then I want you all to walk very quietly home." I was aghast and cried all the way home, he was never going to come and sing to me again. He seemed very grown up to me but I don't suppose he would be any more than twenty-four or twenty-five.'

In a society brought up on the outward suppression of emotions, particularly among men, the news that a son or brother had been killed often elicited in an extraordinary way the calm repression of natural feelings. These emotions must have been difficult to repress, but to the outside world appeared like a consummate example of the stiff upper lip. On the Western Front, the death of a brother or friend could result in the furious exaction of revenge; at home there was nobody to attack, nobody from whom to exact retribution. When the war ended two years later, it was the civilians at home who were most vitriolic in their hatred of all things Teutonic, not the majority of soldiers in France or occupied Germany, who were often shocked at the tirades heaped upon the defeated enemy by politicians and public alike. It was an outpouring of pent-up anger and emotion suppressed while the outcome of the war was still in doubt.

That suppression is nowhere better illustrated than when Len

Whitehead had to break the news that his brother, his father's eldest son, was not coming home. Len's father was working in the fields, ploughing.

> 'I waited for him to finish a bout with his plough and two horses. "George has been killed," I told him. He stood for a moment. He didn't answer, didn't say a word, but left his horses all steaming in the early November weather and together we walked back in silence to the house. When we got home my father went to the bottom of the stairs and called up "That's right, ain't it?" He made no attempt to go up and comfort my mother but went into the kitchen, sat in his wooden armchair and put his arms on the table and his head on his arms for a little while – wept for a few moments, I think. But that sticks in my memory, that he didn't go upstairs to comfort my mother.'

London-born Madge Maindonald was eleven years old when her brother was killed on the Somme. Her memory of her father's reaction to the news was startlingly similar to that of Len. Madge's mother had died in early 1915 and this had deeply affected family life at their home in Vauxhall, just south of the River Thames in London. 'It was a house of misery after that because father was terribly fond of my mother, they were very happy together. Anyway I don't think my brother could stand the atmosphere any more.' To escape the unhappiness, Madge's brother Edwin had enlisted under age – he was only eighteen when he was sent to France to join the 11th Royal West Kent Regiment. In September 1916, a few weeks after arriving, he was killed in action and his body lost. 'My father was sent a telegram, but I was at school and didn't know anything about it until I came home. He was in the bedroom, I think he had been very upset. He called to me and, facing the door, simply said, "Your brother's dead." I think my father was so pent up with it all.'

When the brother of Joyce Crow died, the family would not allow itself to openly mourn. Now aged ninety-three, Joyce recalls the day when news came that Arthur had been killed.

'I was in the bathroom when my sister came up the stairs
to speak to me, she said, and I remember the words to this
day, "Don't say anything about Arthur, Mother has had
terribly bad news, but she's had a lovely letter from his
captain." I went to speak to my other sister to tell her
what had happened; we wouldn't have spoken much, then
I went downstairs and found Mum looking terrible but
still managing to do the washing up. I gave Mum a hug
and simply said, "Shall I take Daddy's breakfast up on a
tray?"'

Madge's response was equally calm.

'I said, "Oh yes." I don't think I took it in – you can only
bear so much and then your mind refuses it. There had
been so many deaths it was just another one and he'd been
gone for such a while, in the army. I was sorry when I'd
got quiet to myself but I couldn't do things in public, not
in front of people, I couldn't get showing emotion in front
of people.'

The response was not unusual. There was a strong tendency for
children to take their lead from adults and refuse to weep, staying
strong for parents who were inwardly devastated themselves. The
enormity of death was often too great for a child to comprehend,
but there were other factors too. In large extended families in
which a twenty-year age range might exist between siblings, a
young child might not feel the death so keenly should the eldest
be killed. 'I don't remember shedding any tears,' recalls Len
Whitehead. 'I was sad that we wouldn't see him again but he
wasn't one of my favourite brothers as he was the oldest in the
family, he was twenty-five, and inclined to tease us, and I was just
eight. I was more concerned about my mother, because she was
so upset.' Madge Maindonald had seen her brother only for short

intervals, and the difference in age had limited the contact, but there was another reason too. 'I think being brought up with brothers and no mother, and being treated like a boy, was why I couldn't be a little girl who cried her eyes out. I did grieve for him privately but I think you didn't want to distress anybody else. Edwin was gone, that was all, Edwin was gone.'

There was an inevitable void after a soldier was killed, a void that was not only spiritual but physical, for whether a soldier was blown to pieces or killed intact there was no body to bury for his family back home. As Len Whitehead recalls, his father went back to work after a brief pause for grief. 'There was nothing much to be done, you see, there were no funeral arrangements to be made. So he went back to his ploughing.' In the Whitehead family, as in so many others, there was only the question of contacting other members of the family, so an elder brother was dispatched to the post office to send two telegrams to Len's sisters, both of whom were working in London. They simply read, 'George killed – come if you can, Mother.'

Early in the war, there had been a great deal of public pressure on the government to bring bodies home. But so many men had been lost that the government decided as early as 1915 not to repatriate any of the fallen. For almost half the families there was no body as the soldier had been blown to pieces or, through lack of surviving identification, rendered unrecognisable. It was not until September 1916 that soldiers were given a second identity disc, one to be taken as proof of death, the other to be left with the body for later recognition. In time only one body was brought back to represent all those who would remain abroad, the Unknown Warrior. A few wartime visits to the graves of relatives were granted by the military authorities, but the vast majority had to wait until after the war, to see the resting place of a loved one or the field in which he fell. Len Whitehead's brother George, killed on 29 October 1915, has no grave and is commemorated on the Loos Memorial to the missing, along with over 20,000 other men who vanished in the area. Madge Maindonald's brother Edwin, and Joyce Crow's brother Arthur were also never found and are commemorated on the Thiepval Memorial to the Missing of the Somme, along with Harold Butler and 73,500 others.

The industrialisation of war led to a centralisation of death, in stark contrast to the Victorian era when death and the grieving process was a major and elaborate affair. Then people, children included, were invited to see the body, which would lie in the home before burial; in Cornwall children were encouraged to kiss the hand of the deceased to aid, it was believed, their own longevity. Traditions were followed as a matter of course. Black horses resplendent with plumes drew the coach carrying the coffin to the cemetery; an old soldier who faded away had his polished black boots turned back to front in the stirrups of the horse leading the cortège. And of course there was mourning dress worn by all, including the youngest children. Until the First World War, people continued to observe the Victorian rites of mourning the dead.

However with the onset of war, the observance of rituals built up over the previous hundred years suddenly declined. Pre-eminent in undermining those traditions during the war was the increasing use of heavy artillery, in which millions of shells were used by both sides to pulverise men in the line. Artillery was the big killer in the war, shattering, dismembering and burying bodies. With so many men abroad having no burial whatsoever, traditional funerals at home were felt to be indulgent and extravagant in the light of wartime economic shortages and restrictions. Desperate grief remained but had fewer outlets for public expression. The prevalent code of conduct was to 'carry on': it was a wartime necessity, and a recipe for intense isolation.

Sixteen-year-old Florence Billington was working as a house-maid in Buxton when she received news that her boyfriend Ted Felton was dead.

'My heart sank when I saw the letter. I told the other girls and they were sorry, but they were getting used to hearing that relatives and friends had been killed. So much was happening that I went away from them, just to grieve quietly on my own. I couldn't really imagine him not being around. I thought maybe one day the army would find out they had made a mistake and perhaps he might turn up. I just wanted to hide somewhere where it was quiet and not to bother to talk to anybody.'

Ted's body was lost and without a body and without a grave there was for Florence, as for so many families, no proper 'closure'. Instead, suffering continued behind closed doors.

As a consequence of the breakdown in funeral customs, children were no longer an integral part of the grieving process; instead, they took their lead from their parents as to how to carry on. Londoner Ellen Elston was nearly nine years old and the eldest of six children when her father, Sergeant John Tanner, was killed serving with the 9th Royal East Surrey Regiment. In the aftermath of the terrible news, Ellen was unwilling to display any emotion in public. Like her mother, she felt the weight of responsibility towards the rest of the family and the need to display strength to the wider community. Ellen recalls:

'Good neighbours would come round and offer their sympathy, feeling sorry for us, bringing us sweets and biscuits to cheer us up. But that was all. In no time at all Mother had made black-and-white check dresses with a black belt for all the girls, and I can see us now, all walking down the street together and people looking at us because Father was well known in the community. I never cried in front of other people. You are too proud to let people see that things reach you, you are taught that. I wanted to cry, inwardly, but you didn't want anybody to see it, especially being the eldest. I kept everything inside because I daren't let the other children see me break down because they looked up to me, so I waited until I got to bed then had a good cry, just as I'm sure Mum did when she was on her own.'

One of the consequences of the break with tradition was that expression of grief was deemed no longer a personal issue but became societal, a collective process overseen by the political and military authorities. Private memorials to dead relatives, a last throwback to the Victorian rites of grieving, began to spring up in the earliest days of the war. At first these were tolerated but then banned, to be replaced by official monuments, dedicated to collective loss. At the apex in managing the grief was the Church of England, which held an exalted position but one that became increasingly invidious as the war dragged on and popular support for the fighting grew stale.

Endorsement for the war by the established faiths had been more or less unquestioning at home in 1914, while abroad clergymen representing many denominations struggled for the souls of the fighting men: nearly 2,000 from the Church of England, 650 Catholics, as well as another 1,000 made up of Wesleyans, Baptists, Methodists and Presbyterians. The unholy scramble to France sickened some, and made many clergymen the butt of soldiers' jokes at the front, although a good few won the admiration and respect of all.

In 1914, the Church had the ear of the nation, with at least 30 million people or 90 per cent of the population notionally members of one of the mainstream faiths, and church attendance a weekly ritual, particularly among the middle classes. There was, however, an acknowledgement that much religious observance was mere convention and that the war was a modern crusade that could be harnessed to reawaken the dormant faith of the masses, especially among those in the industrial working class. Aligning the Church with a popular cause – and in 1914 there were relatively few who cautioned against the war – seemed a sensible stance to take. The belligerence of clergymen varied greatly across the country, although few were as defiant as the Bishop of London who called upon the nation's men 'To kill Germans, not [thankfully] for the sake of killing, but to save the world; to kill the good as well as the bad . . . lest the civilisation of the world should itself be killed.' In such a climate, 'Fight the Good Fight', and 'Onward Christian Soldiers' were particularly apposite, popular hymns that had built-in confirmation of the war's legitimate aspirations.

The bellicose attitude of a few in the Church could taint those others who attempted to give genuine pastoral care. With deaths in every parish across the country, it was up to the rank and file clergyman to make his rounds, comforting the bereaved, as Len Whitehead describes:

'The village vicar arrived, as he did, I suppose, with most families who had lost someone. He came in and I was sent out of the room when prayers were to be said. I stood outside the door and heard him say, "When two or three are gathered together . . ." part of the prayers, of course. My mother and sisters came out of the room, tearful, red-eyed, and the old vicar made his way homeward up the farm chase, stooping slightly. He was a frequent visitor from then onwards but always the same procedure, there would be prayers and it made my mother terribly sad. We used to wish, perhaps, he wouldn't come.'

The effects of war were such that they could reaffirm a person's belief in God or shatter it for ever. Ellen Elston's uncle, a monk at a monastery, came to see the family but was ordered from the home by Ellen's mother. 'She wouldn't listen to him. "Don't come telling me there's a God because I don't believe in him any more. God wouldn't have let this happen to me."'

Joyce Crow's mother, Letitia, did not rail against God, and continued to go to church as she had always done, although her children began to drift away from weekly attendance. Letitia carried on going to Remembrance Sundays, although her weekly attendance declined. She never spoke of her feelings, but years later wrote a fifty-page memoir in which she briefly explained her gradual alienation from the Church: 'But the worst symptom was that often words conveyed no meaning whatsoever. That is really why I gave up going to church. I could hear the words, I could even give the meaning of each one and yet they conveyed nothing. I could feel as it were, the wheels going round and round in my mind and not gripping anything. It was terrifying.'

The Church's outspoken support for the war was a dangerous ploy. As the number of casualties grew, the Church became associated with the causes, yet its role in leading the rituals of grieving was, at the same time, being undermined. There was a problem in traditional, non-Catholic, teaching in Britain, especially among the Nonconformist churches of the day, in that there were no formal liturgical prayers for the dead. Methodists, for example, were taught that it was pointless to pray for the dead because they were already in God's hands.

The belief in the resurrection and eternal life led a significant number of people, if not to abandon traditional methods of prayer, to seek solace elsewhere and in particular to try to make contact with loved ones beyond the grave. The need to make a connection with lost relatives, on at least one spiritual plane, left a vacuum filled in part by the spiritualists and spiritualist societies. During 1916 these groups grew in prominence, undoubtedly helped by high-profile advocates such as Sir Arthur Conan Doyle, the creator of Sherlock Holmes. As a prominent layman of the established Church, he promoted the idea that spiritualism and Christianity were complementary. Such was his interest that by early 1916 Sir Arthur claimed he had positive knowledge of life after death, and later began an extensive national and international lecture tour on the subject.

Another exponent was a leading scientist, Sir Oliver Lodge, whose son Raymond was killed at the front in 1915. His séances with the well-known medium Gladys Leonard, during which she 'contacted' Sir Oliver's son, helped convince him of the afterlife and, because of his impeccable scientific credentials (a former Professor of Physics at University College, Liverpool), a good many others besides. His book, *Raymond, or Life and Death*, was so widely read when it was first published in November 1916 that it was on its fourth reprint before the year was out. In all, there were twelve printings, reflecting the public's desire to believe in the ability to contact the dead. 'There is no real breach of continuity between the dead and the living,' he wrote, 'and methods of intercommunication across what has seemed to be a gulf can be set going in response to the urgent demand of affection.'

In every walk of life there were charlatans, and spiritualism attracted more than most when there was money to be made, although there were practitioners who clearly believed in what they were doing. Florence Billington met a spiritualist in Leeds.

'He came to lunch with his wife, and while we were having a cup of tea, this man told me that he could see a very young boy in khaki standing behind me. "He says he was killed in the war – have you any idea who that is?" I said, "Yes, I know who it is." He said, "Well, this young man is showing an awful lot of love towards you. He's here for you and he wants me to tell you that he loved you with all his heart and soul and had hoped to make his life with you, if he could have done." On occasions since, I have felt his spirit visit me; that he was thinking of me and was somewhere near.'

Spiritualism helped Florence deal with her loss, but for the vast majority there was no quick remedy to deal with the pain. Each family coped as well as they could over the following weeks, months and years. Joyce Crow's brother Arthur was the most popular boy in the family, a great storyteller, and news that he had died was greeted with silence from that moment onwards. His name would not be mentioned in the house again.

'No one wanted to talk about him, it was an unspoken understanding, I am not sure I was even really conscious about it at the time, it was an atmosphere. I think we all felt that Mother would want us to carry on as normal. We had a neighbour, called Arthur, and from 1916 onwards he was nicknamed "Jimmy", when he came to the house, as

was a later boyfriend of mine also, coincidentally, called
the same name as my brother. From the time that Arthur
was killed in France there was an unspoken understanding
among the rest of the children that we must support
Mother in every way that we could. If there was a job to
be done by one of us, it was done and done to the best of
our ability. We wanted to be a happy family and there
would be no quarrelling. You must understand and not
intrude, that was very important. If someone doesn't want
to talk about something you didn't ask questions; that was
the feeling that we gave one another about our brother.'

In the dining room of the home of Ellen Elston was a picture of
her father, John Tanner.

'It was the fashion to have a big head and shoulders
photograph of your loved one hung on the wall. It was a
beautiful picture in a gold frame, a picture of Dad wearing
a peaked hat with a flat top. Well, Mum turned that
picture around to face the wall because when she went
into that room she could not bear to look at it, I can't
remember how long it stayed like that.'

There was at least a grave for the Tanner family to visit, Plot IV,
Row E, Grave 9 of Brandhoek New Military Cemetery, Ypres;
while the family of Joyce Crow had pictures and letters sent by
Arthur from France. For Florence Billington there was nothing,
for they were only boyfriend and girlfriend and any of Ted's
belongings, if they survived, were returned to his parents.
Incapable of expressing her sadness, Florence recalls that her life
became a 'rollercoaster' after Ted's death.

'I was always chopping and changing. I would get a job,
then I would want to go home. But I was thinking of
him, that's what it was. Before I met the spiritualist I
hoped maybe one day the army would find out that they

had made a mistake and perhaps he might turn up. And over the years when missing soldiers did turn up, I thought, "Wouldn't it be wonderful if it was Ted." '

Joyce Crow's mother could not forget Arthur, despite the wall of silence at home.

'Our letter said "Missing presumed killed" and that was the awfulness, not knowing. That glimmer of hope affected her tremendously. Many, many years later she revealed that she had felt that there was a tight band around her forehead and that if it broke she would go mad. She found it difficult to stay still, or sleep, and would often go out with one of my sisters and they would just walk around the streets of Hornsey. I was conscious of hearing the front door shut night after night, and because Mum bottled her emotions up it made the pain much worse.'

Around two-thirds of men who were killed in the fighting that summer were under the age of thirty. The numbers ensured that the pain suffered by Joyce's mother was similarly felt in every corner of Britain after the Battle of the Somme. The British public had come to learn what attrition truly meant.

And the pain is still there for those who so comprehensively bottled up the sadness and anxiety, as Madge Maindonald acknowledges.

'He was dead, the poor boy, he was dead and I've thought about him a lot − even now I think about him − not even got his own grave, poor little boy. I think to myself he was at the beginning of his life, what did he know, he knew nothing did he, he knew nothing and there he was eighteen years old and dead. He was full of life and he was full of laughter and he did love chasing the girls.'

CHAPTER FIVE

Caring for the Wounded

T HE DAILY CONDUCT OF WAR HAD, BY LATE 1916, changed out of all recognition from that of two years earlier. The rapid industrialisation of the fighting had brought new horrors to the battlefield, unimaginable in 1914. The advent of gas as a tactical weapon and the irregular use of flamethrowers were but overtures to longer and more destructive artillery duels, with the PBI (the self-named Poor Bloody Infantry) stuck somewhere in the middle, enduring bombardments from howitzers and heavy guns. In the four and a half months of fighting in 1914, British casualties had totalled 92,000; in the equivalent time on the Somme in 1916, the figures were 420,000.

Trench warfare was the ultimate test of human resolve, and those who escaped through injury could have as many demons in their minds as wounds on their bodies. Nurse Mary Jollie was working at the Notts County War Hospital, caring for soldiers who were both mentally and physically sick.

'There was one soldier who was afraid of sleeping and I couldn't help trying to ease his situation, and I said, "What did you see?" And he said, "Well, I saw wounded men on the ground and our tanks coming along and just mowing through them." He said it was very terrible. I did see it as part of my job, sitting talking with them, trying to make them forget, but they couldn't forget.'

The tank had been the latest British addition to the weapons of war. Its introduction midway through the Battle of the Somme, in September 1916, had appeared to herald a new dawn, a winning aspect in the war's equation. On first sight, the weapon had terrorised the enemy, and large numbers had fled from their trenches. But as the tank crews knew, there was no chance of picking a way through their own wounded; a tank's course never deviated for anything except a target. It was not just the enemy who had been terrorised by what they had seen.

Mary Jollie had been drawn to serve as a nurse, in part, by the emergency of war. She recalled a famous poster that had shown two women, a mother and her daughter, standing at the window of their home waving to the boys as they marched off to war. Above the women was the slogan 'Women of Britain say, Go!' It was one of the many hundreds of posters produced during the war to entice men into the army, but this poster in particular had another, equally important, message: by implication, the women were saying that they could and would look after the country while the men were away. It was Mary's duty to help if she could.

The enrolment of women into war service was by no means widespread or comprehensive in the early days of war. Rather, initial economic uncertainty forced tens of thousands of women out of work. Even when it became apparent that there was a shortage of labour in crucial war industries, there was no rush to employ women unless the powerful trade unions agreed to the 'dilution' of jobs traditionally undertaken by men. Before the war, by far the largest sector for female employment was domestic service. With the advent of war, other areas were gradually opened up, primarily the typical white-collar jobs such as secretarial and clerical work in offices. In July 1914, for example, there were only 1,500 women employed in banking. By 1916, this had risen to over 30,000. During the war, more than 1.5 million women eventually replaced men in the workplace, allowing the men to leave for the army and subsequently the front.

In the nursing profession there was less urgency for women to replace men. The job, inherently associated with caring, was part of the woman's domain, and was one of the few careers to which women could aspire in civilian life without raising eyebrows. Of the 33,000 women in nursing before the war, 27,000 worked in civil hospitals, a number that altered little during the course of the conflict. Not surprisingly, it was in the military hospitals that the number of nurses burgeoned. There were only 700 women employed in War Office, Admiralty and Territorial hospitals in July 1914, a number that rose to 13,600 by 1918. Supporting the trained nurses of the Queen Mary's Imperial Nursing Service was a small army of VADs, voluntary nurses who had enlisted in the new Voluntary Aid Detachments. These detachments had been set up in 1910 to supplement the established nursing services, and were organised through the Red Cross and the Order of St John.

By July 1914, around 5,300 women had volunteered to help in hospitals, while another 47,000 had enlisted into 2,500 VAD branches dotted across the country. Then, just before hostilities broke out, the first VADs had been allowed to join the Territorial Army's annual summer camp to provide food, dressings and transport, as the need arose. For girls looking for new and exciting challenges, the Voluntary Aid Detachments were a truly appealing choice. When war broke out, thousands more enlisted, primarily young women from middle-class and wealthy back-grounds, who flocked to help look after the wounded.

Although girls joining the Red Cross or the Order of St John as VADs were meant to be nineteen years old, many could not wait to enlist. Marjorie Grigsby was one such volunteer.

'I was sick and tired of my father talking about his sons in France, so when I came home from boarding school I went to the Red Cross Hospital, saw the matron and told her I'd like to join the VADs please, and she said, "Oh yes, how old are you?" So I said, "Seventeen." She said, "I'm sorry, my dear, you must come back in two years' time, you're too young." I said, "But you've got Freda Allen here." She said, "Nurse Allen? She's twenty." I said, "Oh no she's not. She and I were in the kindergarten together and when I went to boarding school she was still at the high school, and if she's here she's still seventeen." So she said, "But she's a very good nurse." "I'm quite sure she is," I agreed. "So you've got two choices: you either get rid of your very good Nurse Allen or you must take me on." That was it, I was in. I went home and asked mother for a cheque for £22 to go and buy a uniform, and although she was furious about me joining, I'd won and that was all that mattered.'

Marjorie's desire to join was born partly out of a sense of adventure; for others, it was a sense of duty. Lesley Leigh-Jones was born into a well-off middle-class family.

'I was at home, having left school aged about nineteen, and my elder sister was nursing. I led a very gay life; playing tennis was all the rage, and my sister said to me, "How can you live like that when there's a war on, when men are being killed? You ought to join up and do war work," and that set my conscience ticking, so I joined up as a VAD.'

Another whose conscience was 'set ticking' was seventeen-year-old Doris Neve.

'I was going to be a teacher at Cheltenham Ladies' College, but when the war broke out my father said, "You know, wouldn't you be much more use doing some nursing and helping with the war effort?" and I thought about it. The hospitals were desperate for staff and were taking anyone they could get; mostly they were doctors' wives and people of that sort of vintage and they really didn't know much more than I did. So I started at the Racecourse Hospital at Cheltenham, a totally makeshift hospital. The sister there said, "Oh, you're a born nurse, you'll be fine," so I stayed.'

From the earliest days of the war, the arrival of wounded soldiers drew a crowd of spectators and sympathisers: it wasn't possible to tell the difference or necessarily distinguish the two. At railway stations such as Victoria and Waterloo, hundreds of civilians gathered close to the main entrance to watch the wounded being carried on to waiting ambulances. Many more would hang around at the other end to watch men disgorged into the waiting hospitals. In Brighton, for example, at the 2nd Eastern General Hospital, hundreds regularly lined the railings outside the hospital grounds to catch a glimpse of the heroes who were returning from such epic engagements as Mons, Le Cateau and the fighting on the Marne, while beyond the gates sash windows were lifted as homeowners watched from nearby houses. Some people were family members, trying to catch a glimpse of wounded relatives, but more often civilians were simply fascinated to see and to cheer brave heroes.

As a child, Penny Feiwel watched endless processions of the wounded arrive at her local hospital in London.

'Our road ended in a dead end where the railway ran along to the station by Harrow Gardens. We used to watch over the fence as the trains came in and then we could see men, I suppose they were orderlies, climb on to the train, some with stretchers, others with chairs, and you'd see the carriage doors open and then the Tommies would appear, some on crutches and some being taken on stretchers. From there, further across, we could see the ambulances waiting on a little green to take the wounded men to North Middlesex Hospital. We watched this operation many, many times.'

The public didn't just stand and stare; cigarettes and chocolate were handed out in profusion, as Liverpool-born Sydney Bond recalls with pride.

'The war, which for a long time was far away, was brought very close to everybody because there were train loads of wounded that came into Lime Street Station. These men would be taken to many of the hospitals nearby that were being used as war hospitals, and I remember going with my dad to one of these places. He used to buy packets of Woodbine cigarettes in paper packets of five, and he used to walk along next to a ward and he would throw these packets to the soldiers that were either in bed or up walking around, and to me that was a great thrill.'

Wounded men rarely cared at the time where they went when they left the hospital ships. In theory an effort was made to direct men to hospitals near home, contrary to the belief of many old soldiers who thought quite the opposite. It was almost a standing joke, as 104-year-old Harry Patch recalls.

'We landed at Southampton and the Red Cross came round: "Which was our nearest military hospital?" Well, the Royal United at Bath was at that time a military hospital so I said, "Bath," and I thought, "This is it, I'm going home." So anyway we got on the train, I suppose half asleep, and I thought, "Well damn it, this train's a long time reaching Bath," so I said to the orderly when he unloaded us, "Where are we?" and he said, "Lime Street Liverpool." And that was as near as I got to Bath.'

For most, the knowledge that they were back in Blighty was a source of great joy, which was matched only by the grief of those who were forced to stay at base hospitals in France. Ted Francis, a private in the Royal Warwickshire Regiment, was wounded by shrapnel.

***

'Everybody was looking for a Blighty wound. I was fortunate with my wound because they thought it was
more serious than it was. I was hit in the ankle, and
the fellow in the next bed to mine in the base hospital
said, "You're for England in the morning," and that was
the most beautiful sentence I ever heard throughout the
entire war.'

A Blighty wound was a wound serious enough to result in a trip
home, and ideally not one likely to affect the long-term
prospects of the injured man. For those more seriously wounded,
a ticket home was almost guaranteed as long as the injury was not
deemed so critical that undertaking the journey might prove
fatal. So it was that the severity and the variety of wounds seen
by the medical staff in Britain differed greatly as the men bound
for Blighty finally arrived at hospital.

Phyllis Dry, a professional nurse working at Clacton-on-Sea
Hospital, recalls:

'The soldiers came straight to us from the boat, on to a
train and straight to hospital. Headquarters would be
notified that a convoy of ninety or a hundred would be
arriving at a certain time, so that all the beds would be
made ready to receive stretcher patients downstairs with
walking cases going upstairs. Oh, some soldiers were
simply dreadful, splattered with blood and dirt and mud.
They were still in their khaki, very muddy, very bloody
and terribly, terribly tired, some very distressed by gas. The
orderlies dealt with the men in the first instance, getting
them into bed.

'Those that were helped were so grateful generally,
though not all by any manner of means, because they
were angry. Some were very angry that they had gone
through all they had, and were rather disturbed mentally.
They wouldn't mind swearing at us or anything like that,
they'd gone through so much over there, they had no

control at first, but in time they settled and were much
milder in their behaviour; very much kinder in their
thoughts and words. I was shocked by all of this because
I had lived a very sheltered life, but I was not going to
be deflected.'

Grace Butler was working in a hospital in London. The soldiers
she met were very different from the wounded Tommies pictured
in the daily newspapers, cheerful and smiling.

'They used to be very quiet when they first arrived. You
could see them sort of getting accustomed to not being in
the trenches, it had been a terrible time for them, all the
slaughter out there. They were really terribly depressed.
They wouldn't say anything; they were not used to nurses
looking after them, and they would resent it rather. They
would turn their backs on you and wouldn't speak to you
and you'd put their tea down and they wouldn't look at it
to begin with, and then when you went away they would
turn round and have their tea. You see, most of them
would never have been in hospital before and suddenly to
have all these women dressed up in nursing clothes was
quite funny for them, in fact I think they were shy. In
time they gradually came out of their shells and became
quite friendly, but they did take a bit of working on at
first.'

The shock for young nurses on coming into contact with
wounded soldiers was often intense, but rarely impinged on the
quality of their work. Lesley Leigh-Jones remembers:

'They shipped the soldiers straight from France to
Southmead, up the River Avon, because they could take
them straight off the boat and bring them into hospital.
While the beds were got ready, the men were laid on the
hard cold floor and we had to go round and take off their

field ticket on which was written their name and injury. A lot of them were badly wounded, of course, moaning and screaming. We had to step over them, they were so close together, and lean down and cut this label off, after which they were gradually moved on to the wards.'

Doris Neve, the daughter of a vicar, was working in the temporary huts built on Cheltenham racecourse.

'We were told that the first convoy was coming along, and I had not been there long enough to know anything. I just did what I was told. The men were brought in by the ambulance men and dumped as they were on the beds and there were some awful sights to look at, with all filth and bad wounds. I looked at the man in front of me and I said to the sister, "I can't undress him, Sister, I've never seen a man naked in my life." So she said, "Well, if you don't do it, nobody will, 'cos there's nobody else," and I stood and looked at him and I thought, "I can't," he looked so awful in his dirt and filth and mud and I just looked at him. "Come on, get on with it," he said to me quite cheerfully.

'I had to peel off those awful clothes, days of dirt on them, caked on, and I was told to put everything out in a heap on the floor and the orderlies came and took them away to be burnt. I could hardly bear it at first but I kept saying to myself, "Well, if I don't do it, nobody will and I must help if I can." And so I did my best and it was all I could do. I remember another very young chap that day, and he had to lie on his front because he had sword cuts all the way down his back. He was only a boy really. We tried to wash their wounds and put a sterilised dressing on them and a bandage. You had to do the best you could until the sister had time to come and do a little extra.'

Many of the young VADs were thrown, out of necessity, into the deep end and mistakes were easily made. Eighteen-year-old Harry Wells, who had been gassed in France, was treated by one inexperienced nurse.

'She had syringed me but she got a bit close to the lung, because I found some liquid was coming up my throat. It frightened me, almost as much as it frightened this girl, because she knew she wasn't doing it right and she was nervous. There was a bit of bleeding and I ended up swallowing much of the liquid, but it was one of those things, and it wouldn't have been fair to blame her. The soldiers found by experience that the harder the nurse was, the better she did her job. They would tell you not to be a baby, or that's nothing much. We didn't care for these nurses, but if she took no notice of whether she hurt you or not, she was generally much more efficient than the nervous girl who feared causing you pain.'

The new VADs found conditions appalling. 'I'd never seen lice before,' recalls Doris Neve.

'It was awful. And then some of the men had such great open wounds. I was afraid to touch them in case I hurt them more. I didn't see myself as anything heroic; it was a job that had to be done. The men were marvellous, all telling you, as far as they could, what to do for their comfort. Eventually, when they were clean and in bed, they loved to have a cigarette and a cup of tea; that was what they wanted most of all and, of course, they all hoped to see their wives and mothers.'

The ignorance of many new nurses was often profound. 'The first time I was on the ward,' recalls Phyllis Dry, 'I heard a voice and it said, "Nurse, please bring me a swab." I had no idea what a swab was, it might have been something you swept the floor

with. I really didn't know. You just learnt as you went along.'
Lesley Leigh-Jones recalls a similar experience when she began
work.

'The sister said, "Nurse Arnold" – that was my maiden
name then – "Nurse Arnold, you are to go and blanket
bath Private so and so." Blanket bath, never heard of the
words. So I looked absolutely like a fool. I remember she
had great difficulty not smiling at the look on my face. So
she said to another nurse, "Take her and show her what to
do." I was shown how to blanket bath a soldier and I'd
never even seen my father undressed or anything remotely
like it. I think I was so dazed.'

Lesley's first job was working on a ward full of men suffering
from dysentery.

'These men had come back from Gallipoli and they
couldn't keep anything down, not a thing. They put me to
the test, as they do all young ones, to see if you could
stand it and they didn't think I could, a man with
perpetual diarrhoea, and you were changing beds and
cleaning up all the time. Anyway, before any dressings
were done, the patient had to be got ready for inspection.
We had some new VADs and I saw them strip this soldier
and he was coffee-coloured, and these nurses said, "Well,
we'll have to clean this man up," and they started to scrub
and scrub, and I could see that the men on either side
were laughing up their sleeves. The man was sunburnt,
that was all.'

The stoicism among wounded soldiers constantly amazed many
nurses. Violet Cullen was in her mid-twenties when she volunteered to become a VAD. Brought up on a 365-acre farm, the
only girl in a family of boys, she was hardly the delicate young
thing that so many of her contemporaries were.

'They wanted auxiliary nurses, so I and a friend, we both said we'd be a nurse. I knew nothing, only to be patient and kind. To see them in pain was terrible, but they'd got to put up with it. Well, you're a nurse; you've got to be a little bit hard, or rather, stern with yourself. If you cried over them they wouldn't like that. They'd laugh and say, "It's me that's got to cry, not you." It did upset us sometimes on our own and I'd have a little weep, then I felt much better. Some of the soldiers did cry, because they hadn't seen their family. Sometimes it was because they hadn't had a letter from home and they got frustrated being in bed for so long. It was natural, they're human beings and some were tender-hearted. I'd give them a cuddle, put my arms round their neck, tell them it won't be so bad presently, you'll hear from your family in the morning, anything to quieten them down. You did natural things, what you'd do in your own home. You can't go about with a straight back as if they don't belong to you, no, they all belong to you if you're a nurse.'

Mabel Booth worked on a military ward.

'You couldn't help fretting about it, it was dreadful to see a fine healthy man knocked about and their courage was fantastic. There was no point showing you were upset, though. If you showed you were upset, you simply distressed the other men, you had a standard to keep up, the same as they did. Of course you gave feelings of sympathy but you don't make a song and dance about it. The men would get fits of depression, any of them would, but they'd always try and hide it, I mean their courage was beyond words. It's almost a sacrilege to talk about it. They always remained cheerful to other people and we always tried to crack a joke, but you were too busy to stand there talking, I mean the sister would jolly well be after you.'

There were always jobs to do. Many were repetitive, others gruesome, and dressing the men's wounds was both. 'There would be a man having his wound dressed under a part-anaesthetic and it was very painful, and it was painful for me,' recalls Mary Jollie. 'You tried hard to control yourself because my suffering was imaginary – what they had suffered was very real. Some of the nurses were very near tears, all the time. I was one of them, but you had a job to do.'

The bravery shown by many men while their wounds were dressed stands out in the minds of their nurses, and there is no doubt that many soldiers showed enormous resilience and fortitude. A few, like Ted Françis, were phlegmatic about their injuries and the daily dressing was accepted as an occupational hazard if he was to keep out of the army's clutches.

'I couldn't get out of the army quick enough, and here was a splendid thing, although it was painful, I didn't mind having a badly broken ankle. In England they did an operation but it wasn't really successful and just gave me extra pain. I looked at my ankle and thought, well, surely even if I get well I won't be sent to France again. They bandaged it tight and I screamed the place down, forcing them to take the bandage off and put a piece of wood either side of the bones and put the bandage round that instead.'

The nurses' common recollection of stoicism is, nevertheless, a partial memory. Reginald Spraggins lost his arm at the front. He was later sent to St Albans hospital.

'Every day they brought round the dressing trolley, the Agony Wagon as we called it. Some of the men would scream out when the nurses came to strip then re-dress the wounds, in fact some used to start screaming before the nurse even started on them because they knew the pain they were going to be in. Others would try and hold back. I know I tried to prevent myself making too much noise although it was very painful, because it was hard for the nurses to put up with it. The nurses had to be strong and they had to be ruthless in a sense, to not take much notice when you were shouting out, otherwise they may not have dressed the wound properly. The nurses were very good. I can't complain because my arm was practically shot off, and so they put these hot poultices on to keep the wound fresh, to enable it to heal up. The dressings had to be renewed every day, sometimes twice a day, and it took several weeks before it healed up sufficiently.'

Horace Gaffron was another who had lost a limb, in his case a foot and part of his leg. He was sent to the Rowntree's Convalescent Hospital in York, where, like Reginald, he suffered the daily round of dressings.

'I did not look at the dressings. I wasn't too happy about looking at the rawness so I just let them do what was necessary. The hot poultices were incredibly painful and then there were the dressings. These used to terrify me in every way because the nurse had to pull off the blood-soaked bandages and they stuck to the wound and tugging on them only took away some more of the flesh. You could hear other men having their bandages done too, and you could hear them yell and moan. Aye, it was a rotten job, that, an ordeal I dreaded.

'I was nineteen years old and I had just received this injury which would finish me throughout my life from quite a few things. At my age, to have that injury was quite a shock. It meant I would have to adapt my life in many ways. While I came to terms with what had happened, I was forced to have further amputations higher and higher up the leg; the second one took my leg off to within four inches of the knee and that was very, very sore, I can assure you. Once again there was a lot more crying. Good hefty blubbering, for it was more than I could stand.'

'The most disturbed were those who were coming round after an operation, for there were no recovery wards, and men were brought back into the ward direct from the operating table,' recalls Ben Clouting, who was himself recovering from a wound to his ankle.

'There was one man, a quiet fellow, who had both feet amputated during a particularly difficult operation and was taking a long time to come round from the anaesthetic. On finally waking, he launched, most unexpectedly, into a tirade of language that was just so awful the men on the ward held a handkerchief over his mouth, to protect the nurses. He had difficulty accepting what had happened and became delirious, blaming everyone around him for his loss.'

'The loss of a limb was always a profound shock to men,' remembers General Nurse Norah Claye.

'When someone has an amputation, it's a long time before they know that the limb has gone. I would try and get him to accept what had happened and tell him how good artificial limbs were. The reaction to the loss depended very much on the particular man. Some were prepared to accept – they were so glad to get rid of a limb that had been painful and difficult to cure. Then there were those who bemoaned the loss. I tried to put the best side, the fact that he wouldn't get that pain once the stump had settled down, and how the artificial limb would fit comfortably. Gradually, the man would come round to himself again.'

No nurse, professional or volunteer, could help feel anything but enormous pity for the men under their supervision. Yet, despite the common bond of humanity, there was, more often than not, a world of difference between the trained nurses and sisters, and the young VADs who came under their charge. Just as the army could not hope overnight to mould an enthusiastic civilian into a regular soldier, so the nursing profession could not make a professional nurse out of a willing young girl, who was, nevertheless, ignorant of nursing. There was a crucial difference, however. In the army it was highly unusual for an Other Rank to come from the upper echelons of society. This was not the case in nursing, as Norman Collins, the apprentice in Hartlepool during the bombardment and now an officer, witnessed while being treated in hospital in 1917.

> 'The VADs we met were often from well-to-do families, whereas the general nurses were often from quite humble backgrounds, and had spent many years working their way up the nursing ladder. Many of the VADs were the daughters of aristocratic families, or people out of the top drawer, as the saying goes, and they were obviously – I hate to use the word – a different class, a different social standing to the nurses.'

Seventeen-year-old Alf Pearson had tried to enlist in the army under age but had been rejected. By 1916, he had found a job working as an orderly for the Red Cross at a convalescent hospital in Staffordshire. He was amazed at what he saw.

> 'I worked at Sandon Hall, the home of the Earl of Araby. You went through the main gates and then you saw the hall, a beautiful building, magnificent place, beautiful pictures and it had all been left as it was, to be used as a hospital. The VADs working here were all wealthy people, Staffordshire ladies: Miss Paget, the daughter of Lord and Lady Paget, Lady Parker Jervis

who lived at Bedford Hall – I believe she was related in some way to Lord Kitchener. Anyway, none of these ladies received any pay at all. They used to stay for four weeks and it was my job to meet them at the railway station to carry their luggage. Miss Paget came from a very wealthy Northumberland family and was no doubt used to being waited on herself. Yet in the morning, I usually found her scraping out the ashes from the fireplace from the day before. I never expected to meet such people who were above me in station socially. I didn't raise myself to their level, but they of their own initiative brought themselves to my level and I thought that was rather wonderful. These VADs would be washing up after dinner and I used to do the wiping and they were talking to me all the time, asking me about where I went to school. They were always polite, they never ordered me about, they said would you mind, and would you help me here, and similar expressions.'

Professional nurse Phyllis Dry remembered the VADs with affection.

'The VADs acquitted themselves very well indeed. They worked as hard as we did very often, and they were pleasant with it. They often came from very good families who'd never done anything probably all their lives. One VAD we had was the Honorable Pamela Bruce who became Lady Digby, and she didn't mind the work at all. Even so, to our mind, these girls did have the habit of doing some strange things, such as waking a patient to give him a sleeping tablet.'

The distinction in experience, social standing and expectations caused significant problems. Many who joined did not see their new job as a calling or vocation, but rather simply as an extension of the voluntary work they had undertaken in peace-time, when charitable work was part of the social scene. Doris Neve recalls:

'At Christmas it was a difficult time because most of the older VADs said, "We've got our families, we can't possibly leave them for Christmas, you must just manage." The sister said to me, "You won't desert me, will you?" I said, "No, I never thought of getting off at Christmas, I'll be here, of course." We who remained at the racecourse gave the soldiers a good Christmas dinner and just stayed with them.'

For the younger VADs, with little or no experience of life outside the home, there was a desire to please the professional nurses, come what may. Many young girls were intimidated by the professional nurses, sisters and matrons, as Lesley Leigh-Jones explains.

'We were all scared of the matron and if you did anything wrong, you were sent for, it was called being on the mat and the matron would give you a lecture and be awful. There were a lot of professional nurses, and a lot of the VADs came off the ward crying. The first time I saw this, I said to a trained nurse, "Why do all these VADs cry so?" And she said, "When we trained we went through it – now we're trained, we see you go through it too." I thought this very unfair.

'I think there was so much jealousy between the VADs and the other nurses. One really only saw the trained nurses on duty, not off it. The trained nurses were great friends among themselves. We would follow a nurse in with the trolley with all the equipment for the dressing on it and the trained nurse would say, "Hand me so and so," and I knew before she said what I had to hand her and I think I was rather fortunate in that way. These nurses were much older than we were and there was a sort of division between them and us because of their age and their experience.'

Not all VADs were willing to be intimidated. Older VADs knew their worth and refused to be pushed around, especially when their work was so desperately needed. Violet Cullen was in her mid-twenties and stood her ground, as she had had to do so many times with her boisterous brothers.

'We were told by the matron not to pity the shell-shocked soldiers, to help them, but not to pity them. One day I was tying a tie for one of these men and the matron came along and said, "Nurse, you're not here to dress these boys, you are here to look after them." I said, "Matron, he can't use his hand so he asked me to tie his tie and I'll do it again whether you like it or not. While they're under my care I'll do what I think is right." So she didn't have much more to say to me because I meant what I said. I knew I was right, there was nothing wrong in what I did, his hands were shaking and he wanted to be tidy. I knew I was under her authority but I wasn't scared, and she knew I wasn't scared. I did my duty and she couldn't grumble at that. If she grumbled at what I'd done, I'd tell her to come and do it herself. They wanted my help and they were short-staffed as it was. And that is how I nursed. If the matron came along and said, "Haven't you finished yet?" I'd say, "I'll come when I'm finished." I did as long as I saw fit and if they interfered, I'd tell them to go away. I wasn't breaking rules, just breaking time, taking too much time over my job. Well, I didn't care.'

It was equally important for trained nurses to stand their ground and not give way to VADs who might seek to usurp the authority of the professional nurse or sister. Mary Jollie (née Clarke) was attending a cricket match held for the benefit of recuperating soldiers. The game was over when:

'The sister came over and said that one of us, one of the general nurses, would have to go back to the ward. I said I would go and speak to a VAD. This VAD was older than I was and I said to her, "Will you give me the keys and I'll go back to the ward and give out the medicines." She said, "Miss Clarke, I'll give the medicines out if you'll go and check the dirty laundry." I said, "No, Miss Brown, I'll give out the medicine and you will go and check the laundry and do you mind doing it now!" That was one episode, a VAD trying it on, bossing a staff nurse around.'

Given the pressure that the nursing profession was under, it is hardly surprising that there was some friction between the nurses, as Phyllis Dry (née Lloyd) asserts.

'Sometimes tempers frayed. The matron was a grand old army woman, Georgina Morgan, and she would send her maid Maggie to find me and then I'd go and see her. "Nurse Lloyd, Sister Parker isn't very good-natured this morning, she's a bit bad tempered. Here's half a crown, take her into the village this afternoon and give her tea." You were a female crowd. There was Matron, Sister and the nurses and VADs and you had everything to do except those jobs given to the orderlies. The nurses were doing the dressings, giving treatment, taking temperatures and doing the daily routine. It was their responsibility to see that the dressings were done and that the medicines were given regularly, ensuring the bodily comfort of the patient. We all worked incredibly hard and sharp words now and again were only natural.'

Mabel Booth had an extra incentive to work hard. She had lost her father in 1917 after a long and expensive illness. Funds had largely run out, necessitating the sale of the family home, forcing Mabel to find work. She had entered nursing because, as she says:

'Nursing was the only thing I could start without a training and paying a premium. I worked hard, not least because I was frightened of not being able to continue my job, that they would tell me to go home, because I'd nowhere to go. I had never worked so hard in my life before. During the war, we were short-handed all the time and we'd extra beds. I was sweeping floors, and polishing, I mean we were absolutely crippled by the hard floor, which caused innumerable blisters on my heels. I was on duty eight until eight, two hours off in between. I was completely worn out, and just flopped on to my bed as soon as I was off duty.'

Ward sisters ran their domains with unbridled strictness. Nurses commonly suffered from dropped arches as they covered mile after mile around the ward in low-heeled, laced shoes. Even before they came on to the wards, their dress had to be impeccable, skirts no higher than eight inches off the floor, the cap exactly as it should be perched on the head, high stiff collars, stiff cuffs, stiff belt; if anything was wrong, the sister would tell the nurse in no uncertain terms. Once on the ward there was unending work to be done. The beds were all cast-iron and they all had to be dusted. The ward had to be swept on both sides, the lockers cleaned, the tops of them being washed down with a wet cloth, the castors of the beds had to be pointing the same way, and the ward made fresh and ready for the ward sister's inspection. Then she would come on to the ward from her sitting room, uniform absolutely immaculate, and she would try the tops of the shelves to see if there was any dust. 'It might not have been terrifically hard work mentally,' recalls Phyllis Dry, 'but you were there on duty and you always had things to do, making beds, washing patients, sterilising bandages, serving meals, dressing wounds, giving out medication, and there were stairs to go up and down all the while, so the hours were very long, very often.'

Mary Jollie learnt every aspect of the daily routine.

'The sister would come on to the ward and look down
the beds, and each bed had to be precisely in line with the
others. She would take out of her pocket a handkerchief
to measure the distance the beds came out from the wall,
and then ensure all the castors at the bottom of the bed
pointed the same way. There were so many rules attached
to the giving of medicine, too. A nurse did not just lift a
bottle and pour it out, there were half a dozen specific
movements to be gone through. You lifted the bottle so
that the label was in the palm of your hand and your
forefinger was touching the cork. You read the label,
shook the bottle and poured out the required dose.'

Such uniformity in standards and procedure was hardly foreign to
the wounded soldiers, who watched in admiration while these
young nurses worked to keep the ward spotless just as the men
had been charged to keep their barracks clean. The strict
hierarchy, the clockwork routine, were all par for the course as
far as soldiers were concerned. They hardly blinked an eye,
either, when the professional nurses maintained a professional
distance. Mabel Booth took great pride in her work.

'The standard I maintained, it never slipped. In some
places, there was perhaps a staff nurse and sister and they
were always addressed by their rank. A patient would speak
to a nurse as "nurse", not a surname. It's so much easier,
think of the bother of having to remember what
somebody's name was before you called to them. Similarly,
every soldier's bed was numbered and so often the person
was addressed by the number. How did they feel about
that? Nobody ever asked them. It was a rule.'

The military nurses were a breed apart from the VADs. They
could appear hard and uncaring, but while formality rather than
familiarity was their style, most were not without humanity.
Mabel Booth was working on a ward when she was told by the

night sister that two men had just been admitted.

'They'd both been sent back as nervous breakdowns, and
when I did my rounds I came to these two men. I just
spoke to them and one man started to say how they'd been
transported back to England while the other man in the
next bed just snarled. So I just put my hand on the arm of
each man and I said, "Look, lads, you can no more help
your nervous system giving way than your pals can help
stop flying shrapnel." There was a great shame in shell shock
and men very often just kept repeating that they couldn't
help their nerves. Anyway, those two men grew into
soldiers in front of me because of that understanding word.'

At night, on any ward there would be noise when the war
returned to invade men's dreams, taking them back to the line
and the moments of greatest fear. Men, even those not suffering
from shell shock, would constantly shout out in their sleep,
sometimes kicking out with their feet, or jerking their arms
wildly. Many men refused to sleep, fearful of what they might
recollect.

Mary Jollie had been made a sister at the Notts County War
Hospital and had been appointed to the shell-shock ward.

'These men were nearly all convalescent and they could go
out as much as they liked. Many suffered from nightmares,
and I would read about them from the nightly report.
A lot of them feared sleeping at night because of the
nightmares and some could get quite violent. There was
only one orderly at night on each ward, but he had a
bell that he could ring to summon help to control the
patient, to physically control him so that he did not hurt
himself. Some of the dreams were very terrible and there
were tearful moments when the patients woke up, shaking
with fear at what they had seen in their mind's eye.
Occasionally a man would have facial tremors, hands

trembling. Sometimes during the day they would be asked to help in putting out dinners, and in the middle they would just have a shaking fit that they couldn't control.'

Guy Botwright, a nineteen-year-old subaltern in the Army Service Corps, had never wanted to participate in the war, but eventually he had gone to France where he narrowly survived a shell explosion. Although lightly injured, he was returned to England and a ward for shell-shocked officers.

'I didn't care whether I lived or not. In the first stages, you're much more likely to shed a tear, to feel the depression, oh yes, the depression. The nurses were wonderful, they'd ask a question and by what sort of answer they got, they'd know exactly what was in the air. I did not venture from the bed for anything, good gracious, no fear, not until things began to settle down, then I might be told to get up for ten minutes and somebody would come and help me out of bed to a chair. They would force you to do it, and rightly, too. They'd stay there and help because my legs would flop, your legs would let you down; you never quite knew when they were going to let you down. Luckily I was never in one room alone, thank goodness, because it helped to be in a ward with other people, even if they are ill too, it is a help, you know that you are not on your own.'

The shell-shocked soldiers nursed by Grace Butler were separated from the other wounded men, being kept all together for their treatment on a side ward. Their collective plight was pitiful to see, made all the more poignant by an unbroken desire to still protect the nurses during air raids on the capital in 1917.

'The first time the planes ever came over one Sunday morning, there was fighting, you could see them in the sky, and the men in the beds – the shell-shocked ones – it all came back to them, although they were being brave, trying to cheer us up. They thought we would all be very scared. Their beds had been pulled out on to the balcony because it was a bright sunny day and of course we all came out to have a look at it all, and they kept saying, "It's all right, Nurse, you're quite safe, they are a long way away," and their iron beds were shaking all the while.'

Not all nurses liked working with the shell-shocked. VAD Marjorie Grigsby was sent to Kensington in London where she had to look after several officers, including some who were shell shocked. She remained at the hospital for three months before applying for a transfer.

'We had an officer there who suffered from shell shock. He was perfectly normal apparently, but directly there was any signal that a Zeppelin was en route he got out of bed, if he was reading or eating his meal, and he'd ask you to hold his tray while he got under the bed. You gave him his tray and then you just left him there to get on with it. He was quite happy eating under the bed and when it was all over he'd come out again and get back into bed.

'I didn't enjoy the work at all, it's no good pretending that I did. I did not like mentally disturbed people; I was always scared of them.'

Marjorie eventually went to France to work at a casualty clearing station close to the front line.

Overall, the VADs performed admirably, caring for soldiers and using any free time they might have to talk with men who were desperate for human and, particularly, female contact. 'It was the VADs who did the entertaining, not the nurse,' recalls Norman Collins.

'The nurse was very professional and got on with her job. The VAD was allowed a little time to fraternise with the patient. I remember one of the VADs made a point of coming and reading to me and showing me photographs taken in her home and I thought this was very nice. It was looked upon possibly as part of her duties and the matron didn't seem to object. I remember one particular VAD, very much out of the top drawer, who used to tell me all about her childhood, where she lived and so forth. You felt you were living – you were back living in a normal, civilised world and it helped to get you back from the horror of war and I think it helped me to avoid any real trauma later in life. These VADs, in a sense you can call them counsellors, played a very great part towards the resuscitation of the wounded soldier. I salute them for everything they did in that way.'

The sensitivity and charm of many VADs cheered up soldiers, and was a great antidote to the tiredness that pervaded a soldier's spirit, sick as many of them were of the wholly male company of life in the trenches. Ted Francis recalled:

'There were a lot of silly jokes about the nurses – when we'd recovered enough to make them, mind. There were a lot of lewd jokes too, and I was ashamed of some of the things the men said, which were quite unnecessary. But the nurses knew what they'd got to deal with; they didn't take it too badly. I was respectful to them and grateful as well.'

The men may have been taken out of the trenches, but the trenches hadn't quite been taken out of the men, and the crude, rude world in which they had lived for months was difficult to eliminate straight away. 'Many men were of very rough lives, very rough upbringings, coarse in speech and thought,' agreed Phyllis Dry, 'but that made no difference to us, we were there to help their bodies, you let swearing pass over you, although you'd probably not heard some of the words before.'

In the first instance, it was almost too easy for soldiers to shock some of the more 'delicate' nurses like Lesley Leigh-Jones (née Arnold).

'I blushed very easily at first. I soon got hardened to it, but they had great fun making up stories trying to embarrass me, make me blush. I can recall that the first thing that a VAD did when she came on duty was to go round and empty all the ashtrays, everybody smoked then. Well, before I came on duty all these soldiers had told a man called Lewis, "Now, Lewis, when that little Nurse Arnold comes to empty your ashtray, you're to throw your arms round her neck and kiss her." Well, I'd not been used to this so I gaily went round emptying people's ashtrays, got to this bed when he flung his arms round me and hung on. Lewis had a terrible heart complaint, and he was propped up very high on cushions and the sister who then sat in the middle of the ward could see what was going on. She rushed up and said, "Nurse Arnold, give in, give in, give in, let him, he'll die, he'll die," but I didn't give in. And as we went on struggling, she intervened and separated us. She said I should have let him kiss me.'

Practical jokes of this nature were endemic among men who had had scant chance to relax and laugh while they had been in the trenches. Ben Clouting had enlisted under age and was just seventeen years old when he was wounded in the ankle. Back in Britain, he was sent to Graylingwell War Hospital in Sussex. During the summer, as his recovery progressed, he was allowed to join a group of wounded soldiers invited to a local garden party.

'Walking around the garden, I found a grass snake. Asking for a jam jar, I managed to bottle the snake up, with the idea of taking it back to the hospital. It was only about a foot long, so there was little difficulty getting it on to the ward or concealing my activities, as I tied a bit of bandage round its neck and roped it to the rear leg of my bed. All the soldiers loved to play tricks on the nurses and I was no exception. I knew that last thing at night a nurse would come round to tuck us into bed. Keeping a straight face, I asked the nurse earnestly, "Do please be careful and try not to step on my watchdog." This particular nurse was well known for her nervousness and timidity and I eagerly followed the path of her eyes as she looked down, gave a yelp, and promptly fainted on top of me. I had not quite expected this reaction, and while another nurse slapped her face to bring her round, the sister was called.'

In this instance, Ben was given a reprimand, told to get dressed and to take the snake down the end of the garden.

Such pranks were typical of young men, irrespective of rank. Lieutenant Norman Collins was only a few months older than Ben Clouting. In 1917, he was recovering at Buckfastleigh Convalescent Hospital in Devon and, while hardly causing mayhem, was rapidly bringing the matron to the end of her tether. Norman spent days ferreting, shooting and organising dinners at a local farmhouse for a few of the officers and VADs. His justification was simple: they were young officers with wholly uncertain futures for they did not know if they were going to go back to France within weeks, there to be killed in a month. 'I don't think we cared about any repercussions. We didn't worry about trivial things,' he asserted. In a letter to his brother, dated 29 October, Norman described his latest escapade: 'Last night a raiding party left our trenches (via Billiard room window) at 11pm and entered enemy orchard, returning with numerous prisoners in the shape of best Devonshires.' Such behaviour, while seemingly inoffensive, was too much for the matron. 'I've been threatened six times [in six weeks] by the matron to be sent to Plymouth for "bad conduct",' noted Norman, before a final letter that recorded the inevitable. 'I left Buckfastleigh on Monday morning. I couldn't get on very well

with the matron and so I was sent here for further treatment.'
Further treatment for Norman was the Royal Military Hospital
at Devonport, 'a very austere hospital altogether'.

For men who, until a few weeks before, had maintained highly
active lives in France, there was now a great deal of frustration in
being confined to bed. Rest, on their arrival back in England,
and most of all sleep, was essential but after a while the men
needed entertainment. Teasing the nurses was one expression of
that fun, but it could also be evidence of frustration. To keep the
men occupied, VADs often pooled their own talents, presenting
little skits for the soldiers' entertainment. Lesley Leigh-Jones
found she 'had a very good singing voice and in the afternoon,
when all the men relaxed in their beds, one of the soldiers who
could play the piano got up and I would sing all the popular
songs such as "Roll out the Barrel" and "It's a Long Way to
Tipperary".'

However, for those men who could manage to get about, it
was important to be taken out of hospital for some fresh air and
a change of scenery. There was no shortage of invitations for the
soldiers, who in their hospital blue uniforms were easily
recognisable and fêted by local people. All public transport was
made available to soldiers for free, as was entry to zoos, cinemas
and most theatres. Horace Gaffron, who had lost a leg during
the Battle of the Somme, was delighted to take part in these
trips.

'The nurses were very proud of their uniforms and loved
the occasion of taking us out, a dozen of us wounded
boys, on a trip to the cinema, and of course we got in for
nothing. Being a wounded soldier, you were a bit of an
eye-catcher. Crowds would watch soldiers being moved,
and the nurses felt very much appreciated. The uniforms
were very important; it gave them a sense of purpose, a
challenge. People would stop you in the street, or come
up and talk to you, get you a packet of cigarettes or
chocolate.'

One popular day out was to the homes of local dignitaries, or wealthy aristocrats who opened up their estates for garden parties. Ben Clouting had been to the home of Sir James Horlix near Goodwood on more than one occasion.

'There were plenty of invitations for wounded soldiers to attend various functions laid on for their benefit. Twenty of us were picked up in a charabanc and taken over to Sir James's home for the afternoon, where we were met at the door by the butler and shown into the garden. We sat on garden seats to chat, while Sir James walked round to talk to each group of soldiers. Lemonade was served, and a tea of bread, butter and jam, as we sat around a large wooden table taken outside for the occasion.'

Another wounded soldier, Londoner Vic Cole, recalls a similar occasion.

'We visited Arundel Castle and were guests of the young Duke of Norfolk, who gave me a pipe and tobacco pouch which I kept for many years. The Duke was, I believe, eleven years old at the time, and was being managed by Lord Esmond Talbot with whom I chatted for half an hour thinking he was one of the gardeners.'

Given the often prolonged period of time in which soldiers and nurses came into contact, there was bound to be a certain amount of flirting and, inevitably, romance, particularly between VADs and young soldiers, as Doris Neve recalls.

'Well, it was a hard life, shut up with a lot of women, and one of the men said to me, "There's an awfully good show on at the Hippodrome in Bristol, would you like to go?" And I said, "Rather." The nurses' quarters were near the gates in Southmead Hospital, I could slip out easily from my sleeping quarters and he said, "I'll meet you outside the gate and I'll

take you." I enjoyed it very much but when we got back all
the gates were locked. We couldn't get in. It was dark and we
walked along the wall looking for a stone that was sticking
out of the wall. We found one and I had to hang on to the
stone while he got hold of my feet and pushed me over. I
managed to walk back to the sleeping quarters and I got into
bed and thought I'd had a jolly good time.

'Later, when I was working at the Royal United
Hospital, we young nurses, when we were on night duty,
used to sneak off to the men's wards, the soldiers' wards,
and we used to have a great time down there with them
and we loved it. They loved us coming down but we had
to be very careful to be out of the hearing of the night
sisters or else we should have been for it. They'd say,
"Come and give me a kiss, lassie," that kind of thing, but
we were never serious. I think it cheered them a lot. We
would give them a quick kiss, because many of these
chaps hadn't got their own people, they hadn't got their
mothers and their wives, I don't think it was wrong at all.
We used to get to know the sister's hours for visiting each
ward and we used to wait until she'd been and then we'd
sneak down.'

Violet Cullen was very matter-of-fact about the nature of ward
relationships.

'A lot of those nurses weren't married and they wanted to
get married and that was why they chose to nurse. If I
wanted to get married I should find a husband on my
own, I shouldn't want one pushed on me like that. Some
nurses were working to get husbands. If the boys wanted
to get frivolous, I just put them down in their place. I
wasn't stern or rude and I enjoyed their jokes, but I didn't
go any further. I didn't ask them to take me out, but there
was quite a lot of romance on the wards and I can
understand that. My friend, a girl called Partington, she

married one soldier when he got better, and he was very ill. She nursed him back to health and he married her.'

In most cases, affection, even love, went unrequited. Soldiers often loved from afar, and in time, almost inevitably, they were moved on to another hospital or discharged to return to their regiments. Phyllis Dry was working at a hospital where none of the patients stayed for very long.

'At Clacton-on-Sea we were just a clearing station, so most of the men would only be with us for a few days at most and then passed on and were sent to a specialist hospital, so our relationships with the soldiers were not close, really and truly. Sometimes they'd be there a month but that would be with a bad wound, bad enough that we couldn't risk moving him. There was one New Zealander, and why I cannot think, but he seemed to be very attached to me, and when he was sent on from us he sent me a very delightful little silver card case. Long after the war, his mother wrote to me from New Zealand and the letter came with the old-fashioned mourning paper with black edging, and it said that her son had been killed fighting in France and that among his papers were words saying how fond he had been of me. It was really very nice of her to write.'

The First Blitz

O N THE NIGHT OF 2 SEPTEMBER 1916, SEVEN-YEAR-
old Penny Feiwel was sitting on her bedroom windowsill, peering into the night. She was watching the
searchlights of London as they illuminated the sky, flicking
backwards and forwards in an apparently fruitless bid to find the
enemy. There might have been an air-raid warning but, as on so
many nights before, the call to 'Take Cover' had been a precursor
to nothing much. Frequently, over days and weeks, the public,
right across the capital, had been roused from their beds, and sent
scrambling for cover. They would then spend a frustrating night,
often in cold, damp conditions, waiting for the 'All Clear' to be
given. Penny recalls:

'Living where we did, with all the factories nearby and
the Woolwich Arsenal, we were a target for the raids.
When there was a raid warning, we used to go down
the big arches, that is, where the railway ran across the
end of the road, taking a blanket with us. We'd go out
and they would say, "Get in, get in," because the
searchlights were going all round. There was hay under
the arches there and we'd try and sleep on the floor
until the "All Clear", when we would go home. But
on this night, Mother said that we were not going to
go to the air-raid shelter yet again. We were to stay in
our rooms instead, because very often there wasn't a
bomb dropped anywhere near us. So instead of going

to bed I was sat looking out of the window. It was a clear cloudless night, very bright because of the moon, when, all of a sudden, I saw a Zeppelin caught in the searchlights that criss-crossed the sky. I watched, transfixed by this huge silvery object in the sky, then suddenly there was a flash and a terrible explosion and then I saw the flames coming down. The Zeppelin was falling and everyone began coming out of the arches, shouting and clapping and cheering. I've never forgotten it.'

The sight was spectacular and brought an almost universal reaction of joy among people living in the vicinity. Railway whistles blew, factory hooters were sounded, while people poured on to the street, singing and dancing. People broke out into spontaneous renditions of 'God Save the King' and 'Rule Britannia'. Sitting in her bedroom, Penny was one of only a handful of people who gave any thought to the crew.

'I felt very sorry, the fact that there were people in that Zeppelin, and to have been burnt like that, all in flames coming down. It made a very great impression on my mind and I spoke to my brother a few days afterwards and he said he was quite adamant that they were the Germans and if we hadn't done anything, they would have killed us.'

Zeppelins came to symbolise German technology and prowess in the first years of the First World War, before an adequate response was formulated to combat such raids and the first of the airships was shot down. Yet, in purely military terms, Zeppelins were a costly experiment, incapable of targeting enemy positions accurately. The Germans might have aimed for barracks, docks and oil installations but any damage caused was more by luck than judgement. Instead, bombs were dropped almost at random, making their attacks brutal, if short, and killing men, women and children without discrimination. They were quickly nicknamed the 'baby killers' and further undermined any residual respect anyone had for the enemy.

The advantage of Zeppelins was in sowing fear and anxiety in the civil population. To a generation that had hardly become accustomed to the idea of flight, the vision of a giant airship, well over 500 feet long, hovering overhead, was incredible as well as singularly terrifying. In time, in order to ease public disquiet and even panic, the government at home was forced to redirect resources which would otherwise have been bound for the Continent.

Paradoxically, while the number of Zeppelin raids was in fact few, the number of people claiming to have seen one during the war was legion. Just over fifty raids were mounted over forty-five months, and there were fewer than a dozen airships in any single attack. Yet this is not a case of false memory on the part of scared civilians. The Essex clergyman, the Reverend Andrew Clark, added a very interesting detail in his diary when he noted that a local butcher from Little Waltham was absolutely positive that during one raid a Zeppelin had passed 'directly over *his* house'. Yet on the following two days the butcher was to find that 'within a radius of three and a half miles', every house he came to claimed exactly the same distinction. In truth, the sheer size of a Zeppelin could give the impression that it was floating directly overhead. Coupled with that fact, Zeppelins were slow craft, liable to wander hundreds of miles off course. Driven by prevailing winds, they could pass over the north coast of England, crossing Newcastle, before travelling west as far as Liverpool, or south to Nottingham or Birmingham. They might leave the country over London; this meant that great swaths of the country would have the opportunity of marvelling at these great beasts of the sky, and, in the early days at least, their appearance seemed to confirm German power. For those who saw the great airships, the moment was never forgotten.

At home in Methil, Fifeshire, Maud Cox's first experience of a Zeppelin was awe-inspiring.

'The first I heard was everybody shouting outside. My sister Flora and I both jumped out of bed and ran out on to the landing to hear this woman next door screaming her head off. "Take to the fields, get out of here! Take to the fields, the Germans are coming, they will be dropping bombs." We ran outside to look. It was a very, very windy night, a freezing cold night, bright moon, and you could see everything, you could see this Zeppelin quite clearly and it looked beautiful. My granny came out and she grabbed the two of us and pulled us into the house saying, "You can be just as dead with pneumonia as you can with a bomb so get back into bed." We heard next day that it had blown off course.'

Zeppelins had first been flown in 1900 and had, before the war, travelled over 100,000 miles without incident. The German military, realising the airship's potential for warfare, ordered several, the first entering service in March 1909, three years before the advent of the Royal Flying Corps in Britain. At the outbreak of war, a total of eleven Zeppelins were in operation and were used almost immediately, offensively bombing the Belgian city of Liège on the night of 6 August 1914. At the time, the Zeppelins were the only means available for the delivery of long-range bombing, and it was only a matter of time before they were used against Britain.

The first raid over British soil took place on 19 January 1915, when, at 8.00 p.m., an attack was launched on Great Yarmouth in Norfolk. It was a pinprick by anyone's standards and hardly justified the effort. The target had been the Humber, but the Zeppelin arrived close to Great Yarmouth, where it first dropped a bomb harmlessly in a field before venturing over the town, dropping several bombs and killing two people, Miss Martha

Taylor aged seventy-two and Samuel Smith, fifty-three, a shoe-maker. They were Britain's very first air-raid victims in an attack that lasted no more than ten minutes – though it took the Zeppelin twenty-three hours to make the round trip back to Germany.

There were a further twenty six attacks in 1915, accounting for just over half of all Zeppelin raids in the war, and with each raid public foreboding grew. Liverpudlian Sydney Bond remembers the nervousness.

'There was a lot of fear built up about these Zeppelins because of the publicity they gave them. In a sense, the papers were supporting the idea that the Germans could demoralise us, the civilian population, by using these airships. The people picked that up and the slightest funny noise from then on and it was an airship coming. I can remember actually lying in bed frightened after hearing the sound of what might have been, only might have been, a Zeppelin overhead. Everyone exaggerated about them and that added to the fright, there wasn't one but a dozen overhead, so morally Jerry did have a very good weapon.'

The press and the government were in a quandary, incapable of deciding whether to highlight the attacks in order to condemn the killing of women and children, or to keep such reports low key for fear of fuelling public anxiety. The Defence of the Realm Act had included restrictions on the press, forbidding the reporting of news liable to cause alarm and despondency. Yet, when the first raid over London took place on 31 May 1915, newspapers such as the *Daily News* ran front-page headlines: 'Zeppelin Raid Over Outer London'. A second reported raid on London brought concerted and immediate demands for security. The problem lay with the government, which had starved the press of a regular flow of information from the Western Front. A generally patriotic press was, invariably, desperate for stories. If news, encouraging or otherwise, was not available to fill the columns of the daily papers – and there were sixteen newspapers serving London alone – then the editors of such papers were liable to utilise the stories most readily accessible, namely those produced at home.

News reporting improved later in the war, although acts of crass stupidity were still common. After one serious raid on the town of Folkestone, a government communiqué was issued stating only that a raid had occurred in the south-east and that one town had been badly hit. Without naming the town – for fear of handing the Germans useful intelligence – the communiqué had served only to spread anxiety among those people whose loved ones lived in that rather large and heavily populated corner of England. In the end, *The Times* reproduced the Germans' own communiqué which, without hesitation, named Folkestone as the town attacked.

As a general rule, the press blew out of all proportion the significance of air raids at home and this, in turn, had a small knock-on effect in the prosecution of the war in France and Flanders. Apart from soldiers kept on home defence for fear of invasion, a raft of policies was introduced in time to provide London, as well as other cities, with an adequate defence against attack. Eight Warning Control Centres were built in major cities to receive reports from the police and coastal stations. These centres would rapidly pass on any reports to Home Defence Squadrons, aircraft stationed in Britain to combat the aerial threat. Searchlight stations were also constructed along the eastern side of Britain stretching from Edinburgh to Dover, and supported by a ring of anti-aircraft guns. In all, over 17,300 men were retained in Britain purely for anti-aircraft duties of one form or another.

Ironically, the searchlights, the most visible of the defensive measures taken, were more about finding and blinding the Zeppelin crews, hindering accurate navigation, than they were about pinpointing the huge airships so they could be shot down by ground fire. At the start of the war these guns, primarily of

Boer War vintage, were hopelessly inadequate, the shells exploding well below the height of the airships, peppering the
surrounding streets and buildings with shards of metal. Even
when anti-aircraft guns were supplied with longer ranges, they
were generally incapable of reaching a Zeppelin's cruising
height, and were fired more to quell public disquiet over raids
than to realistically down the enemy.

Frieda Sawden had an anti-aircraft gun sited near her home
just outside Hull. Two NCOs and one officer who served the
gun were billeted at her home.

> 'The sergeant and the corporal were at the top of the
> house in an attic and they had to go to bed in their full
> equipment, ready to service the gun. The captain was in
> another room and as soon as the Zeppelins were reported
> he got a phone call. He then went to the bottom of the
> stairs and yelled up, "Stand by the gun." Of course they
> woke up at once and clattered down the steps and woke
> up the whole house as they all streamed down to the gun
> and got it going. They were always in a tearing hurry; one
> time the sergeant left a boot behind as he ran and my
> father, grabbing it, threw it in the general direction where
> he thought the sergeant would pick it up, only it hit the
> officer in the back. He was not amused. The shells, you
> could see them bursting but about a mile below the
> Zeppelin, they never got any nearer. Of course the
> Zeppelin wasn't aiming at a little place like ours, they
> were aiming at Hull, the docks and the railway, so we
> didn't really worry on that account.'

As the raids intensified during 1915, simple air-raid precautions
were introduced. On 7 June a large raid underlined the seriousness of the situation, so that on the 18th the police for the first
time issued instructions as to what to do in a raid. However,
air-raid precautions remained piecemeal, for Regulation 12 of
the Defence of the Realm Act meant that it was up to local

military authorities to decide what to do, such as imposing a blackout, which often amounted to the dimming of lights just before an attack.

The introduction of a blackout had serious, unexpected results: there was a marked increase in public accidents, as people were unable to see where they were going. Sydney Bond was an early victim.

'When the blackout started all they did was colour the tops of the lamps with a kind of pinky paint so that any residual light was shining downwards. They were still old gas lamps in the first war and they were no good in any case. People don't realise that in the first war there was more danger because there was no provision for painting pavement edges, or tree trunks.

'I was out with the bread van with a lad called Jack Butler, when a Zeppelin raid occurred. It was still early evening and there were people delivering, then suddenly in unison they shouted "Zeppelin!" They were fearful, no doubt about it, "It's a Zeppelin!" I stood to look for it and then I heard it, nothing like a plane noise; a Zeppelin had its own distinctive sound, a funny droning. I had been told not to run in the blackout but this time I ran like the blazes right into one of those cast-iron lamps, knocking myself clean out. It's instinctive when you're frightened, you run, but I don't think I was frightened by the Zeppelin, it was the people talking, frightened like, that made me run.

'The next minute I'm awake in somebody's house and being looked at in a worrying way. I remember the lump I had. You know, when you are a kid you always show your injuries to your friends at school and I remember showing my big lump till it went black and blue, and I said to them, "The Zeppelin did this, ha!"'

The sudden loss of light was not a disadvantage for everyone.

Eight-year-old Bert Smith found that, along with the danger, there came golden moments for personal profit.

'In Nottingham there was a store called Penny Cohen and they used to sell all bits and bobs for a penny. About four or five of us kids were in there one night, a Friday night. It would have been about seven in the evening and the lights went out because an air raid was coming, so they shouted, "Air raid, Zeppelins, air raid." Everybody was running around, there was a lot of commotion and all the staff in the shop got under the counters. So we were in this store looking around and of course we lifted our jerseys up and put as much under as we could, off the counter, and ran out with all this stuff into the street. As we left the shop I looked up and out of my right eye I could just see this big black cloud, a big black shape going past. I was instantly very frightened, so I ran the other way. I've always wished I'd stopped and had a good look.'

Ruth Armstrong was living in the small village of Tilshead, in itself hardly an objective for the enemy, but it was close to Salisbury Plain, and there were numerous military targets in the area. One evening:

'We were sitting indoors playing games on the table, snakes and ladders, that sort of thing, and we heard a lot of screaming, a terrible row in the street, and we all ran out. "Oh, there's a Zeppelin coming. Oh, the Kaiser's coming!" Everybody got out in the road, screaming, they didn't know what to make of it. We could quite see the airship all lit up, all lit up as it went over the village. My brother got all worried about it and he said, "The Kaiser's going to jump out of the Zeppelin and take the lot of us, what are we going to do?" and he ran back indoors and got under the table. Well, he'd want a big Zeppelin to take all the people of Tilshead. We quite thought the old Kaiser was in there and he was going to drop down and shoot us all. My little friend said we ought to go and get the policeman and I said, "What can a policeman do?" I said, "If the Kaiser comes down he'll take the policeman as well."

'There was so much talk about the Kaiser, I used to spit at photos of him. But really, I wondered who in the world was this man, and his son, Little Willie, who was half as tall as the Kaiser and was a very wicked man. I remember my brother coming in one day with a toy gun and he said, "I got this, I could hit them with it, couldn't I?" We quite thought they were coming. My mother used to say that if he, the Kaiser, was to come over here and take England, "I would kill you all and kill myself. I won't live under Germany." I thought that it was a terrible thing for my mother to say.'

Children were in an invidious position. Quite old enough to experience fear and anxiety, many were still too young to comprehend fully what was happening. Londoner Margery Porter was just seven years old when the word Zeppelin first entered her vocabulary.

'I did hear that something called a Zeppelin was going to bomb us. These raids always took place at night, so I was mostly taken out of bed and snuggled in a chair. I did hear the odd bomb drop and I was taken the very next day to have a look at the damage. We walked to Brixton Hill, and I remember looking up at a house and on the first floor I saw a bit of bed hanging out of the window and I thought it rather funny. My parents wanted me to realise that this was a very serious thing, and people might be killed, so I took it on board that it was serious and that it was a dreadful thing. But at seven you didn't realise what being killed was; people being killed by bombs didn't really register as a serious incident.'

Above left: A poster urging women to enlist as nurses in the new Voluntary Aid Detachments. (*Imperial War Museum*)

Above right: Mary Jollie as a newly trained nurse. Later she worked on a ward for shell-shocked soldiers and heard harrowing stories of how British tanks had ploughed through wounded men lying on the battlefield.

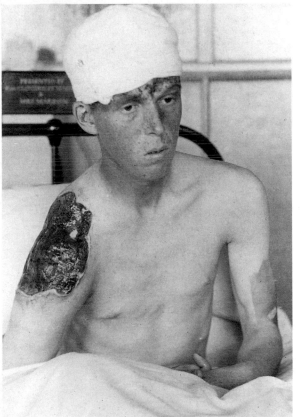

Left: 1916. A patient at the King George V Military Hospital in London. The extensive wound to his shoulder would have required plastic surgery, a new medical technique developed during the war. Such sights appalled young VADs thrust on to the ward with little or no nursing knowledge.

zeppelin. L11 Leaving the Sheds for a raid to England 1916. But never returned.

Above: A remarkable photograph of a Zeppelin passing close by the Schneidemuhl prisoner-of-war camp in Germany. The picture, dated 1916, says that the Zeppelin, L11, 'never returned' giving the impression that it was shot down. However, this is not the famous SL11 airship shot down by Leefe Robinson over Cuffley, Hertfordshire, in September 1916, but is in fact a Zeppelin that was finally dismantled in November 1917.

Above right: A Zeppelin is caught in searchlights. In reality anti-aircraft guns lacked the range to shoot them down. Sights such as this both fascinated and terrified the civilians below, and reinforced the idea that the Germans were more technologically advanced than the British.

Right: A dramatic picture of a Zeppelin as it falls in flames. One witness estimated that it took a Zeppelin three to four minutes to come to earth. Raids over London and the east coast were frequent in 1915 and 1916 and hundreds of civilians were killed and wounded. When the first airship was shot down it was greeted by cheering and renditions of 'God Save The King'. The public relief was enormous.

Top: The remains of SL11 at Cuffley. Lieutenant William Leefe Robinson (inset) won the Victoria Cross for shooting the airship down and saving the lives of many. He sadly died in the influenza pandemic at the end of the war.

Centre: Incendiary bombs collected for disposal after a Zeppelin raid. In the forefront of the picture a sandbag displays a collection of jagged shell fragments.

Left: A privately taken photograph of a home-owner's war souvenir. It was dropped by a Gotha bomber near Harwich Church on 4 July 1917. Seventeen people were killed, and thirty injured, in the raid.

The number of Victims in this raid constitutes a new record in Air Raid casualties.

The Germans don't kill women and little children from the sky for the mere fun of the thing. It is part of their scheme of frightfulness. They believe that the murder of the little ones will cause the parents to revolt and overthrow authority, and by that means peace will come. Of course, they are wrong again.

Half the profits will be given to the Lord Mayor's Relief Fund.

In Sacred Memory of

THE VICTIMS

of the Hun death-dealers

in the great AIR RAID on London,
Wednesday June 13th, 1917.

IN SINCERE SYMPATHY FOR THE RELATIVES AND SUFFERERS

May God Rest Their Souls.

Top: A classroom in the Upper North Street School in Poplar, east London. Rose Moorhouse was buried alive here for several days after the raid on 13 June 1917 in which eighteen of her school friends were killed.

Centre: Cards such as this one remembering the children killed during the raid on Poplar were frequently distributed. The card was printed locally and sold to raise money for the victims of air raids.

Left: A few of the uninjured children lay flowers as a mark of respect for their dead school friends.

A remarkable picture showing the passage of a 12-inch naval shell through terraced houses in Lowestoft. Amazingly, no one was killed or injured.

Very few municipal air-raid shelters were available, and so most people had to shelter in cellars, tube stations, or under railway arches. (*Hulton Getty*)

THIS HOUSE contains a fairly good sized **CELLAR,** in the event of an **AIR RAID** passers by are welcome to what shelter it affords.

Above: With the men away at the front and food imports severely restricted by German blockades, women were recruited to work the land. However, despite their enduring reputation, there were only ever 16,000 of the so-called land girls.

Right: A postcard encouraging the widespread cultivation of allotments in order to beat the food shortage caused by the German's submarine blockade.

Below: German prisoners of war working hard for their keep. Over 30,000 were employed on farms. (*Rural History Centre, The University of Reading*)

OUT FOR VICTORY.

THE ALLOTMENT HOLDER.
Too old to fight, but doing his bit to beat the U boats.

Right: During the war nothing went to waste. Here, naval cadets collect domestic food scraps in Ilford, Essex, to make in to pig swill. (*Hulton Getty*)

Below: A policeman stands at the head of a long queue awaiting a delivery of food. A sign in the window says 'SOLD OUT BUTTER'. (*Imperial War Museum*)

Children queuing up for penny meals at a soup kitchen in Bermondsey, south London. The food distribution is overseen by a Salvation Army officer. (*Hulton Getty*)

Hungry children, most without shoes, await a food handout. In 1917, food shortages became so critical that children were dying from the effects of severe malnutrition. In the northern pit villages of Usworth and Washington, children went on strike, refusing to go to school until they were properly fed. (*Hulton Getty*)

After Maud Cox and her sister Flora had been hastily pulled inside the house by their grandmother during the first raid over their village, the children discussed what they'd seen.

'We were frightened and got into bed, pulling the bedclothes and blankets right over our heads so that if the Germans came they wouldn't see us. We were cuddling up to each other and Flora kept saying, "I'm not frightened, are you?" And I said, "No, I'm not frightened." But we were shivering because we expected the Germans to be running up the stairs at any moment. The next day we heard it had been shot down over the North Sea.'

The date was 2 February 1916 and the airship they had seen was probably a Zeppelin numbered L19, a new addition to the German fleet. This Zeppelin was one of several that had taken part in the raid, of which two, including L19, had lost their bearings. If L19 was the one seen by Maud, then it had indeed been brought down in the sea, although seemingly not by Allied fire; rather, the Zeppelin had suffered from prolonged and persistent engine trouble throughout the flight. The loss of L19 was to cause a storm of protest in Germany, for when she finally ditched in the sea the crew was still alive and seen holding on to the crippled remains, awaiting rescue. It was approached by a British trawler, the *King Stephen*, the captain actually speaking to the men on the stricken airship. However, the seven-man crew of the boat was unwilling to pick up the survivors for fear of being overwhelmed by the fifteen-strong crew of the Zeppelin, and against maritime convention the boat left the scene, reputedly to look for a ship of the Royal Navy to lend assistance.

The Zeppelin crew all drowned on the afternoon of 2 February, although not before members wrote final notes home which were placed in a bottle and plugged. This bottle was washed up on the Swedish coast six months later and among the correspondence was the name of the British boat that had left them behind. The men of the *King Stephen* had already been lucky. In April their boat was sunk by a U-boat, the entire crew being picked up by the attacking submarine. Had the U-boat's commander known their identity, he might have felt less inclined to help.

The German raid on 2 February, although only partially successful, was still an embarrassment for the British government. Nine Zeppelins had taken part in the attack and none had been driven off or shot down by any of the aircraft scrambled to intercept. The assault had been the largest raid on Britain, killing seventy people in the Midlands. A week later, public alarm grew into widespread panic, when on 10 February there were rumours, which proved unfounded, of another imminent attack on an unprecedented scale.

Warnings of enemy raids were inadequate, owing to technical limitations. One primitive early-warning system was built, a concrete sound mirror invented by the Munitions Inventions Department. This was a concave structure that amplified the sound of the thrum of the Zeppelin's engines, akin to cupping a giant ear. But in truth the inability to know when a raid would take place or indeed predict where a Zeppelin might turn up was seemingly insoluble. If the crews of the airships themselves were near slaves to the prevailing wind, what hope had those on land? As the cumbersome Zeppelins could not afford to attack in the day but only at night, so accurate navigation was made doubly difficult. As one former Zeppelin crew member, Kurt Dehn, later acknowledged, 'So-called targets were no targets. They thought they were over, say, the estuary of the Thames, and in reality they were near Portsmouth.' Bombing was almost random: 'It is rubbish to say that this was the so-and-so building and we dropped our bombs over that building. You were happy enough if you found London, and you were even happier if you could drop your bombs and go home as soon as possible.'

The random nature of the attacks led to Heath-Robinson style air-raid warnings. Madge Maindonald recalled that in London, 'There was no siren. To begin with, a policeman came round on a bike with a notice on him saying "Take Cover" and ringing his bicycle bell.' Margery Porter recollects, 'There were constables walking round the streets shouting out, "Take cover, take cover." We waited until we heard the wardens call "All clear" and then we went back to bed.' Emma Cussons recalls that in Hartlepool, 'When the Zeppelins were coming they sounded the air-raid warning which amounted to people simply blowing whistles.' Penny Feiwel remembers that the warning was given by hooters positioned at the end of the road. In his diary, the Essex clergyman the Reverend Andrew Clark noted: 'Special constables are to have long poles, with pads at the end, to reach up to rap upon upper-storey windows. Major Brown says that this is utter folly, because the first action of every sleeper so aroused will be to light gas or candle, and every street will be alight in a moment.'

There never was any universal system of raising the alarm prior to a raid: klaxons, hooters, flares, whistles – they were all used. Other proposals under consideration included the mass ringing of telephones, on the basis that those with such modern appliances would alert those neighbours without. This, of course, meant all of the working class and large swaths of the lower-middle classes, and so the idea was abandoned. In the end, gas provided one solution whereby large numbers of the population could be contacted at once. Warnings could be given by altering the gas pressure, so that when lights rose or fell twice in quick succession, the blackout curtains should be drawn. For those wealthier homes that had installed electricity, an announcement was made in London that suppliers would be ordered to cut power to generating stations in the event of a raid, thereby 'turning-off' every light bulb in the capital.

In the early days of the war, Londoners had been warned of possible attacks, and lighting restrictions had been introduced as early as 11 September 1914, although not until a raid had occurred were they more rigorously enforced. The first memorandum on lighting was not issued by the Home Office until April 1915, but there was still uncertainty. In essence, street lights could be left unlit, while others could be dimmed or shaded. The brightness of lights on trams, buses and trains was also reduced, and was usually extinguished during a raid. In homes, blinds or blackout curtains were to be used and the police cracked down severely on those who were careless. In court cases brought against civilians in Enfield, for example, stiff fines of typically between £5 and £9 (or alternatively five to seven weeks in prison) were levied against those found guilty.

While air-raid precautions continued to vary from town to town, only much later in the war was there even a half-hearted attempt to provide a form of municipal shelter. During the Zeppelin raids, people were left largely to their own devices, being advised to take to cellars as the safest precaution, or to lie down if they were caught in the open. Margery Porter's family simply moved into the main hallway, close to the staircase, traditionally the strongest part of the building.

'There were quite a few raids. We all lived in flats where there was a long passage at the bottom and all the people from the three storeys above us used to come down and we all sat in there. I remember we were just chatting in armchairs and some people dozed off to sleep. I wouldn't say people were really frightened, they would rather say, "Oh dear, let's hope this soon goes over." This was the first time we'd had bombs on London and I think people were a bit awe-struck; they were still talking of the Boer War, after all.'

Cora Tucker's father 'was a special constable and they used to go round making sure people had their windows closed, not a chink of light. We had big heavy curtains to pull across.' Only at night, when the last family members were going to bed, would the blackout curtains be drawn back, enabling anyone who needed to get up at night to see by the half-light of the moon, or the dullest light of first dawn. If a raid was on, a well-concealed lamp or candle might lead the whole family downstairs to take cover.

'We had a very big kitchen table with a leaf in, we pulled that out and I had to go underneath with the dog, and my father used to stagger down with a feather bed and put it on top of the table so that it would take the shock should anything fall down. The poor dog, she was a white Highland terrier, used to shake because she would hear the whining of the Zeppelin long before we heard it; she knew something was not quite right. She was very frightened and used to shiver in my arms. We didn't feel frightened; we were more annoyed that we had to go through all this palaver.'

Madge Maindonald lived in an upper-floor flat in a council block in London. After vacating the flat on many occasions during air raids, she finally resolved to stay put.

'My father would come over from the goods yard and say there was going to be a raid and we would then go under cover until the "All Clear". There was a man living above us and, when the raids started, his children would come out and scream and yell and Hail Mary and God knows what else. I remember we came outside the flat and I said, "Listen to that lot up there, crying and screaming and carrying on, I mean, nobody could sleep with the noise," so I said, "I'm going back to bed," and Dad said, "So am I," and we never went outside any more during a raid, we stayed in the flat. I thought to myself, well, if we are going to get killed, we are going to get killed, but in truth I was really frightened and I used to get into bed and pull the covers up tight. I was terrified but I could say nothing, there was no one I could say that to, since my mother had already died.'

Not everyone was fearful. Many children, who were old enough to know what was happening but young enough not to care, were more interested in seeing the huge beasts of the air than running to hide. If the Zeppelin was some distance away but was picked up in the searchlights it could be very easy to see, yet presented no imminent danger. In a series of remarkable letters written during or shortly after a series of Zeppelin raids, one fifteen-year-old girl, Leila Champ, wrote of the wonderment and excitement. The letters also reveal the extent to which rumour and gossip were part and parcel of daily life.

October 13th 1915
10 o'clock Wednesday evening

My dear Eleanor

Great excitement!!! I've just seen a Zeppelin!!! About 9.30 mother and I were sitting working and father reclining on the sofa. We were talking about Zeps saying they had not paid us a visit lately. Mother was telling us that a lady she was talking to today had heard from very good authority that they are coming over in <u>force</u>, when we suddenly heard Bang. Bang. Bang. Bomb. Bomb. Bomb. I ran upstairs and looked out at the back and saw nothing then ran into mother's room and gazed out of the window and spotted the Zep almost immediately. Len and I are happy now we have seen one.

Father only just got home in time. If he had been a little later we should not have seen him until about 3 in the morning. All trains were stopped at Liverpool [Street Station] about 8 o'clock. (Zeps were over London about 8.30.) The officials evidently knew the beasts were on the way. The station was all shut up and all lights put out, and the people were advised to go down the subways of the Tube.

Yours, Leila

It was dangerous to become blasé about the Zeppelin threat. As Zeppelins became larger and the payload of bombs increased, so the risk of greater damage and loss of life also grew. The results could be horrifying. Frieda Sawden was on her way to school from her small village of Cottingham, just four miles from Hull city centre. Each day, she arrived at the train station and walked a short distance to the school gates, but this morning was different. A Zeppelin raid had occurred in the early hours.

'I happened to walk down a short street which was parallel to the railway to get to my school, and the Germans had been after the station close by and it was really a near miss. They had simply destroyed the road down which I walked and there were bits of bodies all over and whole bodies and heads and arms and legs, bits blown into trees, just everywhere and nobody about, there wasn't any organisation at all, it was pathetic. I walked on to school and I just walked into my classroom and sat down and, if you please, trigonometry was the first lesson. I was in severe shock when I got to my desk, I wasn't all there, I was vague, thoroughly vague, I could hardly speak at all. I didn't tell my parents about what I had seen. It was not until some time later that I even mentioned it. It might have relieved me if I could have done, but I couldn't get a word out.'

For eighteen months the German airships had bombed Britain with seeming impunity, but in September 1916 this unlimited success ended dramatically. The first airship to be shot down over England was numbered SL11 and it was one of the most widely seen events on the home front during the war. After a chase across London, the airship was eventually attacked by Lieutenant William Leefe Robinson, who machine-gunned SL11 with new incendiary bullets, setting it alight. The airship's demise could be seen for over thirty-five miles in every direction and therefore was witnessed by millions of civilians, including young Penny Feiwel, sitting on her bedroom windowsill. Another who saw the event was twenty-two-year-old Grace Butler, who had been nursing in a military hospital but was now working in a children's hospital on Upper Bridge Road in central London. When the airship came over:

'All the nurses rushed up to the operating theatre in the roof where there was a very large window. The matron was furious because there was shrapnel actually coming down around us from the anti-aircraft guns. And there was this man, Robinson, who went up in his plane to shoot it down. He was up there like a little fly, you could see him picked out by the searchlights every now and again, and underneath there was this great Zeppelin, and you could see Robinson shooting into it, and then suddenly the Zeppelin folded up and came slowly, slowly, slowly down to the ground. It was extraordinary, this great cigar-shaped object, all ablaze with light.'

Another who witnessed the events was keen letter-writer Leila Champ. Almost immediately after the incident she wrote once again to her friend.

3rd September
Sunday Afternoon

Dear Eleanor

We were roused by terrific gun-firing about 2 o'clock. The first thing I always do is to rush to the window to see what there is to be seen. A Zep was visible, very much so, it was lower than I've seen one before and shells busting all round it. It gradually went higher heading northwards, meanwhile the search-lights keeping all round it. It went right overhead, [I] thought every minute that shrapnel from the guns would come through the roof. By this time after much grovelling about I had managed to put a few clothes on and then bundled into your room, we were all in there, Zep still going north then turned a little to the west. We lost sight of it now and again in an extra thick bit of mist or some of its own smoke. Then we lost it altogether for a minute or two, but guns were still firing. Then suddenly over in the direction where Zep had disappeared we saw a huge object falling slowly one mass of flames. It did not appear to fall very quickly and disappeared behind some trees and when, as we thought, it had touched the ground we heard a terrific explosion and saw a vivid flash. You can't think how it lit up everywhere as it came down. Father was rather doubtful as to whether it was the Zep, but I said it must be it was so huge. I couldn't help feeling sorry for the crew.

Next morning there was the extraordinary sight of literally hundreds of people converging on the Hertfordshire village of Cuffley, where SL11 had finally landed. News had spread so fast that roads were quickly clogged with sightseers coming from every direction and on every form of transportation. Civilians from miles around wanted to see the wreckage and, if they could, grab a little piece of history, a souvenir of the great occasion.

Joyce Crow's family lived in Hornsey in north London and had heard the raid, although there was no question of watching the attack. 'Whenever there was a raid we went wherever my mother had most recently read the safest place to go was, and in this case it was under the kitchen table.' The family had no idea at the time what had happened, but they were soon to hear more.

'My youngest brother was working at Park Farm at Cuffley, where he had been employed since leaving school. In 1916 he was seventeen, and he came back, when he had some time off, and brought a piece of German blanket home from the wreck, about a foot square. He had it wrapped up in his pocket but Mother wouldn't have it in the house and he was told to get rid of it. He told us that after the Zeppelin had come down hundreds and hundreds of people came to gawp at the wreck, and that the farmer then the police had had to guard it, to stop people wandering round trying to get mementoes. They had come by train, walking on foot, riding bicycles, all to see this Zeppelin. I think he found it all a bit distasteful. The crowds had apparently come for several days in a row and the farmer had had a job stopping people damaging the farm or scaring the animals.'

Lieutenant Robinson was a national hero, being awarded a Victoria Cross for his action. His attack was celebrated in numerous postcards portraying, in various stages, the airship being brought to earth. The sight of a Zeppelin bursting into flames was now an enormous boost to morale for those living on the home front, puncturing the Germans' apparent invincibility. The demise of SL11 preceded a string of successes, when consecutively numbered Zeppelins L31, L32 and L33 were destroyed over England all within a month of Robinson's success at Cuffley, L32 and L33 both on the same night, 24 September. Leila Champ described the attack, only this time it was far more frightening. The letter, of which only part exists, was begun as the raid was still taking place.

It was a perfect evening and Jim said, 'We shall have a raid tonight.' Sure enough, we had no sooner had our supper and settled down in the dining room, than a very suspicious humming noise began and I went out of the door and said I thought it was a very powerful engine at a great height. About a minute later, Dad and I were just going to look out again, when bang! Crash! Bang! started. We went upstairs and watched the shells bursting over Woolwich way, crowds of them. Some looked like shooting stars until they burst and the others were just a flash of light against the dark blue. My word! There wasn't half a hell of a din when the beasts were about over Leytonstone as far as we could judge. The guns were thundering away like mad and bombs shook the house, with a horrid sort of shattering roar, peculiar to them. We all congregated in the hall by the drawing-room door, and

I took poor little frightened Vic in my arms. Dad wanted us to lie down by the wainscoting, but we none of us did. There was a slight lull, broken suddenly by the most terrifying explosions that made the back door rattle like anything. That went on for some minutes, then there was some distant firing and a little buzzing and all was quiet again and is still so now, while I'm writing this.

The demise, later on that evening, of Zeppelins L32 and L33 was a stunning double success, while L31 was destroyed days later in another raid. The loss of consecutively numbered Zeppelins could not have augured well for the crew of L34, when they launched an attack over the north-east of England on the night of 27 November 1916. As fate would have it, the Zeppelin crossed over the coast at Hartlepool where German ships had wreaked so much havoc nearly two years before.

As the airship arrived over the town at 11.30 p.m., it was caught by a searchlight and, shortly afterwards, was attacked from beneath by aeroplane. The Zeppelin dropped some bombs on West Hartlepool in a bid to gain height, but was machine-gunned along its left flank and burst into flames, falling into the sea about a mile off-shore. The fire was so bright that it was seen over seventy miles away by another Zeppelin making its own attack.

Eight-year-old Emma Cussons, whose mother had been so badly hurt in the German bombardment of the town in 1914, saw the last moments of L34.

'We heard it come over, and so Dad got us all out of bed and said, "If we have got to be killed, we'll all go together." We sat round the fire, when all of a sudden we heard terrible screams and we assumed the Zeppelin had dropped a bomb nearby, but then Dad said to my Mother, "My God, I think they've hit something." Mum said, "Don't go out," but he opened the back kitchen door and it was absolutely red, like a ball of fire, and he said,

"They've got it, they've hit it. Come on, kids, come out and have a look at this, you'll never see anything like this again." All us kids went out and there were pieces of this Zeppelin dropping off in flames, and Dad said to Mum, "Come on, come and have a look." But she said, "No, I can't, they're somebody's lads, aren't they?" Dad later brought a piece of the airship back, a bit of metal, just thick aluminium. I think we were supposed to hand it into the police station but he said, "I'm keeping that for a souvenir," but Mother told him to take it out and get rid of it. She said, "I don't want that in my house, it smells of death. If you want a souvenir," she said, "look at my scars." She had sympathy for the crew. I mean, these lads were just doing their duty, same as our lads were, but to us kids it was excitement, really like a party.'

Further inland, Cora Tucker was also watching as the ship blazed.

'I was under the table with the dog when my father dashed in and said, "Come on quick, the Zeppelin's coming down, when you're a big girl you can say you saw it." By this time everyone had rushed out to see it. One poor man was in his nightshirt and when the Zeppelin was coming down he threw his arms up and said, "Let them burn in hell." Well, of course, as his arms went up his nightshirt went up, much to the delight of the women, and they kept saying to him, "Say it again, Mr so and so," and so he'd throw his arms up and say, "Let them burn in hell," and they howled with laughter. I had no thought of the men in the Zeppelin, serve them right, they shouldn't be over bombing us, should they?'

Many children were shocked at the wild expressions of joy. One young girl, eight-year-old Millicent Hetherington, watched as one neighbour, Mr Pounder, who was already the worse for drink, shouted obscenities at the Zeppelin when it fell close to

Hartlepool. He was 'flinging his hands up in the air as he yelled, "Burn, you buggers, burn." I thought, "How cruel," although I was more surprised by his language, which I didn't quite understand.' Kathleen Barron was fourteen when she had a similar experience.

'The neighbours had come out of their houses and were shouting "hurray", that was the end of them, that was a victory for England, but I had rather a strong imagination and I said, "But there are men burning alive," and I rushed indoors, I couldn't stand it, they were human beings. As a little girl you'd got a very sweet mind as a rule, haven't you, and these people were saying that they were only Germans and I couldn't understand that.'

Owing to increasing losses, Zeppelin operations were restricted not only to night attacks, but ones that were also moonless. However, by the end of 1916 the Zeppelin had had its day as an effective weapon, with senior German officers tacitly admitting that raids over Britain by airships had 'become impossible'. Ever-improving methods of defence had rendered the slow, poorly armed airships largely redundant, although the decision to halt airship raids entirely was very late in coming.

One of the last large-scale raids took place in late October 1917, when eleven Zeppelins launched an audacious raid that went horribly wrong. Of all the attackers, only one managed to drop its bombs on London, killing thirty-three people, while a further four were blown off course by high winds. One of these was shot down over France, while another was wrecked on landing. One was forced to land over enemy territory and was captured intact, while another was destroyed by its crew before it could be seized by the French. A fifth managed to land, but suddenly rose again and was, incredibly, swept south into the Mediterranean. The raid was an abysmal failure, and only four more small-scale and largely ineffectual raids were launched in the following months.

In all, the German army and navy had built eighty Zeppelins for war service, of which twenty-three had been shot down or destroyed in the hangars during enemy raids. However, a further thirty-one had been destroyed in accidents or simply by the vagaries of the weather. Over 400 crewmen had died, or around 40 per cent of all those who had served in the airships. The image of the huge cigar-shaped Zeppelin might have come to symbolise the fighting on the home front, yet ironically their giant size ran in roughly inverse proportion to the damage they actually caused. Between the first Zeppelin raid in January 1915 and the last raid in August 1918, only 556 people were killed as a direct result of their bombs, or fewer than three people a week.

By mid-1917, the Zeppelin's role of attacking Britain had been largely superseded by aeroplanes, and in particular the new breed of bomber known as the Gotha. This plane was capable of targeted bombing over a long distance, and could attack during daylight or night-time hours. It was a fearsome and sinister-looking plane, having a huge wingspan of some 77 feet (about twice as long as its fuselage), and when it began to make its first appearance over Britain it caused widespread public alarm.

Ironically, the very first raid on Britain had not been undertaken by a Zeppelin but by a German aircraft, which on 24 December 1914 had managed a brief bombing run over Dover, when a 22-pound bomb aimed at the castle landed in a cabbage patch. The raid on Christmas Eve, and one subsequent attack on Christmas Day, were worse than ineffectual for they were used by the British as valuable propaganda, underlining the Germans' lack of Christian values on the holiest day of the year.

Vic Cole witnessed one of the raids while training in England.

'While having dinner in camp with other men who had failed to get leave we heard the sound of an aircraft and, running outside, saw our first enemy plane go lurching across the sky! Black crosses on yellow wings gave us our first thrill of the war. A few archie [anti-aircraft] bursts from the gun on Purfleet bank followed the plane but it got quite a distance before being turned by heavier gunfire and then sent crashing down into the Thames.'

Such attacks by small aircraft, when attempted, were no more than the mildest shock tactics, for no planes were sufficiently advanced to cover any great distance laden with bombs. Any raids that did occur were often hit-and-run attacks, causing marginal collateral damage. Indeed, public panic on the ground was often a greater cause of destruction through simple contributory accidents.

William Pain was returning from France on leave when he witnessed the first aeroplane 'raid' over London in November 1916. He was just leaving the train at Victoria when he saw 'a lot of commotion going on at the entrance to the station with people running all over the place'.

'A policeman shouted at me to take cover as there was an air raid going on. I looked up and saw a small plane flying overhead. It wasn't going to damage me at that height. I had been much closer to a plane up the line at Arras. I had shot at the pilot. I could see him sat in his seat then, I had seen the markings clearly, but this one was so high you couldn't see anything. The policeman was waving at a car, when he shouted at me. As I stood there, the car he was waving at drove straight into a lamppost in front of the station. We went to the driver who was unhurt but in shock. He had panicked and was quite annoyed with the policeman.'

It was not until the production of the Gotha IV in 1917 that there was any real potential for the German High Command to contemplate attacking Britain from their bases in occupied Belgium. The first of the Gotha bombers had been produced in 1915, but the new Gotha IV, a biplane, with its three-man crew, marked a major advance in aviation. It could fly for over 400 miles and deliver over 1,100 pounds of bombs. The Gothas were well-armed planes and, because they could fly in formation, gave each other added protection. After trials, thirty Gotha IV were ordered to be ready for a renewed assault on Britain, forming a special squadron for the task, Kampfgeschwader 3. Their mandate: to renew the demoralisation of the civilian population with wave after wave of attacks. The general whose job it was to achieve these goals began to anticipate a raid of eighteen Gothas, during which it would be perfectly possible to deliver 5,400 kilos (nearly 12,000 pounds) of bombs on London, the equivalent of that released by three Zeppelins, 'and so far three airships have never reached London simultaneously', he was quoted as saying.

It was an ambition that was to be aided by British policy at home. For just as the German threat appeared to be reasserting itself, the number of pilots allocated to home defence was thinned out to provide more men for the squadrons at the front. Furthermore, owing to the pressure on resources, an order was issued that no anti-aircraft batteries, other than those located on the coast, were to fire on enemy planes. In other words, once an enemy aircraft had penetrated Britain's meagre defences, it was almost free to carry out its attack on any city or town with impunity.

On 25 May 1917, twenty-three Gothas set off, each carrying thirteen bombs. Soon after passing over the British mainland, they ran into problems. While scrambled Home Defence Squadrons had singularly failed to find the enemy craft, the British weather halted operations. Thick cloud obscured the intended target, London, forcing the commander partially to abort the raid, although secondary targets were always possible.

Ten-year-old Win Reynolds was making her way home from school. She did not want to be too late as her aunt was waiting for her.

'She was going to buy me a pair of shoes, because, you see, I was brought up by my grandparents and auntie. It was a beautifully sunny day, really warm. We were about to set off together and I was standing in the garden

waiting for a moment, when I saw all these aeroplanes,
they flew over and they were flying over at a height where
you could actually see the pilots, and thinking they were
ours, I began to wave. I should think there were
twenty-five planes in all flying about, very low. Other
people came out and waved, as did my grandparents, there
was no bother at all. We'd never seen aircraft like these
before. A while later as we walked into town we could
hear thuds because, as it turned out, they were bombing
other parts of Folkestone. I think they bombed a camp
first and killed a number of Canadians. But the noises I
heard, I still didn't connect it with bombs, not these
thuds.'

The Gothas had continued all the way to Folkestone unmolested,
dropping the odd bomb as they went, on insignificant villages
and hamlets, and even a golf course. Now they saw a clear target,
a camp full of Canadian soldiers waiting to embark for France.
Five bombs were dropped, killing sixteen soldiers, before the
raiders were over the camp and heading for the town. Many
people had heard the thuds in the distance but most attributed
them to live-firing exercises. Certainly no warning of an imminent raid was given in the town as the planes began to drop their
bombs. Win Reynolds remembers:

'We were walking along Tontine Street and we went to a
shop which was about three doors away from Stokes, a
grocery store, when a bomb went off. A man came
outside and dragged us inside the shop and took us down
the cellar, along with a lady and two little fair-haired girls,
I think they were about five. I can remember the man
lighting a gas jet, which looking back now, was rather silly,
and then I saw two other people down there whom I
took to be the manager and the assistant. In the cellar, I
got away from the doorway because my idea of a bomb
was that it had to come through the door, I didn't think

about it coming straight through the roof. I remember going right to the extreme far corner of the cellar.

'We had only been there a few seconds when the lady with the two little children suddenly decided she wanted to leave; she wanted to see that her husband was safe. Well, as she left the shop a bomb fell on Stokes and she got killed along with the two children with her. It was a terrific explosion, it really was, it felt like the end of the world. I don't know how true it was, but I overheard my auntie and grandma discussing the thing and the lady who left was supposed to have been picked up with the two children's hands, one in each of her hands, and the children blown to pieces. It seemed such a shame that they were killed. Her name was Dicker and her husband was the manager of the Maypole Dairy Company which was in Sandgate Road, and he was quite all right, he wasn't touched.'

Further down the road worked fourteen-year-old John Pannett. Now aged 100, he still recalls the bombing with undiminished clarity.

'I was working at a tobacconist's down the bottom of Dover Street when the bombers came. I counted twenty-five planes going over and had heard one or two bangs when I saw what I thought was the last bomb dropped. Then I heard this big bang and I saw all the stuff going up in the air. I ran along the street as fast as I could, and when I got to the point of the impact I saw dead animals and people lying everywhere, a terrible sight. All the gas was blowing out of a fractured main, six or seven feet in the air, and then I saw a lady, Mrs Sheridan, she happened to be standing there with a huge hole in her leg. Hardly anyone to my mind was moving. I've always said I was the first one there, I looked and looked but the damage was so much, I don't think I took it all in. There must have been blood and lots of it, but I can't recall seeing any, it was too much to take in. I can't even recall screaming, it was shock, shock, shock, that I must have been in. There were horses there with all their insides running out. The scene was too awful and I ran back the way I had come as fast as I could.'

There was screaming, and plenty of it. Win Reynolds had waited with her aunt in the cellar until it was safe to emerge.

'As we came out, we could hear all the shouts and yelling and people running and rushing about, and others lying on the ground, there was just confusion and ever such a lot of screaming. I remember shaking, I couldn't stop myself, although my biggest memory is hearing a horse screaming, a horrifying, uncanny sound, because there was a potato ration and they had just had a wagonload of potatoes drawn by horse and cart outside Stokes. You could see all the rubble and the glass in front of the shop and the tiles off. I had a terrible feeling, I felt so bewildered. When we got home, my grandparents were standing outside. They burst into tears because they thought we'd been killed because they knew that was roughly where we would be. We sort of clung on to one another, and then I burst into tears.'

In all, 159 bombs had been dropped, killing sixteen men, thirty women and twenty-five children, with a further 192 injured in or near the town. It was a devastating attack, made much worse by the fact that a queue had formed outside Stokes' shop in the hope of purchasing some of the food that had just arrived. The 50-kilo bomb had brought the roof down on customers in the store, and blasted those waiting patiently outside. Lethal shards of metal and glass flew in every direction; John Pannett's cousin John Clark lost an eye, and many more were critically maimed.

The raid was a terrible awakening, remembers Win Reynolds.

'We thought we would never get bombed because before the war there was a German ship which got into difficulties outside Folkestone and our fishermen and the lifeboat went to rescue them. They rescued some and brought all these dead bodies and they were buried in Cheriton Road Churchyard with a piece of ground set aside for them, about forty of them, so we thought wherever they bomb, it won't be here, not after what we had done for them, saving a lot of sailors.

'I thought how horrible they were to bomb civilians. You expect soldiers to fight and you expect some to be killed but you don't expect poor people going about their daily business, queuing for something to eat. The grown-ups hated them worse and their expression used to be there's only one good German and that's a dead one. Ordinary people getting bombed; you weren't very pleased with them, in fact, if you had had one you'd give him a good shake.

'In any air raids after that, they used a klaxon which was on the Town Hall, and on the fire station in Dover Road, while another was on the drill hall, and one more at the public baths, on the corner of Forde Street and Blackpool Road. There were no air-raid shelters then, but after that we used to all go under the stairs. People say you can't get white hair through shock, but I can assure you that you do, because I had a white streak from the time I was eleven which was a few months after that attack. I had a dozen white hairs and if you pulled them out they still came again. And, do you know, as soon as that klaxon went, my face used to swell right up. It felt like toothache and it would last quite a few hours before it went down again. I looked as if I'd got mumps.'

Although as many as three Gothas were eventually shot down as they retreated over the Belgian coast, this was no compensation for the people of Folkestone, who demanded to know why no warning was given. A delegation from the town was sent to Parliament to find answers, while questions were asked in the Commons. As a result, promises were made to 'make any future raid a very risky operation'. To this end, the quality of aircraft defending Britain was significantly improved, in the hope and expectation that no attacker could expect to escape without engagement in the air. Yet there could be no guarantee that another such raid would be deterred. Sadly, Folkestone was not the last town to suffer catastrophic loss.

Within days, a second attack was launched on Sheerness, when the first Gotha was shot down, crashing into the sea. Then, undeterred, another raid was launched a week later. It was 13 June, a bright, slightly hazy day. The Reverend Andrew Clark was outside, mending a paddock fence, when, as he recorded in his diary, he 'heard an unusual drumming noise in the E. and S.E. It went on for a considerable time . . . I thought it was drums in Terling Camp, or a regiment on a route-march on the road beyond that. My daughter thought it was an aeroplane, but out of order.' His daughter was right, but it was neither out of order nor just one plane. It was, in fact, a squadron and was well on its way to London.

Emily Galbraith was twenty-two at the time and training to be a teacher; she had been visiting a girls' school while on holiday from college.

'The school had a roof garden and while we were up there, a raid occurred. I could see the planes and remember counting them, one, two, three, four, five, six, but before I finished counting the girls were marched down to the gym underneath. I remember they went down in a very orderly, quiet way, down the stairs, no trouble, no fuss. We could hear the sound of two bombs exploding, then shortly afterwards we heard wailing outside the school, making the most unholy noise, and it was Jewish women wailing, mourning, a special sort of moan that only Jewish women can do.

'I left the school soon after, as I had to get home by train from Fenchurch Street Station. I remember walking and I had to pass just where a bomb had fallen on a dray drawn by two shire horses. One of the horses was hit by shrapnel and lay on the ground bleeding and the other horse was standing in the shafts trembling dreadfully, its head down. I had to walk past those horses and, as I did, I put my hand out and touched the horse to try and console it. The poor thing was terrified.'

A couple of miles away, Rose Moorhouse was at the Upper North Street School in Poplar. It was a normal day, and Rose had been at school for about three hours.

'We were in this big classroom having lessons when suddenly the teacher told us to go downstairs and sit and be quiet because she had heard that a raid was on. We all left our desks and went, as asked, down below. We sat there talking among ourselves. I was talking and giggling with a little boy next to me and as we had been told to be quiet, the teacher ordered the boy to move. We didn't hear anything, no noise, no bomb falling. Next thing I remember was that I felt heavy, I could scarcely breathe. I kept falling into unconsciousness, then waking up and going to sleep again, then waking up, to hear the sound of myself moaning. I couldn't speak and I couldn't move. I had bits of debris in my mouth. Things come into your mind, and all I wanted was my mum. I didn't know what had happened; you don't rationalise things but I wondered why I had all this debris on me.'

The attack on the school had occurred just before the children were due to break for lunch. There had not been one explosion but several, as the raiders bombed the houses opposite, one of the last bombs hitting the school. The explosion devastated the buildings, burying many children in the rubble. Several lifeless bodies could be seen, some mutilated by flying shrapnel. Survivors were covered in brick dust and could be seen wandering about in the playground, dazed. A rescue was immediately undertaken by anyone who arrived on the scene, and slowly one child after another was pulled from the wreckage and taken away.

Rose was not found. As the casualties and the rubble were taken away, she continued to lie trapped underneath part of the building still to be excavated. 'The reason why I hadn't died was the ceiling had come down and criss-crossed above me, so that's how I got the air to breathe and keep me alive. I was the only one they couldn't find.'

Rose's elder brother, Jimmy, went to see the bodies of those who had been killed before going on to the hospital to see the badly injured. Finding no trace of his sister, he returned to the school, convinced that his sister was still under the rubble.

'Not finding me, he'd been round the school helping to dig. Each evening after work he came and then, instead of going to bed at night, he'd come down again. He'd go there and say, "She must be there somewhere," but in the end someone said, "It's a waste of time, she must be dead by now." Three nights he was there, listening, because it was very quiet at night, and he thought he might hear some movement. And then I must have come round and moaned because he heard something, so he listened again, then sure of what he heard, he ran and got the police.

'I could hear them trying to get me out, I could hear the noise and hear them talking. One of the men was digging away with this shovel and he caught me under my arm, cut it open. I was really very injured. Then I remember them taking me out of the ground and they got this stretcher. I remember I felt the fresh air when they got me into the open. Then I was placed in an ambulance and taken to Poplar Hospital.'

A total of twenty-two Gothas had set out to attack Britain in what was the first daylight raid on the capital. Two planes had turned back with engine trouble. The rest had caused mayhem, fourteen eventually attacking London, where they wheeled and turned over the city centre, before breaking into two groups, one attacking north and east London, the other the south. In all, 126 bombs were dropped, three tons of explosives hitting not only schools, but stables, breweries, train stations and private homes. Eighteen children died in the attack on Upper North Street School, including the young boy moved from Rose's side moments before the blast. Altogether, 162 people were killed and 432 injured, far and away the greatest number of casualties in one raid, and almost eclipsing the number caused by Zeppelin raids in the whole of 1915.

In the aftermath of the raid, public protest was passionate, and demanded that such a raid be properly dealt with, in just the way that public protest had demanded a response to the Zeppelin raids. In a little over two weeks, 270 people had died in raids, and 660 were injured. It appeared that the Gotha might fatally undermine morale and with it the desire to support the war and fight on. The authorities were nervous. As if to underline this sense of crisis, the government detached two squadrons from overseas action to defend Britain. Their withdrawal to home defence was a short-term fix to pacify public feelings, for both squadrons were soon returned to active service abroad.

Lying in hospital, Rose was visited by her mother.

'The next thing I remember was seeing my mother coming through the ward looking from side to side. She actually went past me because my face was so badly damaged, then I must have dropped off again because I remember her passing but I don't remember her coming to my bed. Mother told me later that the only thing she recognised me by was that I had one of my sister's hand-me-down shoes. I had lost one in the raid but was wearing the other when I was pulled out of the rubble

and this was now kept under my hospital bed. My head
was bound, and I was told not to touch it because I had a
bit of shrapnel lodged in the skull; it wasn't a big piece but
it was deep. They couldn't take the risk of taking it out.
So it is still there to tell the tale, a souvenir.

'Some while later, when I was much better, we heard
that Queen Mary was coming to the hospital to see the
injured children and of course we were excited. I was
beginning to walk around so they dressed me up, among
my bandages as well, in this pretty dress, the like of which
I had never had in my life, and they gave me this bouquet
and I saw the Queen coming up the stairs to where I was
standing, arm in a sling, and I had this big bouquet and I
gave it to her, gave a little curtsey and she bent down and
kissed me on the cheek. Then they undid a big box and
she handed me this lovely doll. She had one for all the
children. No sooner had she gone and all the excitement
was over, than they took the dress off me, which was ever
so disappointing.'

On 7 July, another twenty-two planes raided London and
another 250 people were killed or wounded. Once again, a
fighting squadron was brought back from France, this time to
protect Londoners, but as it turned out, that was the last day raid
on the capital. For the rest of the war the Germans would revert
to night attacks, making coastal anti-aircraft fire almost redundant, the defenders being incapable of picking out an enemy
plane in the night sky. If Gothas were to be stopped, they had to
be shot down, but pilots defending the towns and cities had
severe problems pinpointing the enemy.

The number of deaths in London had tripled in 1917 in
comparison with 1916. As a result, large sections of the civilian
population, estimated at over 300,000, began, in their fright, to
take to the underground stations, a precursor of scenes witnessed
in the Second World War. By September, civilians had begun to
descend on the platforms with bedding, food and the household

pets before a warning had even been given. They went merely as a precaution, camping out until all threat had past. That month there was a total of eight raids, the most active of the whole war. There was no adequate means of defending these people against the attacks, and the public knew it.

One of those who eschewed the use of the underground was Madge Maindonald. She had lost her mother in 1915, and for most of the war was raised by her father and another couple, the Gowers, who were friends of the family.

'Mrs Gower was very frightened of the raids and always carried a bag in which was her marriage certificate, insurance policies and whatever money she had. Before an attack, she would leave with her husband and little dog and go to some flats considered stronger than our little cottage, and I and my brother would go with her. Mrs Gower had a friend who lived in the bottom of these flats, just near Vauxhall Bridge, so we could shelter there. As we waited there one night, I remember Mrs Gower talking in the passageway. There was a Mr Walker there with his lad, a very docile boy, and Mr Gower. I liked Mr Gower, he was a quiet man, very kind, if a little deaf. He used to make round boxes at a time when men wore stiff collars and he used to make and cover them with leather cloth and he was very clever at it. I would sit and watch him and he would talk to me about what he was doing and how he did it. Mrs Gower, on the other hand, was a nagger and I used to keep out of her way if I could.

'We were all standing in or near the passageway when my brother suggested that, as he'd run out of cigarettes, we went round the corner to buy some. Nothing was happening outside so we went round the other side of the flats where there was a shop open. Then he said a strange thing, "Let's go and find Father." He worked nearby, so he took me up to Vauxhall Station, leaving me at the entrance while he went off to find him. At that time the station had a glass roof. Well, we didn't know anything about bombing; we didn't understand a glass roof was not the safest thing to shelter under. It was then that the first bomb dropped in the gasworks and set the place on fire. I heard this dreadful bang. People began rushing past me to get into the station, but I didn't move because my brother had said "Stand there." Moments later he came running back from wherever he was and grabbed my hand. We were running full strength into the station and it was like slow motion. He dragged me in and pushed me near a big stone pillar, holding me there, up tight against it. People were crying and screaming and praying; that was very unnerving. Others were rushing in and some people who had lost each other were trying to shout to each other, it was terrible. Everybody was lying on the floor, some cuddling each other and some people were calling, "John, John, where are you? John, oh for Christ's sake, John, speak to me."

'My father came and found us. We waited for a while and there was a lull, so he said, "Let's go and look at the house," but when we got there the police wouldn't let us through because there was a fire in the gasworks. My father pointed out his house and so they let him pass and we went to the flats. Well, I hadn't heard any other bombs drop but I discovered that there were in fact five, and two had landed either side of the passageway in the block of flats we had left. The blast caught Mr Gower and Mr Walker and killed them both. I was told Mr Gower got up and called his wife's name and fell down dead. The boy wasn't hurt; I think he was terribly shocked because he must have been near his father. Mrs Walker, she'd been injured and taken away, but Mrs Gower was still there. She was always a very prim lady, always very clean and well-dressed, but she stood at the gate, holding on to keep herself up. She'd lost a shoe, her clothes were torn and dirty and bloody. Her hair was down over her face because her hat had been lost and I can see her now – I didn't realise but it must have made a very great impression – this very neat woman in such a terrible mess, blood everywhere. All she said was, "Oh Mr Maindonald, what shall we do?"

'It was a long night and when I woke up I was in my own bed, fully dressed; my brother had carried me home. He had shared his bed with the little Walker boy who had been found wandering around with nowhere to go. I was a very silent child after that. I'd seen things and I never used to tell anybody. I used to keep it all to myself. Had we gone back to the flats like we were supposed to, we would have been dead, we would have been right there, right on the spot. That morning after the raid I dressed myself as best I could and went to school and my brother went to work at a printing place in Charing Cross. I arrived at school after having very little sleep and never said a word about what had happened. I couldn't. I have often thought to myself that the teacher must have thought I was a very strange child.'

The year 1917 was the high point for German aeroplane raids on Britain, with a total of twenty-nine separate attacks, just over half being night raids. These raids had sown considerable fear among the civilian population and in all some 300 aircraft were kept out of the main theatre of war to defend Britain. Yet it was not until the following January that a British pilot managed to down an enemy plane attacking at night. In 1918 small but significant improvements would be made in shooting down raiders although even then it has been calculated that it took the anti-aircraft guns an average of 14,540 shells for each plane they destroyed.

The new year would see a rapid reduction in attacks on Britain as the Germans pinned all their hopes, and concentrated all their energies, on victory with a major offensive on the Western Front. Only five raids took place before the Germans' attack in March. The last of these raids on the night of

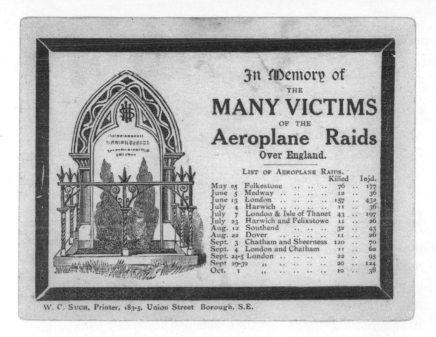

In Memory of
THE
MANY VICTIMS
OF THE
Aeroplane Raids
Over England.

LIST OF AEROPLANE RAIDS.

		Killed		Injd.
May 25	Folkestone	76	..	177
June 5	Medway	12	..	36
June 13	London	157	..	432
July 4	Harwich	11	..	36
July 7	London & Isle of Thanet	43	..	197
July 23	Harwich and Felixstowe	11	..	26
Aug. 12	Southend	32	..	43
Aug. 22	Dover	11	..	26
Sept. 3	Chatham and Sheerness	120	..	70
Sept. 4	London and Chatham	11	..	62
Sept. 24-5	London	22	..	95
Sept 29-30	„	20	..	124
Oct. 1	„	10	..	38

W. C. Such, Printer, 183-5, Union Street Borough, S.E.

A card remembering the victims of the Gotha air raids.

7/8 March caused considerable damage to housing, and twenty-three people died. One of the victims was a fifty-two-year-old American poet, Lena Guilbert Ford. Her death was ironic in the extreme for she was best known and remembered for writing the lyrics to the war song 'Keep the Home Fires Burning'.

After the March raids there would be only one further raid, in May, which met with any success. German desperation was beginning to show and for the final three months of the war there was not a single raid. In all, there had been fifty-three Zeppelin and fifty-seven aeroplane raids during the war, resulting in 1,413 deaths and 3,407 injuries. London had suffered heavily, with over 800 civilians being killed and 1,500 injured in air raids on the capital in 1917 and 1918. Coastal towns such as Ramsgate and Margate in Kent were also heavy sufferers. Dover experienced 113 alarms, and bombs were dropped on twenty-nine occasions. There, people had taken to nearby caves, which could temporarily accommodate up to 25,000. They were essentially making provision for their own safety, in the absence of any co-ordinated government initiatives.

Many of the interviewees who spoke about raids in the First World War often recalled that the attacks in the Second World War were worse. This is true. During the Blitz of 1940 and 1941, 13,000 tons of high explosive were dropped on London, compared with a meagre 280 tons dropped in the whole of the 1914–18 war. The Blitz alone claimed 43,000 lives by mid-1941 and actually outnumbered military deaths at the front. The two wars fought on the home front are clearly not comparable in terms of deaths and damage caused. However, hindsight should not mask the profound shock and horror suffered by the British public when war's brutality was delivered from the air for the very first time. The sense of violation was profound, and the indiscriminate destruction that was wrought appeared fearsome to a people unused to such emotions or witnessing such sights.

CHAPTER SEVEN

The Year of Hunger

I N THE DARKEST HOURS ON THE HOME FRONT, WHEN THE strain of war was beginning to tell, a woman went to her local butcher's shop. As she walked in, she saw the butcher cutting up some meat for sale, though not the kind of meat she normally recognised. 'That looks like cat . . .' she ventured. 'It is,' he replied.

This incident illuminates a new and very real threat to Britain that was apparent by early 1917: starvation. As the war entered its fourth year, the outlook on both battle front and home front was bleak. In France and Belgium there was yet more suffering, best epitomised by the Battles of Arras and later of Passchendaele, both fought in an ever worsening morass of churned-up earth and mud. Meanwhile, as the opposing sides continued to pound each others' trenches on land, German U-boats attacked and sank Allied merchant ships, destroying vital supplies. As Britain depended on imported food and raw materials, it was dangerously vulnerable. On the eve of the war, two-thirds of its food, measured in calories, came from overseas. The war at sea would have a crucial bearing on what – if anything – was on the nation's dinner tables.

It was during the First World War that the submarine was deployed effectively for the first time. The German navy had built up a strong fleet of U-boats, and in 1915 and 1916 had realised that their most profitable use was against merchant shipping rather than warships. Losses mounted rapidly. However, incidents involving the loss of American lives, like the sinking of the *Lusitania* in May 1915, had risked drawing the United States into the war on the side of the Allies; there were orders restricting the activities of German submarine commanders. Now, at the beginning of February 1917, unrestricted submarine warfare against Allied shipping was continued with a vengeance. The German Admiralty believed that their strengthened U-boat fleet could sink 600,000 tons of British shipping every month. This, they calculated, would knock Britain out of the war in six months. Even if America entered the war, which it did in April 1917, they believed it could be won before American military strength took effect. This was warfare against British civilians, aimed at depriving them of food, in the hope and expectation that the British government would eventually capitulate.

In the early part of the war, German U-boats had warned defenceless merchant ships that they were about to be attacked, giving the crew a chance to escape with their lives. By May 1917, the rate of sinkings without warning had tripled to 64 per cent, with a consequent heavy loss of life. The lives of around 3,000 merchant seamen were lost in 1917 alone.

Naval blockade was a strategy used by both sides in the war, but in the spring and summer of 1917 it was spectacularly successful for Germany. In April, enemy action sank 169 British and 204 Allied or neutral ships. This represented 866,000 tons, or a quarter of all the tonnage using British ports. By this measure, the Allied losses in this one month represented 8 per cent of the losses for the entire war. Enormous quantities of meat and grain en route to Britain ended up on the ocean floor. In all, 46,000 tons of meat would be lost at sea in 1917. So, too, was much of the sugar: between February and June, 85,000 tons of sugar were sent to the sea bottom. At one point, only four days' supply was left. Stocks of wheat and flour were so low that they would last only for another two months. A stunned House of Commons was told that the country's food stocks could run out in a matter of weeks. By the autumn of that year, a further 1,500 merchant ships had gone down, with a loss of over 2.25 million tons of goods.

Inevitably, the main victims of food shortages were the poorer members of the working classes in both city and countryside. Because it was cheap, bread was vital to their diet, and 80 per cent of the wheat used to make it was imported. The memory of deprivation remains fresh in the minds of the children who suffered it, such as Ruth Armstrong, now aged ninety-six. She still lives in the tiny Wiltshire village of Tilshead, where she was born and brought up. In 1917 she was eleven. Her father, an agricultural labourer, was fighting in France and her mother – an extraordinarily strong and resourceful woman – was struggling to feed the family.

'It was a terrible time, terrible. We were starving. I can remember my mother going out and picking dandelion leaves and washing them and making sandwiches with them. It tasted like lettuce. Another thing, my mother, my grandmother, my little brother and me used to go out into the fields and pick the greens off the turnips and swedes. You had to pick a lot because they shrunk so. We took them home and cooked them with potatoes and mashed it up with margarine. That was our Sunday dinner. Mother used to say, "When you're eating it, think you've got a nice roast dinner." But we never saw a piece of meat for ages. Many days our mother would make a jug of custard for our dinner, and we ate it with bread and butter. Nothing else. I got sick of the sight of custard. I don't know how my mother managed. It was nothing to see her sitting at the table with an empty plate. "Mummy, you're not eating?" "I'm not hungry," she'd say. Whatever she had was for my brother and myself. If it had gone on for many more months like that I don't know what would have happened to us.'

At least in the countryside there was food for free to help feed families. In the cities, with no such luxury, food shortages were felt even more keenly. Madge Maindonald was twelve in 1917 and lived in Vauxhall, south-west London. She remembers the hunger. 'People starved, do you know, people starved. We nearly starved, didn't we?' But Madge never complained of the lack of food, at the time or since. 'If you were hungry, you didn't tell anybody. People didn't. They had their pride. I wouldn't let people know. No, you don't understand, you've no idea.'

The immediate effect of the shortages was to push up food prices dramatically. By the middle of 1917, bread as well as potatoes – another staple of the working-class diet – had doubled in price, compared to two years earlier. There were similar increases in the cost of sugar, butter, milk, cheese and bacon and even the cheap cuts of meat that had once been affordable to poorer families.

The government was slow to react to the crisis. It was ideologically opposed to a system of compulsory rationing, and preferred a voluntary solution that respected the freedom of each family. In February 1917, Lord Devonport, the new Food Controller, introduced a voluntary rationing scheme. Everyone was encouraged to reduce their consumption, with appeals for restraint and meatless days. Each citizen was implored to eat only four pounds of bread, two and a half pounds of meat and twelve ounces of sugar each week. The aim was to shift consumption away from grain, which was predominantly imported, to meat, which was mostly produced at home. A huge publicity campaign followed in newspapers, on billboard posters and in government propaganda films. Many middle-class families were keen to do their patriotic duty, since they were still able to enjoy a varied diet and were not seriously hit by the inconvenience of food shortages. A survey by the Ministry of Food, undertaken to see how effective its food economy drive was proving, found that in well-to-do Worthing, 92 per cent of those surveyed were committed to voluntary food reduction.

The official strategy, however, revealed a profound ignorance of the diet of working-class families, which was based on a high consumption of bread. Meat, because of its expense, was a luxury. These families were the ones suffering most from increasing food prices and shortages. As bread was still one of the cheapest and most filling foods, their natural response was to eat more, not less, of it. Many were confused and angered by the government's calls for voluntary food restraint. This was vividly illustrated in the Ministry of Food's exhaustive door-to-door survey in the less prosperous market town of King's Lynn in the autumn of 1917. Almost half of all those questioned said they had no intention of eating less.

Journalist Mrs C. S. (Dorothy) Peel worked for the Ministry of Food in 1917. In her book *How We Lived Then*, written ten years after the war, she documents the experience of one Food Campaign speaker whose job was to encourage the working classes to eat less. 'I addressed what I was warned might be a very difficult audience in a poor neighbourhood. Directly I cast an eye over all those in the hall, I realised that here were people who had never had enough to eat, who indeed had never had enough of anything except privation, and of that too much.' The lady was there to ask for goodwill in reducing consumption.

Of those who could not afford too much or even enough [food], I only begged any aid they could give in surmounting difficulties. As, for example, by helping to encourage a determination to bear what had to be borne as a necessary part of the task of winning the war. After the meeting a man shook hands with me. 'I'd two rotten tomatoes in me pocket, I'm glad I didn't feel the need to throw 'em. Ye see, we don't want ladies comin' to tell us to eat less.'

Most poorer families simply were not getting enough food. What bread they did eat was made more palatable by margarine, which, though nutritionally inferior, became the great wartime substitute for butter, now in very short supply. 'Bread and scrape' formed the entire breakfast and tea for millions of families. Agricultural labourers and miners had traditionally enjoyed cheese and bread for their midday meal, but shortages of cheese

No. 67.

Ministry of Food,
Grosvenor House, W.1.

ON HIS MAJESTY'S SERVICE.

I wish to appeal for the immediate help of every man,
woman and child in my effort to reduce the consumption of
bread.

We must all eat less food; especially we must all eat
less bread and none of it must be wasted. The enemy is
trying to take away our daily bread. He is sinking our
wheat ships. If he succeeds in starving us our soldiers
will have died in vain.

In the interests of the country, I call upon you all
to deny yourselves, and so loyally to bridge over the anxious
days between now and the harvest. Every man must deny himself; every mother, for she is the mistress of the home,
must see that her family makes its own sacrifice and that
not a crust or crumb is wasted.

By a strict care of our daily bread we can best help
the men who are gallantly fighting on sea and land to
achieve victory, and so share with them the joys of the
peace which will follow.

No true citizen, no patriotic man or woman will fail
the country in this hour of need.

I ask all the members of your household to pledge
themselves to respond to the King's recent Appeal for
economy and frugality and to wear the purple ribbon as a
token.

29th May, 1917.   Food Controller.

**A letter 'To the Head of the Household' imploring every family to
cut its consumption of bread.**

meant they too had to make do with bread and margarine. Poorer families survived on a diet of bread and potatoes. Amelia Harris was the daughter of a Jewish boot repairer in Hoxton, north-east London. In 1917 she was ten, and remembers that year when there was almost nothing to eat.

> 'Breakfast was tea and bread. At teatime it was bread and
> dripping. For dinner it was boiled potatoes. For vegetables
> we had cabbage leaves that we picked off the floor by the
> market. That was all we survived on. We were very, very
> poor and undernourished. For years I've been very
> anaemic and I think I'm still suffering from it now.'

Children were at the bottom of the food chain in many working-class families. If the family could afford meat or vegetables, they were most likely to be eaten by the man of the house, if he was not away fighting in France. He was the main breadwinner on whom they largely depended for their survival. The children had to wait for leftovers from his plate. Bert Smith, the son of a Nottingham miner, was eight in 1917. They were particularly hard up as there were nine children in the family to feed. 'The war had been going for three years and when my dad had dinner, because he was working we used to stand watching him eat. And he'd get his fork and give me a potato. Then he'd give the other lads one, my brothers. That's all we had to eat.'

The Smith family looked forward to Sunday when they would enjoy their best meal of the week.

> 'On Saturday night I used to go with my dad to the shops
> and he'd get this tanner wrap-up, you'd get bits of meat
> and what have you, used to bring it all home and put it in
> the stew pot and then in the oven. This stew would be
> cooking all Saturday night. That was our breakfast, Sunday
> morning, cow heel stew for nine of us. Now who would
> eat that these days on a Sunday morning? And when you'd
> finished, your fingers were all stuck together, because that

was the goodness out of the cow heel. 'Course we had no knives and forks. You couldn't afford knives and forks. You used to eat it with your fingers and that was it.'

Sunday teatimes were special, too. 'We had bread and lard, as normal, but we had sugar sprinkled on the top of the lot. That was a treat because for the rest of the week you had just bread and lard, no sugar. Margarine, no margarine, I don't think they had it here. And butter was never heard of.' Bert is ninety-three and after such a poor childhood can scarcely believe he has survived so long.

The bread eaten that year was very different from that eaten before the war. From March 1917 onwards, it was doctored. A higher proportion of raw wheat was used and other grains like maize and barley were mixed in. Even potatoes were added. These changes in the milling and production of bread made the limited supplies go further. It was one of the more enlightened government initiatives of early 1917, inspired by the Food Production Department. The new war loaves were more nutritious, but were a mixed blessing, as they tasted unpleasant and were unpopular with the consumer.

'If you'd seen a loaf baked before the First World War, you would have seen something pure white, and people expected their bread to be like that,' says Sydney Bond, whose father ran a small family bakery business in Liverpool.

'There was a period in 1917 when this country had virtually no flour, and it was decided that no loaf would ever be made again with any kind of pure flour. Anyway, eventually the ruling came out, government ruling, that potatoes must supplement any dough being made. That cost Dad quite a lot, because it meant buying equipment to boil potatoes. The next job was to crush them, pummel them and pummel them until they got them down into really a sort of slush because they were continually adding water. Eventually this awful

potato business was tipped over into the trough where
the dough was lying. You can imagine how awful it was
to handle the dough or even to get this potato stuff to
mix in evenly. So it was a very common experience
when cutting a loaf for a piece of potato to shoot out
and that's what the housewives had to put up with. A
black loaf full of bits of potato. Oh, I won't say it was
horrible but it had an unpleasant spongy taste and smell.
It was an awful business, especially to any baker
deserving of the name, because he was so proud of his
bread. My dad had two vans and they had on them
"Bond's Best Bread Beats All Others". I can remember
to this day he was broken-hearted because to him it was
ruining and spoiling what was his life's work.'

Perhaps it was because some of the bread was so unpleasant to eat
that there was always a ready supply to be given away at the
factory gates when the munitions workers came home from
work in the evening. There would usually be a throng of
desperately underfed children waiting to devour the smelly,
crusty remains of the workers' lunches. Among them was
Tottenham girl Penny Feiwel.

'A gang of us used to go up to the factories and wait there
until they came out, and we'd hold out our hands. They
knew what we wanted and they pushed the bits of
sandwiches in your hand as they passed quick to get
home. Perhaps we'd find a huge crust, or a nobbie as we
used to call it in those days. There'd be various titbits,
perhaps a piece of cake, stale cake it might have been, but
it was good, and that's how we survived.'

In many areas, free soup kitchens and penny dinners were
provided for the poorest children by a host of well-meaning
philanthropic organisations. 'You felt so hungry, it was a wonder
you could go to school. Then they started a soup kitchen, you

could get a cup of soup,' remembers Maud Cox, then a schoolgirl in the Scottish mining village of Methil in Fife. 'That was when things were really getting bad. There were ladies, female auxiliary nurses, and they had aprons with red crosses on them. They used to come and open up a big boiler and dish out cups of soup, like in a famine.'

Charlotte Huggett, the daughter of an agricultural labourer, grew up in the Kent village of Wateringbury and in 1917 benefited from the penny dinners provided by the newly formed Women's Institute. Yet even a penny a day was beyond the means of her family. 'The Women's Institute did a dinner, some soup and a pudding for a penny. But my mother could not afford us to have one every day, so we had one three times a week. So you got a good dinner then. Otherwise it was bread and scrape.'

The quality of food provided was sometimes so appalling that it was inedible, even to hungry children like Madge Rutherford. Her main diet in 1917 was bread, margarine and condensed milk.

'Oh yes, I was hungry and I used to go to school dinners, but they were terrible. They were awful, the food was rotten and I couldn't eat them. My father used to pay a few pence for them every week and one day I said I didn't eat them. He said, "You don't eat them, why not?" I said, "The potatoes are bad and the meat's not nice, I can't eat it." I was hungry but they were cooked by the kids that did cookery lessons and they didn't know how to cook. So my father said I wasn't to go there any more, it was a waste of money.'

Another girl who could not eat her school meals was Penny Feiwel.

'The only children who were allowed to go and be given dinners were very very poor and I was one of them. It was called the White Ribbon, a club for teetotallers.

Somehow I didn't like it because I wasn't used to the
food they served. I had only had bread and margarine
and dripping so I just didn't eat the things they gave
you there.'

Small wonder she would fill up on munition workers' leftovers in
the evening.

To make matters worse, the food distribution system was
increasingly unreliable and delivery sporadic. Shops, especially
those in rural areas, kept running out of basic food items. On
18 October, for example, the village shopkeeper of Great Leighs
in Essex had no tea or butter and only eleven pounds of very fat
bacon for sale. He had received only a quarter of his grocery
order for that week from his wholesaler. Over the years, shops
like his had become dependent on food products supplied from
the cities and from abroad. With most imported food now
directed towards the centres of population where it was most
needed, the village store could find itself with little or nothing to
sell, and what it did have was priced beyond the pocket of some.
By the middle of the year there were families facing virtual
starvation – like that of Esther Peel. Esther was born in 1905 and
brought up in the village of Woodford in Northamptonshire. By
1917 her three younger brothers had all died of malnutrition.

'We were very poverty-stricken. Really my baby brothers
starved to death. There was no food for them. I can
remember one kindly doctor coming to see them for
nothing, no money, and he told my mother they had to
have Virol every day. That was kind of a thick, sticky malt
stuff. But, well, we didn't have pennies every day to give to
the babies. I remember when my last brother died, the one
I used to look after. I think I looked on him as a doll,
because I never had a doll, I never had a toy. Then one day
they said he'd died. When I went to bed at night his dead
body was being kept in a coffin in my bedroom before
being buried and my mother said, "Say goodnight to him,

won't you?" I did. I used to kiss him goodnight and he
looked lovely. I did say to my mother one night, "He's ever
so cold, shall I take him in bed with me?" And she said,
"No, you mustn't disturb him." I used to feel sorry that he
was there on his own and I used to think, "They're going to
take him away." To begin with, there was some bubbles of
spittle at the corner of his mouth and I thought, "Well, if he
was ill, if I take those and put them in my mouth I'll
probably die and go with him and so I can look after him
again." I missed him, missed his coughing when he'd gone.
I remember the day he went. Someone gave my mother
and my grandma a lift because she sat in this pony-trap with
this coffin on her lap.'

Families did everything they could to prevent the tragic loss of
young lives. In 1917 the age-old rural traditions of poaching,
pilfering and collecting nature's bounty really came into their
own. The country child had always been a hunter-gatherer. In
the fields and hedgerows there was an abundance of food. Wild
strawberries, hawthorn berries, nuts, blackberries, wild mush-
rooms and apples were some of the most popular. Most would be
eaten raw, though some were taken back for mothers to turn into
pies, jams and jellies. Some of the fruit and vegetables would be
pilfered from farmers' fields, often on the way home from school
in the late afternoon. Although this was a criminal offence, very
few were detected or charged by the village policeman. The
police had been depleted by wartime duties, and country
children usually escaped detection anyway as most knew the lie
of the land. Marian Atkinson, now ninety-seven, grew up in the
Lake District and was a twelve-year-old schoolgirl in 1917.

'We'd see the turnips, potatoes and cabbage and we'd
decide what we'd pinch on the way home. On the way
back, the bigger boys used to say, "Keep your eyes rolling
for the farmer." My parents wouldn't accept anything
stolen – they used to make us take it back – so we used to

sit under a hedge and gnaw the vegetables like a rabbit. If
we could hear the farmers' horses clip-clopping we used
to bung what we'd been eating under the hedge and go
like lightning back home, large as life.'

Maud Cox was just seven, but was no less daring.

'Well, we used to go in and pinch the turnips in the field
and the greens off the top of the turnips. If you cook
them just as you would spinach, they taste not too
different. I didn't like them, they were very bitter. But
turnips, we practically lived on turnips. We used to go in
and pinch the ones that had been thrown in the fields for
the sheep. They were all chewed round the side, and we'd
cut the chewed bits off. We used to eat raw turnip. But
some of the children would come into school in the
morning and they'd had nothing but a slice of raw turnip
for their breakfast. That was when the air got a bit thick
and the teacher had to open the windows.'

Rabbits and birds became a crucial part of the country diet,
helping to keep the poorest families alive. Using nets, ferrets,
sticks and catapults, children – with or without their fathers –
killed many a rabbit for the pot. Joe Risby, born in 1911, grew
up in the Suffolk village of Lavenham. 'I loved the head of rabbit
at dinner. I broke it up so I could suck the pale, white brains out.
We lived on rabbits: rabbit pie, rabbit soup, rabbit dumplings,
every part of the rabbit was used. It was beautiful food.'
Ernie Gray, a young child in the Fens, hunted birds.

'We couldn't get any meat, so what we did – Dad, my
brother and myself – we used to go round the hedges with
a gas lamp or torch. You'd see the birds sitting in the
hedge. If you flashed the light on 'em they wouldn't be
able to see because they'd been in the dark all the while.
Shining the light mesmerised 'em straight away. All you

got to do is make a grab for them and finish 'em off.
Then put 'em in your bag and we'd go home with
perhaps half a dozen birds. Mother'd set to, she'd skin 'em
and feather 'em, and I'll tell you we had lovely bird pie.
Couldn't be better. That was a wintertime job when they'd
be about. That's the best thing we could do. We hadn't got
no other means.'

With no such fall-back in the cities, the poorest families were in
a more desperate state. From spring 1917 onwards, there were
sporadic food riots. Sydney Bond recalls that in the poorer parts
of Liverpool, 'People were literally starving. They would smash
all the plate-glass windows just to get in. They literally went mad
and stormed several shops.' In Hoxton in north-east London
there were similar scenes. Some held the shopkeepers and bakers
responsible, believing they were profiteering. 'Crowds of people
stormed the bread shops, they broke in, beat up the owners and
took what they could. I saw that,' remembers Amelia Harris.

One lady who lived in Fulham, a Mrs Fernside, wrote a letter
to her son Fred on 27 March 1917 describing the chaos:

Over the East End, the food riots began on Saturday
evening and they set fire to some of the shops. There is
almost sure to be some trouble if the food gets scarce. We
have been laying in some stores, for everyone else seems to
be looking after themselves. No – I have not been in any
potato fights yet. Several people got slightly damaged last
Sat in Dawes Rd, while trying to get some.
    Your ever loving mother . . .

Urgent action was needed to deal with the food crisis. One of
the most pressing issues was to break the U-boat stranglehold on
imported food into Britain. In May, Prime Minister Lloyd
George and the Admiralty at last took decisive action to counter
the submarine menace. Until now, the Royal Navy had engaged
in fruitless submarine hunts across the oceans. Now, they

introduced a much more effective strategy: the convoy system.

Convoys had been a time-honoured method of defence, reaching back to the days of sail, but fears that they would tie up large numbers of ships and lead to excessive delays and congestion in ports postponed full adoption of the scheme. On 10 May, the first British convoy of seventeen ships left for Gibraltar. All the ships arrived safely back home twelve days later. After initial successes like this, the convoy system began to be employed on a large scale. It was the beginning of a major turnaround in the war at sea. The evasive routing of convoys made it difficult for submarines to locate them and, when they did, they could be engaged and sunk by the escorts. By late 1917, the number of British ships sunk had been reduced dramatically, while German submarine losses had risen. To replace the ships that went down, Lloyd George ordered a new shipbuilding drive. A crucial success had been achieved, but the British government recognised that convoys could not by themselves solve the nation's food problems.

To ensure that Britain would not be starved into surrender, there had to be an immediate increase in food production at home. But it was not easy. Britain's wealth had been built on industry and commerce. While the cities grew and prospered, the countryside had become a byword for decline and poverty. By the eve of the First World War, agriculture had lost half the farmers and farmworkers it had had a century before and it could not compete with cheap grain from overseas. The migration to the cities and decades of agricultural depression had left a landscape of ruined barns, rambling hedges and fields that were overgrown and uncultivated. It was picturesque but unproductive. One of the few profitable areas was cattle farming and dairy produce, but this was too expensive for almost half of the population.

The complacent assumption that the war would be over quickly meant there had been little government intervention to gear up agriculture for the war effort. There was in any case a reluctance to interfere in the countryside. It was conservative, suspicious of change and dominated by the powerful landowning classes and big food distributors, who were doing well out of the war. Food scarcity ensured higher prices. The profits from agriculture increased five-fold during the first three years of the war, rising to around £100 million by 1917.

To make matters worse, the food production on Britain's farms was actually falling. The calorific value of the food they produced fell from 21.4 billion calories in 1914 to 19.3 billion calories in 1916. There were a number of factors involved. Overseas supplies of artificial fertilisers were cut off and the supply of imported animal feeds disrupted. Large numbers of farmworkers, who were traditionally among the lowest wage earners in the country, followed Kitchener's call to arms. They were lured by the promise of better money, regular meals and military glory. Around 15 per cent of the rural labour force, self-selected from the young and fit, and many of them with vital skills in animal husbandry and ploughing, were lost from the countryside.

The army also commandeered large numbers of horses, mules and donkeys throughout the war for service at the Western Front. Around half a million horses taken by the British army died during the war. This would reduce productivity on many farms where the horse was the major source of power, pulling ploughs, hay carts and binders. It could be especially difficult and upsetting for small family farms, as farmer's son Len Whitehead remembers.

'I think the one thing that affected me, apart from my brother George being killed, was when they took the horses. They used to come from the War Office and say, "We're going to buy three or four of your horses." You had no redress. You couldn't say, "I don't want to sell them." We only had four and two of them were beautiful Shire horses. They took those and another bay mare which wasn't quite as big, and left us with just one horse. It upset me very much. It was a morning before I went to school, oh, I was so sad all day at school, I think I cried myself to

sleep that night. They weren't pets, but I knew them by
their names and they meant an awful lot to us. Boxer,
Duke and Violet were their names. Never saw them again,
of course.

'The men said, "We'll send you some more horses," and
we waited a day or two and a very large mule arrived, that
was their replacement. He was a wonderful mule really.
Lots of the army mules were vicious things but he was as
quiet as a mouse. He turned out to be a good asset, but it
was strange to see my father ploughing with one horse
and one mule, that was the only power on the farm. Poor
old things, they had to work so hard. But it was all part of
the war, I suppose. Animals suffered the same as human
beings.'

The crisis finally pushed the government into action. From June
onwards, under the new Food Controller, Lord Rhondda – who
had replaced the ineffective Lord Devonport – the food supply
system was gradually brought under effective state control. This
led to far greater efficiency on farms, and essential foods were
grown that the nation desperately needed. Wide-ranging administrative machinery was set up, extending from Whitehall to the
villages. The aim was to give a massive boost to arable farming
and the production of wheat, barley and potatoes. Much was
achieved through the Corn Production Act, which established a
guaranteed price for corn – double the prevailing price at the
beginning of the war. Prices were to be held for five years,
reassuring livestock farmers that they could safely invest in the
switchover to crop production.

The Board of Agriculture was empowered to see that land was
properly cultivated. In 1917, 2.1 million acres, formerly devoted
to pasture, were ploughed up for staple crops. Directives were
handed to farmers by the newly formed War Agricultural
Executive Committees. There were sixty-one of these local
executive committees all over rural Britain, and their staff
supervised the farmers and ensured that they did as they were

told. Farmers received a 'Notice to Cultivate' form:

TAKE NOTICE, that should you negligently or wilfully
fail to cultivate, manure, and manage the lands herein
referred to in accordance with the requirements of this
NOTICE and DIRECTION, you become guilty of a
summary offence against the DEFENCE OF THE
REALM ACT . . .

They were threatened with fines and imprisonment if they did
not comply. The vast majority did.

A Wages Board was established to administer a minimum wage
for male farm workers of £1 5s (£1.25) a week. The government
also assisted in making new labour available to work in the
countryside. The most highly publicised group of outsiders
drafted in to replace the missing agricultural workers was the
Women's Land Army, which officially came into being in January
1917. It was essentially made up of town girls – many of them
from a middle- and upper-class background – who were eager to
'do their bit'. There was much propaganda value in this new
army of rosy-cheeked girls, dressed in smocks and breeches, who
were turning their backs on the comforts of suburban life to toil
on the land. Endless government films and newsreels were made
on the subject in order to boost morale.

The farmers were not impressed. Many were suspicious of
outsiders, especially well-heeled women who, in their view, had
never done an honest day's labour in their lives. They poured
scorn on them, assuming work in the fields was too arduous for
ladies with dainty hands and lily-white skin. It was indeed very
tough. Hard manual labour, dirty and dangerous conditions, long
hours, primitive accommodation, low pay and strict regimenta-
tion were the order of the day, but the old male prejudices just
made it worse.

Those who had illusions about the romance of the countryside
or who had been lured by pastoral fantasies often didn't last long.
Neither did those who were seriously unfit or who had health

problems. Edith Storey from Sheffield got a shock when she answered the call of the Land Army.

'I had a good job in a factory, I'd taken the foreman's place, and had a lot of girls under me. But I wanted to help on the land. I was so proud to do my bit for the war effort, and I was so proud of my uniform. I had no idea how hard it was going to be. That winter it was bitterly cold, it was very bad and it seemed to rain all day, every day. The farmer was hard and he had me cutting cabbages in the fields and driving a horse wagon around. I got soaked through, there was no shelter, no escape from the rain, I just had to keep on working. Well, as a child I'd been a delicate, petite girl and the wet and the cold started to make me very ill. I got a severe chest problem, bronchitis it was, I couldn't do anything. It stayed with me for years. So after a few months I ended up coming back to Sheffield. That was the end of the Land Army for me.'

Most stuck at it and some even came to enjoy farm labour. Dorothy Chalmers, working on a farm near Nantwich, wrote:

We do have fun, though the most part is really heavy, dirty work. I was knocked over by a calf this morning, and my hand is pretty badly hurt, but the experience did not equal that of being chased by the old sow, as I was the other day; she took a dislike to me as I was carrying a huge sack of potatoes up the field. Of course I ran as fast as I could, but she kept up with me until I backed through a hedge, tearing my dress on a piece of barbed wire. My revenge was complete, though. Yesterday we went (the farmer and his wife and I) to the market and sold the offensive animal for £9 and ten shillings. My farmer is also the village blacksmith and I am learning to shoe a horse and blow the bellows: the sparks fly from the anvil and make holes in your clothes – not to mention yourself. Some people tell me that I shall not be able to go on with my farm work in the winter because it will make my hands so bad. But I intend to stick to it. Our men don't stop fighting in the cold weather and neither shall I. My only brother is in the trenches – so you know how I feel!

One of the most exciting challenges for the young women was driving a tractor. In an age when driving was a novelty and cars were virtually the exclusive preserve of men, the sight of a woman tractor driver could cause a stir in the villages. The tractor was seen as a solution to the desperate shortage of horses on the farms, and thousands of the new Fordson tractors were imported from the United States, together with American advisers. They were a revelation: light, reliable, easy to drive and much faster than using horses. The land girls were among those given a hasty training and then set to work in the fields. As well as ploughing, tractors were used for harrowing, seed drilling and mowing. Jessica Godwin, at the age of 105, still remembered the ironic song the tractor girls would sing:

'You ought to join, you ought to join, the Women's
    Land Army,
Eighteen bob a week and very little to eat,
Bloomin' great boots make blisters on your feet,
You ought to join, you ought to join,
The Women's Land Army.

'My word, the boots were terrible. I joined the tractor section and I was with the tractor girls and it was very nice indeed. We only had six weeks' training but the mechanic was very clever. He took the tractor to pieces and showed us every part of it and put it together again. Not that we ever took it apart, but I could do all my running repairs, you know. I was very proud of that. The farmer, Mr Oldwinkle, funny name isn't it, Mr Oldwinkle, he came to me and he said, "I've got eighteen acres, do you think you can plough that?" "Oh yes," I said, "I'll do it in about a week." With a horse-drawn plough it probably would have taken two or three weeks. He said, "What, will you? You're joking." He was so excited, he'd get on the back of the tractor. Anyway, I did it in a week and he was pleased.'

Young women like Jessica took great pride in ploughing a straight furrow. To suggest that their furrows were inferior to those of the horse ploughman was taken as a grave insult.

'We used to step out twenty-two yards, then stick a yardstick in the ground, then go a little further down, another twenty-two yards, and put another stick in, so that we got it straight the first time. I remember a man saying, "She'll have a half-moon by the time she's finished." I was furious. I never had a half-moon. It was straight as a die.'

The Women's Land Army did some heroic work, helping to feed the nation and to change male prejudices about what work a woman could do. But the Land Army's contribution to the home front has been much exaggerated by subsequent historians, partly because of the effectiveness of the wartime propaganda. It has been claimed that as many as a quarter of a million women left their homes in the cities to work on the land. In fact, the true figure is a small fraction of that. Even in 1918, when the Land Army numbers peaked, they were only 16,000 strong. Most of the women land workers were not the uniformed, predominantly middle-class members of the Land Army. They were in fact countrywomen, often the wives of farm labourers and village craftsmen, or village girls, who had traditionally acted as a reserve army of labour at harvest time. Now that there was more work for them to do, they made the most of it, and outnumbered the ladies from the towns by almost twenty to one. Many were organised through the Women's Section of the Food Production Department's Labour Division, which had around 300,000 part-time workers on its books.

If the Women's Land Army aroused suspicion in the country-side, this was nothing compared to the hostility directed towards another set of newcomers who arrived to work on the land. German prisoners of war had been sanctioned by the govern-ment to work in the countryside from mid-1915. By late 1917, there were 30,000 of them working, around double the number of Land Army women. To begin with, they were housed in camps and policed by armed guards, but soon many were allowed to live and work on the farms. They were involved in all kinds of farm duties such as ploughing, harrowing and drilling. As forced labour, they were often made to do the most menial and backbreaking work, such as bringing waste marshy land into use. Although they played a valuable role in the increased food production in the countryside, they were often viewed as potential troublemakers and spies. Nevertheless, friendships sometimes developed with local villagers, even with the children, many of whom had been taught to believe in the inherent evil of 'the Hun'. Ruth Armstrong remembers:

'We had a lot of German prisoners around the village and they were cleaning out the ditches. Well, one day I was going up the road with a girl called Dulcie, and we ran past them, three or four of them it was, and one of them called us back in perfect English. He said, "Come back, little ones, why are you running away from us? We're not going to hurt you, not at all." He said, "I didn't want to fight your country, that's why I became a prisoner of war so that I wouldn't have to fight you any more. I love all you English people." I thought that was lovely, so every day while they were in the village I used to go round and have a chat with him. He used to say what a lovely village it was, the war wasn't mentioned of course. And I wasn't frightened of him any more.'

The army proved to be the most vital substitute labour force in the countryside. In 1917 it deployed 80,000 men of the Labour Corps to work on the farms. Many were soldiers who had suffered disabilities and injuries that made it impossible for them to return to the front line, but did not prevent them from working on the land in Britain. One of the disabled soldiers discharged from his duties on the Western Front who did his bit on the Dorset farms during the last two years of the war was George Louth, a private in the 15th Hampshire Regiment. 'The guns were firing all night, hundreds of guns. Now one night, we were walking along and the sergeant said, "Stop." I said, "What did you stop for?" He said, "Can't you hear all those shells going across?" I said, "No." So he said, "You're no use to me, you'll have to go back." '

After examination by a doctor, it was discovered that George's hearing had been seriously impaired by the noise of battle. He could just about make out enough words to have a conversation, but was considered a liability in the front line and so he was sent to work in the Labour Corps on the land in England. Like many of the others recruited on to the farms, he had no previous experience of farm work and as a result the first couple of jobs were complete disasters.

'We got to Winchester and the officer started dealing out the jobs. He sent two of us to a farm to go haymaking. I didn't know how a potato grew, let alone about haymaking, and the farmer sent us back. Said we were no good. Then the officer said, "All right, better send you somewhere else." We went near Blandford, stopped another fortnight there, and we weren't any good to this farmer. So he sent us back. Then the officer said, "If you can't do anything on the land, it's no good you stopping here, you'll have to go back to France." I said, "Oh no." '

The threat of returning to the front line was a huge incentive to learn quickly. George Louth's salvation was the tractor. He had always wanted to drive one. With the entry of the Americans into the war, there was a steady stream of Fordson tractors arriving in Britain.

'I said, "Is there some tractor drivers wanted, sir?" He said, "Is that what you want to do?" "Yes, sir." I did a couple of months' training on tractors under Americans at Taunton barracks. They taught us about the engines and how to plough. There was about sixty of us and we went to all parts of the country. I was sent to Blandford. We had to keep our khaki on. I drove the first tractor in that part of the country and to begin with all the farmers came to see it and they said it would never catch on, it would never work properly.

'Well, to begin with it was a cake walk, until the harvest started. We decided to wait until one Sunday morning when nobody would be about. We didn't want to look fools not knowing anything about the machine. Then, after a while, all the people started coming up, they didn't know what it was, because they'd never heard a machine running. They were only used to horses, which were few and far between in Dorset in those days, because they were over in France being killed. Anyway, we finished that thirty-acre field and that was the highlight of our life.'

Disabled soldiers played a vital part in increasing productivity on British farms. The 1917 harvest was the biggest and best ever, with a substantially increased output of cereals and potatoes. There was more food for everyone, and for men like George, country life could start to heal some of the physical and psychological wounds they had suffered in France.

'I felt free after all that trauma. It was quiet. You were on your own, your own governor while doing the job and never any interference from anybody. No, they just brought you your money and you had to find your own way through life. I was lucky. To begin with, in the winter I had to sleep in a hut. It was my first night and it was cold, icy, and I fainted. Then I came round, thought to myself, "I'm not going to stick this after all the torment I've had." So I walked down to the village, Strickland, three miles, and I didn't know what door to knock on. I saw an old lady and she said, "Are you looking for me, son?" I said, "Yes, ma'am, do you take in lodgers?" She said, "Come in, come on in." She'd lost her son from the first flush of fighting, great big six-foot lad, and she told me about it and she was getting a pension of five shillings a week. We was talking and she decided to let me stop there. That was the finest day I ever had with that lady, which was my future mother-in-law.

Back in the towns and cities, the nation's gardeners were also answering the call to increase food production, goaded by the Kaiser's threat 'to starve the British people, until they, who have refused peace, will kneel and plead for it'. This was the cue for an army of the elderly, mothers, housewives, munitions workers and their children to pick up their forks and spades, roll up their sleeves and do battle with the weeds in a million allotments and back gardens. Vegetable growing had long been a popular British pastime, but it was not until now that the government saw its potential value for the war effort. In December 1916, with losses at sea steadily increasing, local authorities had been given powers to take over unoccupied land for allotments without the owner's consent. In the following spring, common land, parks and playing fields were dug up and planted. Horticultural advisers from the government's Food Production Department urged public schools, hospitals and asylums to turn over all available land to help feed the nation. Even the country's leaders made token efforts to encourage the wartime allotment movement. King George V decreed that potatoes, cabbages and other vegetables should replace geraniums in the flowerbeds opposite

Buckingham Palace and in the royal parks. Lloyd George announced that he was growing King Edward potatoes in his garden at Walton Heath, and the Archbishop of Canterbury issued a pastoral letter sanctioning Sunday work.

The allotment campaign was a great success, a miracle of food production celebrated in local newspapers all over the land. They advised the new gardeners – as did instructional government films – how to grow the biggest and the best potatoes. The number of allotments doubled in the year to around 1.3 million. By the end of the war there would be over 90,000 acres under allotments, almost four times the total when war began. Most of the allotments were tended by the working classes who had no back garden or only a back yard. Mothers and fathers often recruited their children to help work with them at weekends or after school. Bert Smith from Nottingham remembers vividly what he and his brothers had to do.

'We had two big barrows, and two of us went along Castle Boulevard and two of us went the other way, collecting horse manure off the roads. Of course all the transport was horses then. We used to shovel this manure up, fill the barrow, then take it down the allotment. Then my dad would examine it. He'd usually tell us we hadn't filled it enough, he was a bit of a stickler. Anyway, he'd spread it on and he used to grow good cabbages and potatoes and beetroot and rhubarb and everything. That was our staple diet.

'A boy saw us with a barrow full of manure one day and he said, "What do you do with that?" I said, "Me dad puts it on his rhubarb." "Oh," he said, "we have custard on ours." '

Every available bit of land was planted with food. Householders were urged to dig up their back lawns and sacrifice their flower borders for the war effort. 'Mum decided she would give up flowers and grow vegetables,' recalls Ruth Armstrong. 'I used to help her. We grew carrots and onions and potatoes and swedes and God knows what, and made soup. Mum used to thicken it with a bit of cornflour. She always put a lump of celery in it to give it flavour. Oh, that was delicious. We loved that.'

Some people consumed every last home-grown leaf with patriotic fervour, in order to achieve a high level of self-sufficiency. But occasionally there were tragic consequences, as the *Enfield Gazette* reported in June 1917. In order not to waste any of their produce, local allotment holders experimented by eating the tops of root crops, cooked and served as a second vegetable. The Reverend W. R. Colville, Minister of St Paul's Presbyterian Church in Enfield, died after eating cooked rhubarb leaves, the recipe for which he apparently obtained from a woman's weekly journal. Some leaves could in fact be highly toxic and dangerous.

Accidents apart, by the autumn and winter of 1917 real progress had been made, ensuring that the nation would not be starved into submission. The U-boat menace was much diminished. Britain was winning the war at sea. Direct government intervention in the food supply system was proving a success. The drive to reduce profiteering, improve productivity on the land and achieve greater self-sufficiency in food was starting to work. The good potato harvest later in 1917 had halved prices. By this time, the shift to grain production and the effectiveness of the convoy system meant that the consumption of bread – the cheapest and most efficient wartime food – was increasing. To boost it further, in September the government introduced a bread subsidy. The tax-paying classes found themselves paying extra to make sure the less well-off could afford to eat. Bread, which had doubled in price since 1914 to one shilling (5p) for a 4-pound loaf, was reduced to ninepence (nearly 4p).

But there remained serious unresolved problems. The food distribution system was still uneven, resulting in shortages in the shops. There was a strong feeling among the working classes that they still weren't getting their fair share of the available food. 'Us and them' attitudes were getting stronger. Many believed there was a middle-class bias on the food control committees set up by the government to oversee food distribution. They were dominated by traders, businessmen and the local great and good, but the co-operative shops and factories that provided for the needs of most working-class families were barely represented. There was a popular perception that the shops in better-off areas were always well stocked, while the working classes had to queue for their food. There were constant allegations of discrimination with 'one law for the rich, another for the poor'.

An article in November in the socialist newspaper *The Herald*, describing 'How they Starve at the Ritz', caused a storm. It was revealed that a *Herald* reporter had been able to buy a six-course meal including four rolls, hors d'oeuvre, smoked salmon, a wide choice of soups, fish, meat entrées and desserts and unlimited servings of cream and cheese. Eating out for pleasure was then a privilege affordable only by the middle and upper classes. There were supposed to be official restrictions on restaurant sales while those who could afford to go were meant to be exercising self-restraint. The article suggested that neither was happening. It was mass-produced as a leaflet and distributed to thousands of factories all over Britain.

The upper and middle classes had to feed not only themselves but also an army of servants. One of the myths of the First World War is that the majority of domestic servants took up jobs in factories, offices and munitions industries. Some did, but many stayed in service, which remained the most common job for a working woman throughout the war. In 1917 the number of women in service was about 1.25 million – admittedly a fall of 400,000 from the 1914 figure, but still a lot of people. This gave those families with servants distinct advantages when coping with food shortages. The lady of the house was advised to take the lead, learning how to cook so that she could instruct her kitchen staff in the most effective ways of preparing food. The *Win The War* cookery book told her that 'the struggle is not only on land and sea; it is in *your* larder, *your* kitchen, and *your* dining room. Every meal *you* serve is now literally a battle.' She was instructed to teach her servants how to make 'patriotic' haricot bean fritters, barley rissoles and nut rolls. It was only families with a cook or a maid who could afford to spend the enormous amount of preparation time these wartime recipes took. They were also able to send out servants to queue for food, ensuring that they got first choice of what was on offer.

In the autumn of 1917, queuing became a major issue. In big cities like Birmingham, Coventry, Manchester and London, there were sometimes hundreds or thousands in the queues. Mrs Dorothy Peel, who worked for the Ministry of Food, recalled:

> In the bitter cold and rain of that depressing winter of 1917, women and children waited outside the shabby shops common to the poor districts of the town. They carried baskets, string bags, bags made of American cloth, and babies, and stood shifting their burdens from one arm to another to ease their aching. Often, in spite of cold, rain and weariness, there was a flow of wit. Sometimes a latecomer would try to sneak in at the head of the line, and there would be trouble, promptly allayed by the policeman or a Special Constable.

On 17 December, over 3,000 people were reported to be waiting for margarine outside a shop in south-east London. Around 1,000 were sent away empty-handed. In the cities, queues were heavily policed for fear of disturbances against shopkeepers when supplies ran out, or quarrels arose among those queuing. House-wives could spend hours every day queuing for essential items. The lines of women outside grocery stores were forming as early as 5 o'clock in the morning. As many were now combining factory work with bringing up their family, their children were frequently used to find and keep a place in the queue. It all proved too much for seven-year-old Maud Cox.

> 'Mum took me up there and put me in the queue and she says, "Now stand still and don't move until I get the other

ones away to school and I'll come back. But keep my
place." Of course I was standing there and the snow was
deep, it was right up over your feet. The next thing I
knew, I was lying on a bench in the dairy. I'd fainted.'

Madge Maindonald remembers how the pressures of work and
school meant that there was nobody in the family to queue for
food. 'We didn't get much food because there was nobody to
queue up for it. Two of my brothers were in France, Reg my
other brother was working, and I went to school. Who was there
to stand in queues for hours? Nobody.'

In every area, there were constant rumours about which shop
had food available. As Sydney Bond remembers, 'It was rumour
that governed how people got extras or in fact got any food at
all. The rumour would go around among people in Liverpool
that Irwin's had margarine, and it was passed on. So what
happened? At every Irwin's branch, a queue formed.' Rumours
sometimes led to disturbances, especially when there was little or
no food to be found. One rumour claimed that the shortages
were due to hoarding by the better off. It was a popular assertion
that gained currency in the West Riding of Yorkshire in early
December and led to rowdy demonstrations.

According to Mrs Dorothy Peel:

The conduct of certain tradespeople who at this time shut
their shops to the general public and sent out meat and
other goods to favoured customers via the back door
infuriated the people and occasionally the luckless butcher
boys were held up and the contents of their basket looted.
The knowledge that some well-to-do folk were hoarding
food also caused discontent. It was these annoyances which
made local authorities adopt rationing schemes before
national compulsory rationing came into force.

By the end of the year, a few areas – most notably Birmingham,
which had endured some of the longest queues in Britain – had

introduced their own rationing system for basic items, controlled by the local Food Committee. In December, ration cards were distributed to 300,000 Birmingham families for tea, sugar, butter and margarine. It was a great success and the queues were reduced accordingly. Nevertheless, with the government still reluctant to introduce rationing on a nationwide basis, popular resentment increased. It was picked up by the censors vetting the letters home written by soldiers to their families – hundreds of thousands of them mentioned the food problem and food queues. The Head Censor at Calais reported, 'It is immediately obvious that the effect on men in France is very serious and that their morale has suffered considerably in consequence. It is clear that this question is very universally discussed. Men hear from their relatives at home and see accounts in the papers, but the greatest effect seems to be produced by men returning from leave.'

What many of the returning soldiers were hearing was that the sacrifices of war were not being shared fairly or equally at home. The problems of a class-divided society were coming back to haunt the government, and in 1917 the divisions and conflicts seemed more damaging than at any time before. Some believed they were so serious that they might undermine the war effort altogether.

CHAPTER EIGHT

Toil and Trouble

THE DESPERATE FOOD SHORTAGES OF 1917 THREW into sharp relief the underlying inequalities of Britain's class-ridden society, which exacerbated the rigours of war on the home front. For how much longer could the government depend on the loyalty of the people, their resilience and commitment to the war effort? Their labour, their moral support and their will to win were vital.

With a third of the population living near or below the poverty line, Lloyd George and his War Cabinet were only too aware of the potential for resentment. In the years before the war, such emotions were expressed in a wave of industrial unrest, partly inspired by revolutionary syndicalism, with its faith in strike action. In 1912, 40 million working days had been lost to strikes. Now, five years on, there were again government fears that damaging industrial action might be renewed, with the possibility of a critical shortage of the materials and munitions needed to win the war.

The government was also alarmed by the collapse in social turmoil of Russia, one of Britain's key allies. The February Revolution led to the abdication of Tsar Nicholas II, followed by the rise to power of Lenin and the Bolsheviks with their proclamation of 'Freedom, Equality and Brotherhood'. The previous year there had been the Easter Rebellion in Ireland, in which Irish nationalists had demanded independence. It had been easily crushed, but it was a reminder that there were deep-rooted social and political divisions on the home front. The government could not take allegiance to their cause for granted; the war could be used as an opportunity to break free from hated authority figures, to demand new rights and to win revenge for the injustices of the past. A few feared a revolution inspired by the Russian example.

Such was the anxiety of the War Cabinet in April 1917 that it set up a special Commission on Industrial Unrest to provide regular reports on the level of morale among the working classes, and their precise grievances. This information was to be used to gauge the mood of the nation in order to placate possible discontent. In the fourth year of war, there were many pressing social problems as well as food shortages and the possibility of industrial conflict. All were areas of increasing government concern and control as the war went on. The overriding aim was to increase the efficiency of the war production drive, while at the same time responding to the basic needs of the people and maintaining their morale.

So much depended on Britain's working classes, but in 1917 they had few reasons to celebrate. High on their list of discontents was housing. Most families lived in rooms and houses rented from private landlords and they struggled to keep a clean and respectable home in conditions of severe overcrowding. Life was made more difficult by a frequent lack of running water and decent sanitation. Housing surveys undertaken before the war found that very few working-class homes had a separate water supply, bath or indoor toilet. Large numbers were cold and damp in the winter, stiflingly hot in the summer and vermin-infested. Despite the best efforts of overworked housewives, they often had a foul smell.

The problem was aggravated by large families. The average family during the First World War included 4.6 children, although a significant proportion had seven or more. Overcrowding often became worse as extended families lived together. Con Gray grew up in the village of Walters Ash in Buckinghamshire, the daughter of a building worker. During the war, to relieve the overcrowding in the family's cottage, their kindly neighbours came to the rescue:

'Our cottage was so small with just the one bedroom and the landing upstairs. I shared a bed with my sister and we slept in the bedroom with Mum and Dad and the baby in the wicker cradle. Then on the landing there was a bed for Gran, my mum's mother, she was a widow. There wasn't enough room for my two older brothers, Bert and George, to sleep in our house at night and they were taken in by some elderly neighbours who had a spare room. My brothers would have supper at home then go there to sleep, coming back to us for breakfast. I think Father gave the neighbours some vegetables from our garden for their trouble; it was payment in kind. I longed for a bed of my own, my own bit of private space, but that was the last thing on Mum's mind during the war.'

The conflict made housing problems worse, especially in the towns and cities. Some had to accommodate a sudden population increase of over 10 per cent, as workers flooded in for jobs in war industries. The Ministry of Munitions tried to provide housing for them, building around 12,000 homes on thirty-eight separate estates. However, 20,000 munitions workers had to live in hostels, usually converted schools or church halls, which offered a spartan, barrack-like existence. Many had the atmosphere and discipline of the workhouse and were avoided at all costs by those they were meant for. One workmen's home in the most crowded part of Port Glasgow had a hundred empty beds every night. The new workers in the war industries preferred to go elsewhere.

Construction in the private sector had ground to a halt during the war – indeed, only thirty private houses were built in London in the first two years of the conflict as both men and materials were urgently needed elsewhere. By the end of the war, the housing shortage would be estimated at some 600,000 dwellings. Private landlords proliferated, bringing back into use houses that had been condemned as unfit for human habitation. As a result, growing families that might have moved and upgraded to bigger homes had to stay where they were and make the best of it. This could make for a tense atmosphere in which tired fathers insisted on a strict discipline in the home and resorted to harsh punishments if their children misbehaved, as Bert Smith from Nottingham remembers.

'Yes, it was very overcrowded, with Mum, Dad and nine of us kids, four girls, five boys. I was the youngest. I shared a bed with all my brothers, three at the top, two at the bottom. All your feet touched in the middle. It took a long time to get to sleep with all the tickling of toes. In the war my dad was a miner and I think that was why he was so strict. With no space you had to behave yourself or there would have been chaos. My dad had fists like blacksmith's aprons, great corns and calluses on his hands through hard work, and he didn't mess about if you stepped out of line. He'd whack you with his leather belt that was four inches wide by a quarter of an inch thick. He'd take it off, double it up and hit our bottoms very hard. We didn't do it again.'

In the spring of 1917, the government tried to alleviate some of the overcrowding in the cities by introducing the Billeting of Civilians Act, which gave local authorities the power to compel home owners with spare rooms to provide accommodation for workers at fixed rates. This met with much resistance, especially among trade unionists who felt that their members were being targeted for an added wartime burden. They pointed to large empty town houses, temporarily vacated by wealthy families who no longer had sufficient servants to run them. Most of these, they argued, were not being commandeered as part of the housing drive. Nevertheless, some working-class tenants were only too keen to take advantage of the demand for homes in the cities by sub-letting their own rooms. Ellen Elston from Lambeth recalls, 'Mum was short of money so she let out the upstairs to lodgers. Because of that we had very little space for our family. Us four girls all had to share the same bed downstairs.'

Added to the problem of overcrowding was the appalling neglect of the housing stock by unscrupulous landlords. In the first year of the war, they had exploited the extra demand for accommodation among new migrants to the cities, with huge rent increases. This provoked the anger of working-class families, which exploded in Glasgow, an area particularly affected by the increases. Twenty thousand tenants staged a rent strike, refusing to pay. Many of those involved were the families of Clydeside shipyard workers, and the agitation resulted in their downing tools in a spate of unofficial strikes. Fearing that further militant action by workers might seriously undermine productivity, the government caved in, rushing through the Rent Restriction Act, which pegged rents to their pre-war level.

This was a triumph for tenants, and many now spent proportionately less of their income on rent. But there was a price to pay. Many landlords refused to provide basic maintenance on their houses, claiming they could no longer afford it. The problem was not helped by wartime damage – repairs to roofs, ceilings and windows were very slow in coming. Bert Tucker from Highbury, north London, remembers that after an air raid in 1917, 'We had slates missing off the roof, a hole in the ceiling and a broken window. I think that remained until the end of the war. There wasn't anybody to put it right.'

Some landlords, however, evaded the new Rent Restriction Act and continued to exploit the housing demand by putting their rents up, with evictions quick to follow when tenants fell behind in their payments. A survey of 150,000 working-class dwellings in Birmingham in 1917 revealed that the rents of more than a third of tenants had been illegally increased.

The Cumbrian shipbuilding town of Barrow-in-Furness also witnessed agitation on the housing issue. After protests and threats by local labour leaders, the Commission on Industrial Unrest paid a visit in the summer. They detected a tense atmosphere and a deep-rooted fear of eviction. Resentment was further exacerbated by the fact that Belgian refugees, 200,000 of whom had escaped from their own country ahead of the advancing Germans in 1914, had been dispersed across Britain, a small but significant number being sent to Barrow-in-Furness to work. These refugees had, in time, bought houses, subsequently applying for warrants to evict the sitting tenants. A local magistrate told the commission, 'This is a very sore point. As sure as you and I are here, there will be Satan's row if Belgian people are allowed to buy houses and the working classes in Barrow-in-Furness are turned out into the streets. There will be a riot.'

The commissioners reported the housing situation as a 'crying scandal'. After threats of strike action by the town's shipyard workers, the government intervened. Tenants were at last given proper protection from unscrupulous landlords, and Barrow was designated a 'special area' in which the building of new, temporary accommodation for workers was to be urgently undertaken. This victory would lead to further improvements elsewhere, as other towns in the industrial north and Scotland queued up to be designated 'special areas'.

In just the same way that news of food shortages had reached the fighting men in France, so too did reports of discontent with housing conditions. There was no censorship of letters leaving Britain for the Western Front and wives were quick to tell their husbands of their fear that they might be turned out on to the streets. Dan Rider, a campaigner for improved housing during the war, recalled:

'Chaplains with the troops at the front started sending me distressing letters from the wives of soldiers in their regiments, containing notices to quit. They said the men were distracted and had come to them for advice and they asked me to look into the matter. The chaplains did not spare themselves on the men's behalf. Several wrote me stinging letters asking what these landlords were up to, as their men were beside themselves upon receipt of such letters from home and they were threatening to return to England and finish off the landlords and then come back to Flanders and polish off the Germans.'

In some cases, he added, these anxieties 'almost led to mutiny'.

If housing was a major cause for concern in 1917, so too was heating. It was a very cold year, with the first few months noted as one of the coldest winters on record. Coal fires were the main source of heating but, to add to the woes of the civilian population, coal prices had risen rapidly since the start of the war and supplies were irregular and often ran out. The problem was caused partly by labour shortages, as so many miners had volunteered for the army, and partly by the increased industrial demand for coal. Some shops were closing early to save on their heating and lighting bills, while families were going to bed earlier for the same reason. The need to conserve fuel led to a Defence of the Realm Act of 1916, banning even Guy Fawkes' Night bonfires. By the following year, the fuel shortage had reached crisis point, with the police having to control crowds at railway distribution centres. An angry mood was reported by the press and government investigators.

Poor families often fared badly. Ellen Elston remembers, 'It was very cold a lot of the time. The bedroom was freezing but at bedtime Mum would warm a brick in the oven and we'd have that in bed to keep us warm.' In rural Wiltshire, it was a similar picture, as Ruth Armstrong describes.

'It was bitterly cold. There were draughts everywhere and Mum put curtains up inside the door to try to keep the cold out. We didn't have much money to buy coal so Mum was very careful about lighting fires. We only had one when it was really cold and it always went out at eight o'clock. That was when we all went to bed to keep warm. All us village children would try to help out by going up the woods and collecting little bundles of wood to bring home. Mum was always very grateful for those sticks to keep the fire going.'

In London it was a different story. In October, the continuing shortage prompted the introduction of coal rationing, under which residents had to register with coal dealers and were guaranteed an allocation of coal. Here, the shortages hit the middle classes, as they could no longer get sufficient supplies to heat their large homes. In contrast, the poor, with only one or two rooms to heat, were now able to enjoy a regular fire.

Yet no fuel ration could compensate for dreadful housing conditions which were breeding grounds for another scourge: ill-health. The chief casualties here were children. The Bishop of London argued in the *Daily Telegraph* of July 1917 that 'while nine soldiers died every hour in 1915, twelve babies died every hour, so that it was more dangerous to be a baby than a soldier'. Around one in ten babies died before they reached their first birthday. Of those who survived babyhood, one in every four died before the age of five. Working-class babies and children were particularly at risk. A host of childhood diseases, which today are prevented by immunisation, were killers. Whooping cough accounted for almost two-fifths of all deaths under five; diphtheria and scarlet fever claimed many lives and were made more acute by overcrowding and bed sharing; tuberculosis, though generally on the decline, was still common among children. Most working-class parents rarely took a sick child to the doctor as they could not afford medical bills. They had little choice but to resort to traditional cures, such as raw onion or onion gruel used to treat sore throats and colds.

There were also 'quack doctors' or even gypsies to whom frantic mothers could turn for advice. In 1917, Con Gray's five-year-old sister Olive was diagnosed with tuberculosis.

'You couldn't afford proper medical treatment then, so a gypsy woman said to my mother it could be cured if we put snails in a muslin bag and rubbed it anti-clockwise around Olive's stomach. That was well known as a supposed cure for TB. It was my job to collect all the snails, which I did. There were loads around the front of our cottage. My mother did this with the snails religiously like the gypsy said and Olive seemed to improve a bit. But I'm afraid she died after just a few months.'

Yet something was to be done about the poor health and early death that blighted British society, and working-class babies and infants were to be surprising beneficiaries of the war. As the grim statistics of the war dead were growing and, with so many men away, the birth rate was falling, greater emphasis was placed on life. Babies came to be highly valued.

Up to the outbreak of war, the average working-class woman experienced ten pregnancies. Of these, three would end in miscarriage, two in death during birth or infancy and only five children would survive. Women could expect to spend around fifteen years either pregnant or nursing babies. According to the Bishop of London, speaking in 1917, all this had to change: 'The loss of life in this war has made every baby's life doubly precious.' The *Daily Telegraph* intoned that with better health care in the past, Britain would have been able to put another half a million good soldiers on the battlefield. Out of this concern came the predominantly middle-class 'Mothercraft movement', which aimed to teach poor mothers the craft of motherhood. Among its main spokespeople were Church leaders and, rather bizarrely, retired army personnel.

This campaign to save babies was heavily influenced by racist and eugenicist ideas. Behind it lay the need for British babies to serve in future armies and to populate the empire. The newly formed Babies of the Empire Society demanded that 'the noble sacrifices on the battlefield, in the air and on the sea, must not be made in vain. Every effort must be directed to securing the future of the race.' National Baby Weeks aimed to 'save every savable child'. Captain Sir William Wiseman told mothers 'not to reprove but to encourage' children who fought in the nursery, as it would stand them in good stead when it came to hand-to-hand fighting against Germans: 'In a rough and tumble with Tommy Atkins, [Germans] always went off in the opposite direction.'

All this rhetoric meant little to working-class mothers, but they did enjoy some real benefits. By 1917, there were 446 infant welfare centres operated by volunteers and another 396 centres run by local authorities. In the same year the number of midwives and full-time health visitors doubled from 600 to over 1,200. As a result of these and other improvements associated with what *The Times* called 'the cult of the child', the infant death rate continued gradually to decrease throughout the war.

Far less was done to look after the health of men and women on the home front. It might be expected that by 1917 the immense stress of living through the war would have taken its toll and resulted in increased illness and death. In fact, among most of the population, except the very poorest, the standards of health had not declined at all. This has been described as 'the paradox of the Great War' and some claim that there was actually a gradual increase in life expectancy through the war years. Although this has been disputed, it is remarkable that there seems to have been no deterioration in the nation's health at a time of such privation. Medical care for civilians was severely restricted owing to the army's demand for doctors. At the front, there was one doctor for every 376 soldiers, while in Britain there was on average one for every 2,344 civilian patients. Almost a quarter of the country had more than 4,000 patients per doctor, while in the poorest areas, like parts of Glasgow, there were 5,000 patients per doctor.

Perhaps the resilience of the nation's health can in part be attributed to the fact that most people were not in any case used to the regular attention of doctors and to hospital treatment. Before the discovery of antibiotics there was little that doctors could do to prevent or cure the diseases that accounted for most deaths. The food shortages meant that the diets of many families – especially the middle and upper-working classes – were actually getting better. They were eating less sugar, fat and meat and compensating by eating more bread, potatoes and vegetables. Lack of adequate nutrition could and did damage the health of the poorest families, making them more vulnerable to disease. But for better-off workers and their families, the chief wartime complaint was that the food was dull and unattractive.

Nevertheless, the life expectancy of civilians was still, at least by today's standards, very low. Most men died in their late forties or early to mid-fifties, while most women died in their mid- to late fifties. For the Gray family, 1917 was a very hard year. Three months after losing her younger sister from tuberculosis, Con lost her father.

'Yes, he died too. He was working on the roads. He was in a reserved occupation helping to build a new road in Wendover. Well, this day in May he was at work and he suddenly collapsed, we think he had a heart attack, and was run over by a steamroller. His body was brought home by the first motor van I'd ever seen. It was a huge blue thing with solid tyres. I can still remember it vividly because Mother was so upset. The funeral was held at the same mission hall where Dad had buried my little sister [Olive] a few months before. And Gran, my father's mother, she took hold of my wrist, not my hand, and gripped it very tightly. I'll always remember that. After that my mum was always singing in the home to try to cheer herself up. We coped, though, we always tried to be cheerful.'

The loss of one or both parents sometimes led to children being placed in orphanages or other foster homes. Their pre-war population of around 30,000 steadily increased during the war years due to the privations of war and the absence of breadwinners, who were either fighting at the front, or had died there. By 1918 some homes were overwhelmed by unwanted children, many of them brought by poor working-class mothers who could no longer cope with all the pressures they had to endure. Sometimes the trigger would be the loss of a husband at the front. But while the government became more involved with encouraging a new generation of healthy babies, it had little time for these forgotten children. Orphans had traditionally been regarded as bad stock, the offspring of feckless parents, who needed strict control and discipline to keep them on the straight and narrow in later life. Before the war, many orphanages had been renowned for their cruelty. Overcrowding, shortages and the absence of trained staff meant that conditions for the children deteriorated still further between 1914 and 1918.

Wartime children's homes had strict regimes that revolved around early rising, cold baths, obsessive cleanliness, tight discipline, drill, and above all, corporal punishment. The staff saw the young inmates as in need of moral reform and training and they set about this task with enthusiasm. Little allowance seems to have been made for the fact that they were dealing with recently bereaved and vulnerable children living through a world war. In 1917, Wilfred Chadwick was living in the Firbank Scattered Homes in Oldham. He had been sent there after his mother's death three years before. 'Scattered Homes' were in theory meant to create more of a family atmosphere by encouraging staff to act as 'house mothers' in smaller units than the old orphanages. But, on the contrary, they seem to have been characterised by a lack of love.

'They never used your name. I was number seven and we had a mother who looked after us. Ooh, she was heartless and cruel! You lived in fear. You had to sleep with your legs straight: the mother would come up when you were asleep and throw your bedclothes back and then cane you across the legs for sleeping with your knees up. We had to do all the work in the home: we had to scrub the stone floors, mop the steps, prepare the food. Everything had to be done in a certain way. You couldn't talk, you couldn't run about, you could only read what they wanted you to read. You never laughed and if you did she'd want to know why. Laughter was something you never heard. We never felt as though we were wanted.'

Even some middle-class children would not be spared the sadism and heartbreak of the wartime orphanage. For those who had enjoyed a protected and loving family life before the war, the experience could be deeply traumatic. In 1917 Phyllis Ing and her twin sister Muriel were inmates in a large orphanage in Wanstead in Essex after losing their father, formerly a solicitor's clerk. Their mother who had once enjoyed a comfortable middle-class life in suburban London could no longer cope. Phyllis remembers:

> I remember Mummy taking us to this big building and saying, "This is your new home." We were terrified. We had all our nice clothes taken away and we had to wear awful clothes. We had black stockings and boots and very coarse navy underwear and a big pinafore. All the other girls were dressed exactly like us. Then they marched us upstairs to bed and they put Muriel in another dormitory. I was crying, "Mu Mu, where's my Mu Mu?" Why they parted us, I've no idea at all. I just can't describe the anguish of it. All I wanted was Mu Mu but all I got was a good spanking. I didn't see her much after that.
>
> 'The nurse who was in charge of us was obsessed with cleanliness. Every Sunday we had to wear our clean pinafores and line up on parade to be inspected. If you had a spot on it you got a good beating. Well, this day I badly wanted to go to the toilet so I put my hand up and said, "Please can I be excused, I want to go to the toilet." She said, "No wonder you want to be excused, you've got a spot on your pinafore and you think you're going to get away with it." So anyway the next thing I knew, she'd turned me over and pulled my drawers down and she was hitting me with a hairbrush. And while she was hitting me I was pooing everywhere, all over the place. I just couldn't stop. I couldn't help it. Oh dear, she was furious. She got hold of me and she

rubbed my face in it and she said, "You filthy little beast." Then she grabbed me and marched me round the building. I was crying all the time. I had all this poo all over my face so I could hardly see where she was taking me. She was taking me to show my sister Muriel. She stopped in front of her and she said, "Look what your filthy sister has done." And I was so cross because I didn't want Muriel to see me like that, my lovely sister was going to see me in that state. It was dreadful. Oh, it was the most disgusting feeling in my life.'

All the drudgery and deprivation of war made many people desperate to escape and enjoy themselves, if only for a few hours. Before the war they had drowned their sorrows with drink, the most popular pleasure of pre-war Britain and now the focus of government attention. Around a sixth of all working-class income had been spent on beer and there was a warm, friendly pub on every street corner. Drinking in a convivial atmosphere provided short-term relief from poverty, and from physical and mental exhaustion, but now it was to become even more difficult to have a drink. In time even 'treating' a friend to a drink was outlawed, as was the publican's 'on the house' offer to a favoured customer.

The government knew when it first regulated opening hours in pubs, in August 1914, that the act would be unpopular, but it was deemed to be essential to winning the war. As Lloyd George – formerly a temperance campaigner – put it in 1915, 'Drink is doing more damage in the war than all the German submarines put together . . . we are fighting Germans, Austrians and Drink, and so far as I can see the deadliest of these foes is Drink.' In 1917, the restrictions that had applied only to centres of the munitions industry and ports were extended all over the country. Many pubs that had once been open eighteen hours a day, closing for business only in the early hours of the morning, were serving customers for just three or four hours a day; most opened only at lunchtime, and some closed in the evenings as early as 9 p.m. Staying open after 11 p.m. was prohibited. In addition, liquor duties, imposed to raise money for the war effort, meant that the price of a pint tripled in three years. At the same time the government progressively lowered the permitted alcohol content of beers and spirits. Some whisky distilleries were even converted to the manufacture of explosives.

Assisting the government in its campaign to stamp out the evils of excessive drinking were the Temperance Movement and the Social Purity Movement, in which the churches played a leading role. The Birmingham branch of the White Ribbon Band, a Christian and teetotal organisation, collected 37,155 signatures from women and girls in the city (equal to 10 per cent of all females in Birmingham) demanding that no drink be served to women aged under twenty-one until three months after the end of the war. Their members, posted outside the pubs, kept detailed records of the numbers of women going in for a drink. They claimed to have counted 7,753 females leaving 150 of the city's pubs within a period of 129 hours and 28 minutes, of whom seventy-nine were drunk. They believed they were witnessing a frightening increase in women's drinking, due to the wartime absence of the 'controlling influence' of a husband. Similarly, in Blackburn the 338 city pubs were closely monitored, each pub being visited on average once a week during the course of a month. A tally was then made.

The results shocked campaigners, for no fewer than 16,146 females had been counted with, on average, eleven women being seen in each pub. Temperance campaigner Mrs Allan Bright, from Liverpool, claimed that, 'Women who drank before, now drink more, and what is infinitely sadder, young wives, many of them mere girls, to whom alcohol must have meant nothing at all, now take it because they are dispirited or lonely, or without resource.'

There is no doubt that drink provided many women with an escape from the grief of bereavement and the pressures of work and family life in overcrowded homes. In some cases an occasional tipple with friends seems to have given desperate mothers the strength to carry on – as is evident from the memories of Penny Feiwel from Tottenham, who in 1917 was eight years old.

'There would be lots of rows going on at home. Us kids would be shouting and screaming and fighting. And my mother would get so fed up she'd say, "I can't bloody well stand it any more, I'm going to drown myself." She'd sling her coat on, put her cap on – it was a man's cap – and she'd wear a coarse apron and button-up boots, and she'd storm out and we'd follow her. There would be Violet, my brother Jim, George and myself, and we'd all be whimpering like goslings following the mother goose. She would go up by the River Lea. Now in the war you'd see quite a lot of women who'd drowned and been fished out of the river being brought in carts covered in tarpaulin to the mortuary. That's what we thought was going to happen to Mum. And she'd always lose us, she'd turn a corner and she'd be gone. We'd wait around for a while and cry, then we'd come back home. Mum would be back a while later and she was always in a much better mood. We wondered why. Then my sister got wise to what she was doing. She managed to follow her one day and she found out she was going to her friend's house to have a drink. You used to get beer in those days in a jug to drink at home. That was why she was always in a better mood when she came back, wasn't it?'

In fact there was little evidence to prove the claims of temperance reformers that there was a dramatic increase in women's drinking. A committee appointed to enquire into fears of the excessive drinking of women in Birmingham, and which examined the evidence presented by the White Ribbon Band, concluded that most of the fears were unfounded. Although there was a rise in moderate drinking by women, drunkenness was decreasing, reflected in a decline in the number of arrests for drink-related offences. Overall, arrests for drunkenness among women in Birmingham went down from 511 between January and June 1914, to 182 between January and June 1915. The committee further claimed that because many of the White Ribbon ladies had not previously ventured into the world of pubs, 'they are naturally shocked at scenes to which they are unaccustomed and therefore tend to exaggerate and confuse rowdyism for intoxication'.

Alcohol consumption was indeed going down. The government had tried a risky piece of social engineering in the name of national efficiency, and it had worked. Although weak beer and early closing were universally derided, they were endured with stoicism. Getting drunk was now not only more difficult, it was regarded as unpatriotic. The habit among some working men of drinking before work, at lunchtime and after work was largely broken, and work discipline on the home front was strengthened.

Drunkenness had been closely associated with street fighting and domestic violence, and could lead to destitution. With the decline in drinking, convictions for drunkenness and assault went down from over 60,000 in 1908 to fewer than 2,000 by the end of 1917. Arrests for drunkenness among women decreased from around 40,000 in 1914 to around 25,000 in 1917. There was also a fall in the number of infant deaths registered at weekends, some of which had resulted from heavy drinking that led to 'overlaying', the accidental smothering of babies who shared beds with their parents.

There were still some cases of extreme violence, and even murder, in which the key factor was drinking to escape from the burden of bringing up children alone and on the breadline. One particularly tragic case involved Private Simpson from Newcastle. The *Hucknall Dispatch and Leen Valley Mercury* reported what happened when Private Simpson came home on leave from the front.

His homecoming was no joyous one. There was no trim,

clean wife to welcome him. She was out drinking; his children neglected, his home all dirt and disease. One of his children, a boy of two, lay dying of water on the brain. Simpson saw his child in agony and wondered what on earth to do. He could not stay and tend the poor little fellow. Simpson felt that he could not go back and leave the poor child to the painful and lingering dying, unattended and uncared for. So, not knowing what to do, and no doubt distracted himself by the terrible situation, the miserable father resolved to save his child from torture by putting an end to his life. He cut his throat.

For this, Private Simpson was sentenced to death, later commuted to penal servitude for life.

Drink and the pressures of war were to play a central role in a tragic case that reached the Central Criminal Court in late 1917. It involved a London couple, Sarah and James Petty, and it was every bit as tragic as the case involving Private Simpson.

Sarah Petty was twenty-five when she had married her sweetheart James in August 1914. James Petty was a regular soldier serving with the 1st East Lancashire Regiment and was under orders to leave for France when he got dispensation to marry, forty-eight hours before his boat was due to embark for Le Havre.

James served on the Western Front until badly wounded, being discharged from the army in June 1916. He returned to civilian life and took a job as a flagman on the Great Western Railway. While James might have escaped the fighting, he had, apparently, not escaped the effects of war. Almost as soon as he came home he had turned to drink and then became violent, beating his wife and giving her frequent cut lips and black eyes. Although he had a young family, he was, as his wife and neighbours claimed, a 'habitual drunkard'. The assaults continued until October the following year when, on the 24th, there was a violent domestic incident during which James Petty threw his dinner into the fire. As he stormed out of the house he threatened his wife, telling

Above: A protest meeting at Tower Hill, London in March 1916. These married men are demanding that single men should be called up for service before those with families. (*Hulton Getty*)

Left: Mounted police stand by as men attack a peace rally in 1918. Serving soldiers appear to be involved in the fray at a north London church. (*Hulton Getty*)

Above: A mother and her six children join a protest demanding milk, and at an affordable price. (*Hulton Getty*)

Left: Phyllis Ing (centre, left) and her twin sister Muriel. After their father's death in 1915, their middle-class family fell on hard times and Phyllis and Muriel found themselves the inmates of a brutal orphanage in Essex.

Left: Daisy Collingwood (left) working in a cordite factory in Shellhaven. In 1915 Daisy was to be slightly injured in an explosion, the force of which blew her out of the building. She never returned. Today, she is nearly 106 years old.

Below: A female munitions worker at the massive Chilwell factory on the outskirts of Nottingham. In July 1918 there was a huge explosion at the site killing 134 women workers. Some of their bodies were removed from the factory on the back of a cart as eight-year-old Bert Smith witnessed. (*Hulton Getty*)

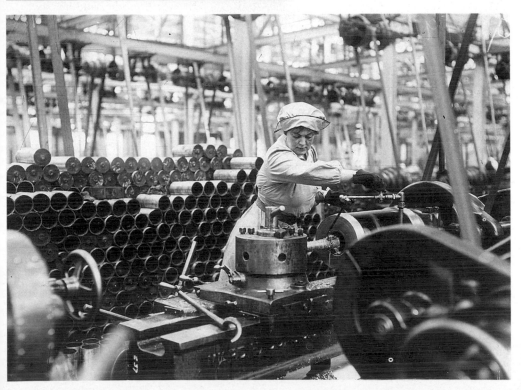

It wasn't only women who were employed to do jobs previously carried out by men. These pictures show a young girl pushing a trolley in a munitions factory (right) and boys working in a factory (below). The boy in the centre looks no older than twelve or thirteen. As many as 600,000 children were working in British industry by 1918. (*Imperial War Museum*)

Left: Florence Billington's permit book allowing her to move freely around Folkestone. The district, and in particular the docks where Florence lived and worked, was a restricted military area.

Below: Charlotte Huggett (left) next to her mother, who suffered a nervous breakdown in 1918, before attempting suicide. As a result she spent the last fifty years of her life in a mental hospital.

Across the country wild jubilation and the waving of flags greeted news of the Armistice at 11.00 a.m. on 11 November 1918. (*Hulton Getty*)

Still today we observe the two-minute silence for the fallen. In the years immediately following the war this had particular poignancy. This photograph shows a farm boy who has halted his plough to show his respects. (*Scottish Life Archive*)

Above: Emily Galbraith, aged 107, holding a picture of her younger brother Peter, who was killed aged twenty on the Somme in 1916.

Left: On returning from the war a soldier kisses his young baby, almost certainly for the first time. (*Imperial War Museum*)

Below left: A woman visits her husband in hospital. The strain of war is evident on both their faces. In the months after the war, the government promised 'A Land Fit for Heroes'. This was soon perceived by many to be little more than a sham. (*Imperial War Museum*)

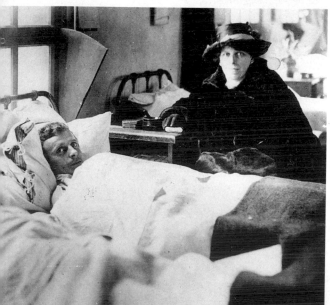

Top left: Irene Rhodes was never to see her father, Sergeant Rhodes, as she was born three months after his death.

Top centre: The grave of Sergeant W. Rhodes DCM in Tyne Cot Cemetery, the largest cemetery in the care of the Commonwealth War Graves Commission with nearly 12,000 graves.

Top right: Irene and her elder sister attended the official dedication of the Tyne Cot Cemetery in 1927.

Bottom left: Final touches are made to the Tyne Cot Cemetery as the dedication is made.

Bottom centre: Irene's sister walks through an old trench during their first visit. Rifles and helmets still litter the battlefield.

Bottom right: Irene Rhodes visits her father's grave every year. This photograph was taken in July 2002, seventy-five years after her first visit.

her, 'Don't be here by teatime or I will kick your guts in.'

This was the final straw for Sarah. Writing a suicide note and tucking it into her pocket, she turned the gas taps on in the living room and, with her children round her, prepared to die. A short while later neighbours, smelling the gas, rushed in and pulled the family outside. All three were unconscious, although Sarah and her baby daughter later revived. Her young son Arthur did not. Sarah Petty was charged with wilful murder and sent for trial.

Apart from several eyewitness accounts, there was only one formal piece of evidence submitted in the entire trial. It was the suicide note discovered by a policeman in Sarah's pocket as she lay unconscious It read:

> Dear sisters
> Jim has been on again and I can't live any longer like this. Don't hide his faults. He is the worst man I could have married. But don't grieve for me, as I shall be happy. I have not had a days happiness since he came home. Will you see that he pays the 10/- I owe, and dear Emma thank God you have got a good husband. If they should bring in that I am insane, tell them it is Jim that is insane and not me. Goodbye and forgive me. I don't know why I should have this life. I don't think I have ever done anyone much harm but God pays debts without money.
> Sarah

Although Sarah Petty was found guilty of murder, she was later released for undisclosed reasons. The judge during the summing up had heavily censured her husband for his drunken assaults, making no allowance for the effect that service in France might have had on his alcoholic state. As for Sarah, she had to live for the rest of her days with the knowledge that she had been the cause of her own son's death.

While generally having a positive effect, the government's efforts to reduce excessive drinking and the problems associated

The suicide note that Sarah Petty tucked into her dress pocket, moments before she attempted to take her own life and the lives of her two children. *(Public Records Office)* with it did not work in all communities, and further action was needed. One such area was around the munitions factories of Carlisle and Gretna. There had been a big influx of migrant workers from Ireland and Scotland; accommodation was poor and there were no other entertainments on offer, with the result that convictions for drunkenness were among the highest in the country. In 1917, all this was to change. In what became known as the 'Carlisle Scheme', the government bought up most of the pubs and breweries in the area, and then closed them down. One hundred and twenty-three pubs were suppressed, and only one brewery was left to supply the region. Some new 'improved' pubs were built, like the Gretna Tavern, but they were designed to slow down people's drinking. There was a small bar area to reduce 'standing up' drinking; customers had to be seated and served by waitresses. Long waits between drinks were built into the system.

When the figures for drunkenness in the Carlisle area went down in 1917, there was a popular clamour among the Temperance Movement for a nationwide extension of the scheme. Sensibly, the government declined to take further action, knowing how deeply unpopular this might be. Drink, even in wartime, was a highly charged political issue and they had pushed the controls as far as they could, though in the post-war years there would be experiments with the Carlisle Scheme on council estates all over the country.

The decline in drink-related crimes was part of an overall reduction in crime. The men who had made up the greater part of the criminal statistics were now on the Western Front, subject to military discipline. But there was one category of offender that was very much on the increase and causing concern: the juvenile delinquent. There was a dramatic rise in the numbers of boys subjected to the 'short sharp shock' of a birching. Birchings, ordered by courts in England and Wales, increased from 2,415 in 1914 to 5,210 in 1917. In some towns and cities, even in genteel Bath, the crime rate of young teenagers doubled during the war years. One survey showed that in seventeen of the largest towns of Britain, the numbers of under sixteen-year-olds charged with offences increased from 2,686 in the three months from December 1914 to February 1915, to 3,596 in the three corresponding months of the following year. In an urgent report requested by the Secretary of State at the Home Office, the Police Commissioner of London wrote that the rise in juvenile crime for the year to February 1916 'shows an increase of something exceeding 50 per cent, while the figures for larceny indicate an even greater increase'.

'The principal cause of the increase is, no doubt, the absence of parental control,' wrote the Commissioner. 'In numerous cases the father is away on service and the mother has obtained employment in a munitions factory or on work of some other description, with the result that no adult is left in charge of the children; this is a factor of very great importance.'

Concern over juvenile crime peaked in 1917. Lurid reports of vicious hooliganism by gangs of young men were common in the popular press. In an article headlined 'The Terrorists of Glasgow – Savagery of Hooligan Gangs', the *Sunday Chronicle* warned that:

> each gang outvies the other in savagery and frightfulness. Ladies are held up and robbed: policemen are clubbed or cut with bottles when trying to take some of the ruffians to prison; and old men are beaten and left lying after their pockets have been gone through. With many districts at night so infested with these brutal ruffians that ladies are afraid to venture out and even men have often to run for their lives, the citizens are demanding that this state of matters must end.

The main gang responsible for the civil disorder in Glasgow was the Redskins. They allegedly modelled themselves on Red Indians from the Wild West, heavily featured in such comics as the *Boys' Own Paper* and in early cinema films. Reports of gangs like these fuelled moral panic in cities suffering from the deprivations of war. A breakdown of law and order seemed an imminent possibility. Although many of the reports were exaggerated, there was some reality to the fears. Working-class youth crime had been a problem in the pre-war years, some centred on other gangs like the Bengal Tigers of Manchester and the Peaky Blinders of Birmingham. Now, with the war on, they became 'folk devils'.

Most of these young rebels came from the poorest, toughest areas in the cities, and the war provided them with more opportunities for crime, especially during the blackout. The police force was depleted, as many officers had been called up for duty at the front; while thousands of special constables had been recruited to take their place, 20,000 in London alone, they were predominantly elderly men and no match for the fleet-footed young thief.

Some people believed that, in addition to the lack of parental control, the problem of youth crime was caused by full employment and higher wages for young workers during the war. They had greater confidence and independence, which broke down discipline and made them less amenable to authority. But they had nothing to spend their money on. Most popular working-class entertainments and sports such as professional football, cricket and racing had been closed down by 1915. There was nothing to do but to roam the streets looking for trouble.

One notorious teenage gang in wartime Manchester was the Napoo. They originated from the Ancoats district and won a reputation for hacking off young women's plaits and claiming them as trophies. At a time when male paternalism towards women was still profound and ingrained in the public psyche, such attacks – which perhaps seem less serious today – were, in post-Edwardian Britain, truly disturbing. Larry Goldstone remembers:

'They'd creep up behind girls and young women in the street. Then they'd grab the long plaited hair which hung down the back, that was the style of the day, and with a sharp pair of scissors cut off the plaited hair and run off with it as a souvenir. They got bolder and bolder hunting the women with plaited hair. Some used to go upstairs on the trams late at night, and if a woman was sitting on her own, they'd cut off her hair, then, like lightning, dash off without being caught. The idea was probably hatched from the pictures of Red Indians scalping the whites. The tough would take the plaits to the public house to show how clever he was at hunting.'

The Napoo wore a distinctive pink neckerchief and razorblades displayed in their waistcoat pockets or in their cloth caps. 'They became notorious and everyone was talking about them,' says Henry Grimshaw.

It must really have been enjoyable to be a Napoo because everybody ran away. At Heaton Park I looked around and saw this gang, must have been about fifty or sixty strong, and they were coming, running like mad, you see. Well, we made for the trams and fortunately one was just on its way and I got on. I don't know what happened to those that didn't get on, but everybody started to run.

Many of the older teenagers in such gangs such as the Napoo would very soon end up on the Western Front. By late 1917 and 1918, the army, desperate for new recruits, was becoming far less choosy about whom it enlisted. Troublesome boys from working-class backgrounds found themselves in khaki, whether they wanted to go or not. The battle charges across Heaton Park had been a kind of rehearsal for what they would shortly be doing when they went over the top in France. Some of these 'folk devils' would, a year on, be remembered as heroes, after giving their lives for their country.

Alongside the pressing social problems, there was always for the government the potentially more damaging threat of industrial action. The war economy depended on the support of workers in key industries such as munitions, engineering, coal mining and shipbuilding. Never had the nation's working class enjoyed such a powerful bargaining position from which to improve pay and conditions. At the beginning of the war they had not used that power. There was then a mood of patriotism throughout the trade union movement and union leaders conceded all the government's main demands in order to ensure industrial harmony for the duration of the war. Under the Treasury Agreement of 1915, they accepted the introduction of dilution (using unskilled and female labour in jobs traditionally regarded as a man's domain), the end of restrictive working practices and arbitration of wartime disputes to avoid any strikes. The assumption that the war would soon be over meant that the sacrifices would be short-lived, and there would be rich rewards for the workers.

But their patriotism soon cost them dear. Wages in many sectors did not keep up with increasing food prices as the cost of living increased by about 27 per cent each year. The issue of pay became even more contentious, because a large number of workers were, for the first time, eligible for income tax. Over the previous three years this tax had been gradually extended to finance the war effort. The standard rate increased eightfold to six shillings (30p) in the pound by the time the war ended. Refusal to pay income tax became a new form of protest, first used by South Wales miners in 1917. Many became convinced, and with some justification, that they were working themselves to the bone while the captains of industry were growing ever richer from lucrative government contracts and a booming war economy. Led by their shop stewards, and often in defiance of the union leadership, workers increasingly turned to unofficial and illegal strike action to get what they wanted.

Industrial relations worsened, with 5.5 million working days lost in 1917 to strikes, the most since the war began. Many were quickly settled with an increase in wage rates by a government desperate to avoid long-drawn-out disputes. Lloyd George wisely refrained from confrontations that might further antagonise a labour force whose goodwill and continued co-operation were crucial to winning the war.

Prominent among the strikers were the miners, who formed one of the largest occupation groups in the country, with over 750,000 men. Gwen Herford was the daughter of a South Wales miner in the village of Pontycymmer in the Garw Valley, and one of nine children.

'Practically all the families were very poor like us. We were all very proud too, but it was very difficult to make ends meet. Dad used to work nights and weekends to get everything he could. We still had to go on the parish to get extra, though. Dad was a quiet, patriotic man and he would rather not have struck especially with the war on. He supported the war, he'd volunteered for the army but they'd told him he would be more useful as a miner. He didn't go to all the meetings that the police tried to break up, but he decided to go along with the majority when they came out on strike. When they were out, I used to get up early to go up the slagheap with my dad and my brother to get coal for the fire. I can't remember how long the strikes lasted, but they got what they wanted. I think they were awarded two shillings a week extra and then Dad had to admit that perhaps it was worth it after all. Everyone was jubilant and we even sang a song at school to celebrate the end of the strike.'

As the war went on, the conscription of growing numbers of skilled workers who had once been in reserved occupations, exempt from military service, made industrial relations even worse. There was an insatiable demand for troops to replace those injured and killed at the front. Conscription, which came into effect in early 1916, began to have a widespread impact on industry a year later. In May 1917, the government abolished Trade Cards that had previously exempted skilled men. Working men in their twenties and thirties, often married with children, who had resisted the pressure to volunteer for military service earlier were now available for the call-up. They were only too aware of the terror and danger that awaited them in the front line. In the distinctly unflattering phrase of the time, they had to be 'combed out'. The new legislation prompted a wave of strikes, with 1.5 million working days lost in disputes involving 200,000 men in May alone. Grievances against conscription, the dilution of skilled trades using cheap unskilled labour, wage differentials, rising food prices and the ever-increasing cost of living all came together. Sheffield, one of the great engines of war production and a centre of the skilled trades, took over from Clydeside as the heartland of militant activity.

Bill Moore remembers the mood in Sheffield at the time.

'People were starting to turn against the government and against the war. In my family, it was heartbreaking. My father had been killed. My mum had died just after I was born and I was brought up by my grandmother, my father's mother. She was devastated by my father's death. Her hair turned white in a couple of weeks. I remember watching her and my grandfather weeping, trying to console each other. And some of my uncles never came back from the war, either. That was what was happening to lots of families in Sheffield. They were exhausted and they were angry. I can only describe it as a dark cloud hanging over us. But Sheffield was a proud city that had fought for its rights, going back to the days of the French Revolution, and that's what it did again in the war. Many times the engineering factories were out on strike.'

One of the unofficial strike leaders in Sheffield was shop steward Albert Sweeting. His memories illustrate how there was a growing mood of confrontation between police and pickets in the city.

'One day I advised them all to bring a big, thick stick

with them because some of the Cossacks [mounted police] had rushed us in Earl Marshall Road. I went to report these Cossacks to the Chief Constable, Major Hall-Dallwood. He said, "Well, you tell me, Mr Sweeting, how it is that your men went out armed yesterday?" "Is it really necessary to tell you?" I asked. "Yes." "Well, don't you know that the best line of defence is to be prepared to attack?" They never attacked us again after that.'

While resistance to conscription was one of the main issues provoking strike action in Sheffield, in County Durham it was hunger. In November 1917, the pit villages of Usworth and Washington staged an extraordinary protest involving miners' children. The background to the dispute was extreme poverty and malnutrition. Albert Walmsley was one of those involved.

'We were getting short of bread, short of supplies. Mother, she had a basin and she'd get a slice of bread. She'd tear it up into little pieces and put hot milk on and give it to us. But we were better off than most. There was some dying from what they called consumption. Oh, it was a terrible thing. It took months before they died, it would bring the tears to anyone's eyes. There were two of my pals, Jimmy Anderson and Jackie Hoff, they lived in Waterloo, just a bit out from Usworth. Their constitution got that low. They had galloping consumption, because they were hungry. There was nothing inside their body to fight. Doctors couldn't help. Their mam gave them sweet water thinking it was medicine. They just more or less lay there and died. You know, it was pitiful. Mind you, there wasn't just one or two. There was quite a lot died during that time.'

On 18 November, the children of Usworth and its neighbouring pit village of Washington came out on strike. They refused to go to school until they had been fed, demanding free school meals.

The strike was initiated by the fathers, most of them trade union men. The *Sunderland Daily Echo* provides a detailed report of the strike and the near starvation of local families:

> At a meeting held in the Alexandria Theatre, New Washington, yesterday and attended by over 1,600 miners employed in the Usworth and Washington district, it was decided to declare a school strike as a protest against the action of the local authorities in not putting into operation the Feeding of the Schoolchildren Act, owing to the poverty existing in the area . . . our representative made careful and thorough inquiries and the facts brought to light lead him to the conclusion that unfortunately the miners' statement that many families are practically starving is not exaggerated. For four to six months there has been very little work in the collieries in and around Usworth and Washington. The result has been that food prices being so high, many men have been unable to buy sufficient of the necessities of life to feed themselves, their wives and their families.

Albert Walmsley recalled that the miners themselves could not strike. Any reduction of the meagre weekly wage earned by the Usworth and Washington miners would have spelt disaster for their families. Their only bargaining power lay in the children.

> 'The children were getting that hungry, they used to cry. Well, it was no good going to school to cry. That's the reason the parents had to take charge. One of the miners would go round with a big rattle, like they used at football matches, and announced a meeting at seven o'clock about the children being starved. The place was packed. They started digging their heels in and said the children are not going to school. If you're not going to give us any aid, that's it. It was up to the council to decide what they were going to do. So we all came out on strike. The school was

empty. There was no point in the School Board man doing anything about that. Our parents were behind us. After a few days they gave in. Every dinner time from then on we had a free dinner bun and soup with good stuff like carrots and turnips and leek in it. We weren't so hungry then, so that was a real victory.'

The Durham pit villages won their soup kitchen, showing what could be achieved through a communal act of solidarity and resistance. But, fortunately for the government, there was rarely a united front of striking workers. Conscription, for example, was extremely divisive in breaking down any working-class solidarity against the government and against the war. Many skilled workers and their trade unions argued that they should be among the last to be called up. They wanted their less skilled brothers, with a comparatively unimportant role, to go before them. During the May strike in Sheffield, a song called 'A Prayer to Lloyd George' was chanted, mocking the elitism of the ASE, the Amalgamated Society of Engineers:

> Don't send me in the army, George,
> I'm in the ASE,
> Take all the bloody labourers,
> But for God's sake don't take me.
> You want me for a soldier?
> Well, that can never be –
> A man of my ability,
> And in the ASE!

Revolutionary ideas failed to take hold in Britain during 1917, in part because of these divisions and conflicts within the working classes. There were too many people with too much to lose in an elaborate hierarchy of income and status. Men like Glasgow socialist John Maclean, who believed that there was 'a spirit of revolution developing in the workshops', were sadly mistaken. For Maclean, the way forward was to 'seize the chance while our enemy was weak, to sweep the capitalist class out of the way and bring about peace'. But there was no stomach for revolution. The Russian Revolution did little to inspire revolutionary fervour in Britain. Most workers were not inclined to embrace a movement whose origins lay in Russia, and calls for the establishment of Workers' and Soldiers' Councils along Russian lines fell on deaf ears. Although the convention 'Follow Russia', called in Leeds by the Independent Labour Party and British Socialist Party on 3 June, caused anxiety within the government, they were soon able to relax in the knowledge that it had been very poorly attended. Only around 1,000 representatives from trade unions, feminist groups and peace societies turned up. There was to be no mass movement to challenge the government and no strong demand that it follow the example of Russia and withdraw from the war.

The pacifist movement had never provided significant opposition. Its weakness was to be exposed when conscription had been extended to the many thousands of men who had no desire to be soldiers. If ever there was a time when the ground was fertile for pacifism, it was in 1917 just as war weariness set in. Yet only 16,100 men and women took advantage of a clause in the Military Service Act to register as conscientious objectors, among them Bertrand Russell, Fenner Brockway and Sylvia Pankhurst. The overwhelming strength of public opinion was behind the war and it took immense courage to become a 'conchie'. Many were subjected to abuse and violence. Pacifist meetings were often broken up by mobs, sometimes with the collusion of the police. At the local tribunals that determined their fate, 80 per cent were granted some form of exemption from military service: 3,300 joined the Non-Combatant Corps; 2,400 worked in ambulances or as stretcher bearers at the front; 3,964 took up work on the home front, many working on road building schemes; 6,261 men were sent to prison.

It was the absolutists who refused to do war work of any sort who suffered most. Some were forcibly sent to the front. If they continued to refuse to obey orders, they could, in theory, be shot. In all, seventy-one pacifists died in prison as a result of injuries sustained there, often after they had been force-fed or buckled in straitjackets and beaten. For the individuals and families involved, it was a terrible tragedy. They became martyrs to the cause but, to the majority of the population, they were just 'shirkers', 'cowards' and 'traitors'.

In the end, the worst fears of the War Cabinet about the people it was leading proved unfounded. Revolution was not around the corner. Official reports on morale and the causes of discontent consistently came to the conclusion that the British people – and in particular the working classes – were determined, despite all their sacrifices and suffering, to struggle on to victory. As a Ministry of Labour report put it, the strikes of 1917 had not 'arisen out of any desire to stop the war. On the one hand [the men] were reluctant to hold up the war to the detriment of their relatives in the trenches. On the other hand, it seemed important to them, in their own interests, to keep their trade privileges intact. One has an impression, in short, of unrest paralysed by patriotism – or, it may be, of patriotism paralysed by unrest.'

Most workers were prepared to fight for a decent wage and working conditions, but ultimately they were loyal to the war effort. This usually meant something very personal. They were working to back up their sons and fathers, their family, friends and neighbours who were fighting at the front.

The Darkness Before the Dawn

ON 9 JANUARY 1918, FIELD MARSHAL DOUGLAS HAIG joined a convivial group of soldiers and politicians for a lunch at 10 Downing Street. 'We had a very cheery party,' he wrote, 'before the conversation turned on the length of the war and some betting took place.' Wagers were offered and quickly taken: Lord Derby gambled 100 cigars against 100 cigarettes with the Prime Minister that the war would be over by the following New Year. Haig, ever the optimist, sided with Derby. Subsequent events ensured that Derby would win his cigarettes, but no one round the table that day could ever have guessed how close Germany would come to winning the war, and in a time far quicker than that allocated by the bet.

The collapse of Russia in 1917, and her subsequent withdrawal from the war, had been a godsend to the stretched forces of Imperial Germany and a severe body blow to the Allies. By early the following year, the Germans were able to move upwards of a million men and hundreds of guns from the Eastern to the Western Front and launch a massive offensive in order to defeat the Allies before America had time to reach the front and tip the balance of the war irretrievably against Germany. Intelligence summaries told the Allies that an offensive was probable; the real question was, could they withstand the onslaught when it arrived? As the talk had turned more serious over lunch, Haig had emphasised 'the critical nature of the coming four months on the Western Front', but he was still undecided as to whether the Germans really would risk their reserves in an all-out assault. If they did, then he was in no doubt 'it would be a gambler's throw . . . We must be prepared for this,' he wrote.

Britain was preparing, and not just for the anticipated offensive. Long gone were the days when Britain could act as if it were still 'business as usual'. For all the bonhomie of the lunch, there were critical issues that had to be faced.

As the mounting casualty lists were posted up, there was a growing sense of anxiety, bewilderment and, among some, despair. There seemed to be no end to the suffering on the home front. Now, in the fifth year of conflict, war weariness was becoming a serious problem as every man, woman and child was asked to sacrifice even more than they had before.

The government's role in this struggle was to strive to maintain the highest level of national efficiency in the war effort. There was ever greater control and interference in work and everyday life – this meant bureaucracy and bullying, but it also meant a greater degree of social justice, epitomised best in the introduction of a nationally co-ordinated scheme of food rationing. There was an anxious need for a sense of shared sacrifice in order to encourage the continued support of workers in the munitions industries. By the middle of the year, this had largely been achieved. However, there were many highs and lows as the last gruelling year of war touched almost every family in Britain.

Fears about war weariness were closely linked to the welfare of women munitions workers. By 1918 there were almost one million of them, providing the guns and ammunition on which the prospects of the British army ultimately depended. In August 1914 there had been only sixteen heavy guns on the Western Front; by March 1918 there were well over 2,000, with a commensurate increase in shells expended. Similarly, well over twice as many shrapnel and high-explosive shells were being produced in Britain's factories by mid-1918 than at the outset of the Battle of the Somme just two years before. Women now played a vital role in Royal Ordnance factories and national

shell-filling factories, as well as in other engineering, metalwork-
ing and aircraft industries.

Since the widespread recruitment of women early in the war,
there had been growing concern about their general aptitude and
whether heavy physical labour in the factories would be too
much for them. Some reports claimed that munitions work had
transformed strong and healthy women into 'pale and anaemic
creatures with no joy in living'. Others voiced the hope that the
hard work was doing them little harm, 'for their eyes are bright,
their cheeks are fresh and there is hardly any evidence of fatigue
among them'. As the pressure to meet production quotas became
more and more intense, it was unpatriotic to worry too much
about limiting hours of work or to be over-demanding about
safety. With the relaxing of the protective legislation governing
factory work by the Home Office, long hours, shift work and
shorter mealtimes all became the norm. Inevitably, fatigue was a
problem, even among younger single women. Their long working hours were exacerbated by often long journeys to munitions
factories that were generally built, for obvious reasons of public
safety, on the outskirts of cities.

Florence Nield had worked since 1915 in a munitions factory
near Swansea.

'The journey to the gun cotton factory would take an
hour and a half on the train, so if I was on the early shift
that started at six in the morning, I'd be up at half-past
three to get to the station. If we were on night shift, at
two o'clock in the morning we'd go down to the special
room where there was a woman cooking our supper.
Afterwards we'd all get under the table or we'd put our
heads on the table, lean on it and try to have a little doze.
There'd be about twenty-five of us. Then all of a sudden
the door would fly open and the policewoman would call
out, "Five minutes more," and we'd all shout out, "Shut
the door." But she wouldn't shut the door. We'd all have
to go back out into the cold, it was really cold, especially

in the wintertime, and we'd have to walk all the way back
to the factory. At the end of your shift you'd be glad to go
to bed. Bed was our refuge. To snuggle down in the
blankets and go to sleep for a few hours, that was lovely.'

Most of the young women in the munitions factories were from
a working-class background. The few middle-class women who
took factory work were usually inspectors. On the shop floor it
was a tough atmosphere, especially for anyone regarded as
coming from a slightly better-off home, as Jenny Johnson from
Newcastle discovered. She was a respectable girl from a lower-
middle-class background who found the work arduous and her
workmates unfriendly.

'I was six months on night work, from six o'clock at night
to six in the morning. Then I had to walk home. In the
winter I'd go up in the dark and come home in the dark.
I had to work on this machine, it was dreadful. I said to
this young girl working with me, she was a few years
older than me, "I'll cry." She said, "Well, cry then. The
more you cry the less you wee." That's what I got. No
sympathy. You didn't do anything apart from work. It was
a miserable existence, it wasn't worth having.'

By the last year of the war there were few young women workers
who had not lost somebody at the front, relative or friend. For
many, this had a double-edged effect. The initial reaction was
often one of despair. Loss and grief added to the general air of
exhaustion. But there were also feelings of anger, shared camaraderie in loss and a sense of duty to keep going to the end. Gladys
Hayhoe was a munitions worker in Colchester.

'I was one of the "Brass Gang". We were six girls who
worked on lathes making depth adjusters for submarines.
It was while I was in the factory that I started going out
with my first real boyfriend. His name was Alfred Watson

but everyone called him "Watsy". He was on the night
shift. I'd met him at a family wedding and he'd escorted
me home afterwards, that's how it all started. He was
about ten years older than me and quite shy. I think I had
a fear of being an old maid, young as I was, I was only
seventeen, and I'd decided to marry him.

'I was very proud when he was called up to join the
navy as a petty officer on the convoys. We wrote to each
other every week but then his letters stopped coming. So I
went round to his parents' home to see what was
happening. His mother was in a terrible state and that's
when they told me that he was dead. I thought it was the
end of the world. The Brass Gang were very, very nice to
me, they gave me a lot of support. Autograph books were
very popular then and one of them wrote in it, "Of all the
sad things of tongue or pen, the saddest of these, it might
have been." It helped to know that so many other women
were going through the same thing. But it made me very
bitter towards the Germans, and it made me work that bit
harder. At one time I'd worried about being involved in
making weapons of war. I didn't care after that.'

Others continued to be troubled by the knowledge that the
weapons they made would one day kill, as Florence Nield
explains.

'We were making something that was going to kill or
maim others. We had relations out there and we were glad
to make the munitions, but we also had to think about the
ones that were going to be on the end of it, you see. They
were youngsters just coming up in life like I was, sixteen
or seventeen. They had parents too. That made me feel sad
sometimes.'

By 1918 the health of the women in the munitions factories
was suffering. This is all too easy to forget when looking at the

black-and-white photographs of them working in armament factories or in the patriotic group poses used for government propaganda. The determined, smiling faces obscure the important fact that many of these women had severely discoloured hair and skin. They were known as 'canary girls', with a strange yellowish coloration that was one of the symptoms of lydite poisoning, along with coughing, swelling, burns and eruptions of the skin that occurred when the girls filled shells with high explosives.

One of the girls who suffered, Caroline Rennles, worked at the famous Woolwich Arsenal. 'It was all bright ginger, all our front hair, and our faces were bright yellow. They used to call us "canaries". Of course the conductors used to say on the trains, "You'll die in two years, cock." So we said, "We don't mind dying for our country." We were so young we didn't realise.' At least 349 cases of serious lydite poisoning were registered across the country and of these 109 died. Many more cases probably went unrecorded. There was no treatment.

The inherent dangers of working with explosive materials meant there were many small-scale accidents. In early 1918, Daisy Collingwood was working in a cordite factory in Shellhaven. She had worked there for two years.

'I thought, I haven't got any brothers to fight in France, so I am going to do the next best thing, work on munitions, and I was quite pleased to do it. I gave it my best, I was a conscientious kind of person. We were proud of our shift. It was hard work and a bit dangerous but you never thought of that. Then one day all that changed. The stove exploded. There was a sudden blast of air that drew me out of the door, down the steps and shot me head first into this gooey mud outside. I didn't really know what had happened at first. I faintly remember seeing a body flying through the air but whose it was I don't know. I think it must have been the chap who was cooking the cordite when the stove blew up. I was just suddenly plonked in ice-cold muddy water and there was this terrible bang. When I look back, I often wonder that the noise didn't kill me, because it was so awful. It was as if the whole world shook with it. I don't know how long I laid there but of course there was always a medical team on duty.

'I was lucky, I only had one or two bruises, nothing serious, but Dad said, "No, that's finished, you're not going back." The after-effects of the shock stayed with me for quite a while. I came out in a terrible rash, with scabby sores all over me. Apparently fright can do that, and I was frightened, I'm not afraid to admit it. A door slamming used to set me trembling. When I look back, I only wonder that I kept my nerve as much as I did.'

There were several large-scale accidents in munitions factories. Housing thousands of tons of explosives in confined areas, they were disasters waiting to happen. In 1917 there had been a huge explosion at the Silvertown munitions factory in east London. It was heard fifty miles away in Cambridge; a huge ball of flame razed the entire factory complex, along with everything within 500 yards, including a fire station, flour mills and two schools. Over 70,000 houses were affected by the blast, with ancillary fires caused by lumps of hot metal thrown for thousands of yards in every direction. Seventy-three people were killed, around 100 were seriously injured and a further 1,000 suffered minor injuries.

On 1 July 1918, there was to be an even more disastrous explosion at the vast Chilwell munitions factory on the outskirts of Nottingham. It employed around 10,000 people, many of them women, producing over 45,000 shells a day. Tragedy struck when eight tons of TNT exploded without warning, killing 134 people; of these, only thirty-two were positively identified. Another 250 were injured. Bert Smith, then aged eight, lived nearby.

'I was having a game of cricket with my friends after school in the local recreation ground and I went to retrieve the ball and there was this almighty bang I felt at the back of my neck. It seemed to push me forward. I turned round to look and there was this huge cloud, a black cloud of smoke from ground level right to the heavens above. It seemed to be rolling and everybody on the recreation ground was looking at it with their mouths wide open. There were two old boys sitting under a tree and one said, "That's Chilwell gone up." The other replied, "And I bet some bugger's done it as well, sabotage." But while I was looking at it I felt this kind of breeze come and the trees started to tremble and the leaves were coming off them. One of the kids came up to me and said, "That bloke says Chilwell has blown up, we're going to have a look, are you coming?"

'We got as far as Beeston and we couldn't get no farther on account of the people milling around the streets. So I sat down on the edge of the pavement and I could see a wagon coming. It must have been one from the factory, and when it got level with me, only two feet away, there was a smell of burning rag. I looked and this wagon was piled up with bodies, stacked with bodies, must have been twenty or more, they were lashed on with ropes. There were half-naked, blackened bodies and the arms and legs were hanging over the side. I noticed there was blood trickling out of the back of the wagon. Then another wagon came, same again. I felt like I had a nest of rats inside my belly, that's how I felt. There was a local bus company nearby and I think they moved quite a lot of these bodies. One of the kids said, "Come on, Bert, let's go home." So I did. But what I saw there I will never forget if I live to be as old as Methuselah.'

While most women munitions workers were single and child-less, there were also growing numbers of wives and mothers. Many had been driven to the factories by the need to supplement their separation or widows' allowances from the government. Separation allowances, payable to all wives with husbands in the armed forces, covered only around half of a family's expenditure, and widows' allowances were also pitifully low. Working-class married women needed to work to make ends meet. Despite the fact that they were generally paid only around half the rate that men received for doing the same job, there were opportunities to earn far more than before the war.

While the state had been quick to encourage them to do war work, it was much slower to recognise the consequent need for childcare. To provide nurseries was seen as a dangerous precedent, as the received wisdom was that a mother's place was in the home. In the last year of the war, the state provided a few crèches and nurseries for munitions workers, but they were regarded as a necessary evil. There were only around 100 nurseries looking after about 4,000 children, and most towns had no crèches or official childcare facilities at all. Mothers made their own arrangements with relatives, friends or neighbours, or more often the eldest daughter was called upon to miss school and play 'little mother'. The great advantage was that she was free, and always available.

One of the little mothers was Ellen Elston from south London.

'I was only nine and I was looking after the family because I was the eldest. There was my brother Bill, my sister Betts, Winnie, Alice and the baby. Five of them. I didn't mind it most of the time. Money was so short that my mum, because she was a war widow, had been given a job at the local army canteen, packing fruit. That left me looking after everybody. I'd do the shopping, go to the butcher's —"Sixpennorth of pieces, please", or "Sixpennorth of bacon bones". My dad, who'd been killed the previous year, had been very popular so I think the shopkeepers felt sorry for us having no father and gave us extra, so we did quite well. Sometimes the butcher would give us half a pig's head, I can see it now with a tongue and everything. We ate well considering there were six of us. The bit I hated most was when the baby cried. I used to make up what they called a sugar tit, a piece of material with some sugar in and make a knob, then stick it in the baby's mouth hoping that it would suck and be quiet. I'd end up crying as well when the baby cried. It worried me because you didn't really know what to do to make her stop, you didn't know what was wrong.'

Penny Feiwel from Tottenham missed a lot of school while helping her mother.

'I had to do lots of jobs for Mum. I never went to school on Mondays; that was washday. I had to look after the little ones and there were lots of errands to do. The School Board man would often come knocking on the door in the afternoons and I'd just hide, I wouldn't let him in. I got terribly behind at school. I was known as the dunce and my mum was threatened with prosecution, but it didn't make any difference, the work had to be done.'

Some mothers found it almost impossible to deal with the strain of juggling the competing demands of work and family in wartime. This was made worse by separation from their husbands. A woman at this time was defined in terms of her man: she was someone's daughter, sweetheart, wife or mother. She now had to cope by herself in a man's world. The constant worry that she might soon get the dreaded news that her husband had been killed drove some to the edge of despair. Sleepless nights, extreme depression and what are now called panic attacks were common. After losing her fiancé earlier in the war, Florence Billington had married and had a baby. By 1918 she was pregnant with a second child, but losing weight and suffering from nervous exhaustion.

'You were worried all the time. My husband Syd was on a hospital ship and I was terrified that I'd lose him, that his ship would hit one of those mines. We lived in Folkestone and you could hear the guns firing over the sea. If you were out in the dark you could see the flashes over France of the actual war going on, so you were constantly reminded of the danger. I'd be tossing and turning in bed at night, worried about what was going on. By then I had a baby and the baby was always crying. I didn't know what was wrong with him, that was a worry. One night the Germans dropped a bomb and I just grabbed the baby and ran out towards this arch where somebody had told me they would shelter if there was any trouble. As I ran I was knocked flat on my back, in the rush, dropping the baby. Thankfully, somebody picked me up and gave the baby back to me and I made it to the shelter, but it all made me ill.'

Florence managed to keep going but, for others, the strain was too much to bear. Much has been written about the shell-shocked troops of the Western Front. Far less is known about mental breakdown on the home front. One of the victims who added to Britain's growing population of mental hospital patients in 1918 was the mother of Charlotte Huggett from Kent.

'It all got too much for her. She used to get these depressions, wanting to do herself in. She'd take poison. Try to drink poison. She had two or three attempts at taking her life. My sister and I used to hide the razor because she'd tried to cut her throat with it. And we'd hide the gun that my father used to have so that she wouldn't shoot herself. I think my mother was a depressed person but the war had made it unbearable for her. We were very poor and life was a terrible struggle. Then my father died in 1915. He was a lovely man, a farm labourer, but he had a bad heart and the work had got too much for him. I had a great love for my father, always had a great love for him.

'After that my mother's brother died. He was in the Marines and that upset Mother a good bit, she was very depressed then. She started trying to drown herself. She was found down by the river twice, and I think it was the third time it happened, her eldest brother put her away in a mental hospital. I'd just started in domestic service in the big house and this all made a terrible impression on me. I used to go regularly to see my mother. When I went she always had her bag packed ready to go but she never went. I thought she might come and live with me one day but no, she'd been there too long. She was there for fifty years.'

As well as physical and mental breakdown, many people were concerned about moral breakdown. Any war sees a loosening of conventional behaviour, frequently arousing panic among respectable society. The strain of war found its most bizarre and hysterical expression in 1918, with an outcry against the supposed decline in British sexual morals. Fears of sexual licence and national betrayal came together in a scandal involving Noel Pemberton Billing, a Conservative MP. He ran the Vigilante Society, which aimed to promote purity in public life and root out German spies and infiltrators known as fifth columnists. In an article he accused the well-known dancer, Maud Allan, of lesbianism. When Maud Allan sued for libel and the case came to court in June 1918, Billing made the sensational accusation that the German Secret Service had compiled a 'Black Book' containing the names of 47,000 British people who could be blackmailed because of their sexual perversity. In the book, he claimed, were the names of former Prime Minister Herbert Asquith, former War Minister Lord Richard Burdon Haldane and many other leading members of society, including the trial judge Justice Darling. The trial fed the nation's hysteria as it passed through a crucial stage of the war. The press had a field day. When Billing was acquitted, pandemonium broke out in court and he was mobbed by over a thousand admirers.

There was also growing concern about the spread of sexually

transmitted diseases. Venereal disease had become a major medical and social problem in Britain. In March 1918, regulation 40D of the Defence of the Realm Act was passed, making it illegal for a woman afflicted with venereal disease to have intercourse with a member of His Majesty's forces – the disease being seen as a scourge inflicted by prostitutes on innocent Tommies. The 1916 Royal Commission had estimated that 8 to 12 per cent of men in working-class areas of London suffered from syphilis, with far more infected with gonorrhoea. In an age before penicillin, syphilis was very difficult to cure, and it killed thousands each year. But in a classic example of double standards, not lost on feminists at the time, it was women who were largely blamed. After this legislation was passed, a wife suffering from VD could be arrested for having sex with her husband, even if he had infected her to begin with.

Such was the shame surrounding venereal disease that very few wives knew their husbands were infected. There was a conspiracy of silence, and they often only found out the painful truth much later. Ruth Evans from Birmingham remembers:

'My husband was in the trenches and I think he caught syphilis from one of the prostitutes that used to meet the men coming out of the trenches. I wrote to his Commanding Officer asking what was wrong with him. I didn't know that they weren't allowed to tell you. He wrote to say my husband was in hospital suffering from strain. It was syphilis. He'd been in hospital for three months with it and he couldn't tell me. I didn't find out until I'd been married ten years and had three children. The eldest tested positive, he had to have twelve months' treatment. The others were all right, thank goodness.'

Much of the blame for wartime immorality and the rise in venereal disease was attached to the 'amateur prostitute'. She was thought to be far more dangerous than the full-time professional. She was simply a single girl who had casual sex or sex before marriage. For this she was attacked in the newspapers as 'the enemy in our midst'. As every respectable girl would deny that her virtue had been compromised, the only ones who could be labelled with absolute certainty as 'amateurs' were those who 'fell for' an illegitimate baby. As a result, they became the main victims of the moral panic about the decline in wartime sexual morals.

Since the beginning of the war, newspapers had been full of stories about the 'khaki fever' that supposedly led 'dizzy' girls to make immodest advances to men in uniform. More than 2,000 special patrols of volunteer women police officers – the Women Police Service – scoured public parks, cinemas, drinking clubs, back alleys and shady lanes, determined to save the pleasure-seekers from themselves. The aim of these high-minded, predominantly middle-aged and middle-class ladies was to prevent the sin of sex before marriage, or, even worse, adultery, which they regarded as a poison that could seriously undermine the nation's war effort. They were particularly active around army and navy bases.

The assumption, from the beginning of the war, was that there was a crisis of 'war babies', the illegitimate offspring of soldiers and sailors. In the wartime atmosphere of living for the present, the illegitimacy rate increased dramatically. The young unmarried mother had always been stigmatised as a 'female temptress' and a 'fallen woman'. During the war the treatment of her became even more cruel and brutal.

In 1917 Gina Baker, a clerk in her early twenties working at the Ministry of Labour in London, fell in love with a naval officer.

'There was a big naval do at Wembley Park and he asked me to bring a friend with me. Well, unfortunately, as he was in charge of the spirits, he got drunk. I waited thinking he would take me home but it got past twelve o' clock. I was scared because I'd never been home late like that before, I was frightened. Well, he'd got another friend with him and he said to us, "Come home to my place, the wife's away and you can have the wife's bedroom if you're frightened to go home." So of course I stayed the night and that was the night I ceased to be a virgin . . . After that it became, not once a week, but every time I went out with him. We used to go into his barracks and into his room. Then another time he took me to his grandmother and I thought, you know, everything was going to be all right, I'd be able to marry him. At Christmastime I stayed at home and it was then I realised I was going to have a baby.'

Gina's boyfriend encouraged her to abort the baby using Epsom Salts and mustard baths. This failed, and it made her so ill she was unable to go to work. She was dismissed from her job.

'I remember it well, it was a Thursday morning and I went across the road to get a newspaper to see if there was any work going. I came in with the paper and my mother said, "What do you want a paper for?" I said, "Well, I want to look for a job." She said, "You want to look for another home. Who's responsible?" That's just how she talked. So I hung my head. She said, "Who is it?" Of course I had to say it was the naval officer I'd been going out with. "Okay, you take your trouble where you got it from then," she said. "You're no longer a daughter of mine. There's the door." So of course I went to pack some things in a bag. I'd got a bank book but my mother had taken it and she wouldn't give it to me. All I'd got was ten shillings. I walked out of that house. My mother stood on the doorstep and she watched me walk up the road.'

For men in the armed forces, who might be dead in a month, there was an increase in a desire for easy and immediate gratification in all its forms. The devil-may-care attitude saw more people willing to risk breaking traditional social practice, even if the law was less willing to turn a blind eye, or sanction such irregularities. The records of the Central Criminal Court for the years before the First World War show, for example, that the crime of bigamy was a small proportion of court cases handled. In 1912, 2.75 per cent of cases – or thirty-four out of 1,232 – dealt with that year were on charges of bigamy. The following year the proportion rose slightly to 3.4 per cent. By the penultimate year of the war, this figure had risen dramatically to just over 13.35 per cent. But even this was dwarfed by the figures for 1918. In this year 20.2 per cent of cases involved bigamous marriages, close to seven times the pre-war average. In April alone, there were twenty-seven cases brought before the Central Criminal Court; twenty-two defendants were found guilty, three were discharged, and two cases were postponed. Of the defendants, the majority, twenty, were married men, of whom a third were serving soldiers. However, seven were women.

Given how many men were in khaki at the time, it is unsurprising that a large proportion of those charged were listed as being soldiers. In April 1918 Joseph Rule, John Milliard, George Turner and John Orange were all convicted of committing bigamy within a few days of each other. Interestingly, the court records also show that a significant number of women involved in war work were charged too. In late 1917, Ada Roe and Jane Bransom were convicted, both munitions workers, as was Mary Barfoot who was found guilty the following year. Another woman, thirty-one-year-old Louisa Casson, was convicted in July, her job title being given as 'carpenter's mate'.

Relationships were put under intense pressure during the war as husbands left for France, and possibly forever. Lovers, caught in the excitement of the moment, could marry without a true and lasting commitment to each other, while the majority of married women were destined to lose their husbands for years on end, with only the very occasional leave to rekindle or reaffirm relationships. At home, the new close proximity in which men and women worked together in industry no doubt helped relationships to blossom. In truth, there were many reasons why bigamous marriages increased during the war, but for those worried about the development of new, scandalous sexual freedoms, there was certainly ammunition to prove their point.

In June 1918, Gina Baker ended up in one of the many Church-run homes for single pregnant women. They were punitive institutions, the last resort for those with nowhere else to go. This one was in Brighton and was run by the Church Army, an offshoot of the Church of England. 'Well, these homes for wayward girls were, I tell you, more or less like prisons. You were treated just as if you were a prisoner. You weren't allowed money, you weren't allowed writing paper, you weren't allowed anything, while the meals were really atrocious. They were very, very strict.'

In an effort to contact the father, Gina wrote a letter on toilet paper, pinching an envelope and asking a local gardener to post the letter. Not having the money even for a stamp, she asked the man if he would help, but instead he reported her 'misdemeanour'. Gina was called before matron and was told that, for stealing the envelope, she would have to leave and return to London. After returning home and again being thrown out on to the streets, this time with her baby, Gina attempted to take her life in the River Thames. She was rescued and eventually took a job as a domestic servant to pay for the upkeep of her daughter.

While the unmarried mother had the most tragic fate, things were hardly any easier for the mother who, after losing her husband at the front, found comfort in the arms of another. In all, 16,000 women had their separation allowances stopped because of allegedly 'immoral behaviour'. Even those who remarried faced unforeseen difficulties. One problem they faced was the children's dislike and rejection of the new man in the house. Esther Peel's mother remarried two years after the death of her first husband.

'Dad had been killed soon after he joined up, and in the last year of the war my mother married again, an Essex man living down in our village. He'd come down to

Northamptonshire to work on the farm because of the war. Well, me and my brother didn't like him. We said, "Bugger off to Essex." I suppose it was because he wasn't Dad. Dad had died fighting for his country and we'd had no man in the house for practically four years and then we had this man there. We disliked the authority coming into the house.'

The anger and fear that lay behind the moral panic informed a new-found sense of national purpose, which would have a more positive outcome. The spectacularly successful German offensive in the spring made many realise there was nothing inevitable about Britain's victory. This could be achieved only through a spirit of unity, manifested in better labour relations. From spring to summer there were virtually no strikes. Only a tiny proportion of working days were lost in April 1918, compared to those lost in May 1917.

If there was a renewed determination to work harder, then there was also a greater desire to settle disputes at this vital hour in Britain's prosecution of the war. Records held at the Public Record Office show that while strikes did take place in early 1918, many were resolved very quickly, often by management; indeed, of the forty-three strikes that involved Welsh miners during 1918, twenty-eight could be said to have been won by the employees or settled amicably to mutual satisfaction. Most of the strikes involved no more than a handful of miners dissatisfied with a particular local issue which was quickly dealt with; in fact, sixteen of the strikes lasted less than one week and many of these just one day.

The desire to work when Britain faced possible defeat was common across industry. As the Minister of Munitions put it, 'The response to the appeal to munitions workers to work over the Easter holiday was excellent and indeed almost embarrassing.' Even the militant shop stewards' movement agreed to put aside old grievances and wholeheartedly back the war effort. Florence Nield captured the spirit: 'It made you work harder when you saw the news was getting bad. When you saw the wounded lists coming in, and the wounded soldiers in their blues, it made you try harder to get more done. Then when you got some good news, it would buck your spirits up.'

The new resolve was also shown in the vital role played by the British people in financing the war. They had already contributed much in the new direct income tax and in a range of indirect taxes, principally on drink and tobacco. Now, with renewed vigour, they invested yet more money in war bonds and loans. Between October 1917 and September 1918, war bonds raised a staggering £1,000 million. There were various special appeals too. In some of the larger cities Tank Weeks were staged, during which the awe-inspiring vehicles were driven through the streets. There would be War Weapons Weeks and Feed the Guns Weeks, many commentators noting how frenzied the devotion to the national cause had become.

The resistance to conscription that had been so marked in 1916 and 1917 declined after the shock of the German offensive. Between April and July, there were 100,000 new recruits from the munitions factories. There were now very few strikes triggered by the conscription of skilled workers compared to the previous year. Even miners and engineers, who until then had been strongly opposed to 'comb-outs' of skilled men, were unusually co-operative in helping the government find new recruits among their numbers. With casualties at the front between late March and early June running at 31,500 a week, Haig needed a constant supply of fresh troops. This was in part supplied by raising the upper age limit of conscription from forty-one to fifty-four years, and by recruiting boys as soon as they reached the age of eighteen for combat overseas six months later. Even so, there was a rush of young men to the colours.

Despite the upsurge of patriotism, the older and wiser ones were not so keen to go. They became the butt of younger men's jokes, as Essex farmer's son Len Whitehead remembers.

'They were calling up much older men and so my father was teased. He was round about fifty-two. In the village

they'd say, "You'll have to go, you'll have to go." We sang a
song about it:

> Forty-nine and in the army,
> Forty-nine, oh isn't it fine,
> Though I'm wheezy across the chest,
> And gouty about the knees,
> I'm learning to shoulder arms,
> But I'd rather be standing at ease,
> Forty-nine and in the army,
> And soon I will be in the fighting line,
> If somebody holds me rifle,
> While I borrow a pair of steps,
> I'll be over the top and at 'em at forty-nine.

'Yes, that was a song we used to sing. My father would
only laugh really. I don't think he ever thought he'd have
to go. He was too important a man on the farm.'

With fewer men available to work on the home front, and
with many women who were willing to work already in jobs,
1918 saw greater numbers of children taking the place of adults
in the workplace as well as in the home. Although children
were meant to remain in full-time education up to the age of
fourteen, there were many loopholes. Those with a good
attendance and proficiency record could leave at the age of
thirteen, and half-timers could, from the age of twelve, work
up to thirty-three hours a week on the condition they attended
school 'half time'. In addition, there were widespread exemptions and abuses of the system. Since the war began, there had
been growing pressure from employers and parents to persuade
the education authorities to relax their restrictions on the use
of child labour. In some areas this had met with surprising
resistance. There were huge differences between cities,
Birmingham determinedly holding out for regular school
attendance. Nevertheless, Education Minister H. A. L. Fisher

admitted as early as 1917 that 600,000 children had been withdrawn from school for employment during the first three years of the war. 'They are working,' he said, 'on munitions, in the fields and in the mines.' Although the figures for 1918 are scanty, the upward trend in child employment seems to have continued.

There was a big exodus of village children from their class-rooms, as many thousands were officially sanctioned to help the war effort. In Huntingdonshire, as early as July 1915, it had been reported that around half of the county's boys between the ages of twelve and fourteen had been granted exemptions. Every pair of hands was welcomed in the fields, most of those exempted being the sons and daughters of agricultural labourers. Even those country children who continued to attend school found that at certain times of the year they would be called from their classroom to do war-related work. Many were only too happy to get out. For Marjorie Riddaway, who grew up on a small farm near the village of Atherington in north Devon, it helped her come to terms with the grief she suffered after the death of her brother Willy.

'Everybody's aim was to win the war, so we children did whatever we could willingly. Every family had lost somebody. We lost my brother, Willy, he was only twenty-eight, in the navy; he was drowned. My mother and father never got over that because he was married and had three little boys. It was devastating, terrible. There was silence, we couldn't even talk to one another, but one thing you could do was work. That was a help. At that time, with all the fighting, our whole country was very short of cotton wool, they hadn't got enough cotton wool to absorb the blood from war injuries. So we children used to be sent out from school two or three times a week to a place called High Biddington. There's a certain moss there that was very absorbent and they used it to make the cotton wool. We used to pick basketfuls, basketfuls in school time. It wasn't hard because moss isn't heavy.'

Len Whitehead was also pulled out of school to help on his father's small farm.

'We were told in school that if we worked, we were helping the war effort. We did lots of jobs that had normally been done by the men but of course they'd all gone. I'd always worked on the farm but I had to work that bit more, working into the evening. My father said, "You work until you see five stars." On a clear night you probably could see five stars but on a cloudy evening you couldn't. So you just stayed out working until after sunset, until it was dark.

'In the war they wanted your help more. You'd have a day off from school, sometimes two or three days. My father called my schoolteacher "the governess" and sometimes he would say, "Ask your governess if it's all right not to go to school tomorrow. I want you to drive the drill horses." And she used to say yes, so I didn't go that day.'

Part-time employment of children before and after school also rose. By 1918 Len had a second job, working for the local vicar.

'One day the vicar and his wife arrived at the farm and I was called in and told that I'd been found a job at the vicarage. Get there at six in the morning and work till half-past eight. I had to clean out the grate in the kitchen, light the fire, clean the boots and shoes, and then go to school. Then in the afternoon, go back to the vicarage at four o'clock and work till six as a kitchen boy, which meant emptying the ashes from the range and chopping wood ready for the morning. As well as that, I was supposed to work in the garden. Their gardener had been directed to work on the farm and the garden had gone to pot as the vicar had had to do it himself. He was incapable of doing anything, so they had me.'

Much of the work done on the farms was undertaken by local children, though by no means all. During the war, children from the towns and cities also took employment in the country at weekends and in the summer holidays. Among these were a few middle-class girls, following the example set by the Women's Land Army. For Kathleen Leek Roe, the young daughter of a Bristol lawyer, the war was a liberation. She quickly discovered that she loved farm life and much preferred it to the fussy etiquette and childish games that characterised her middle-class suburban childhood.

'I was nine or ten in 1918. I'd been working on the farm since I was six. By then I was doing more than ever. Every weekend I'd go out with my brother and mother on the train from Bristol to Pensford, it was about five miles, that's where the farm was. During the holidays, especially the summer holidays, we'd stay out there all the time, living on the farm. I did everything that was needed and there was a great deal to do. There were six of us children on this farm, three farm children and three helpers. I really loved it, I loved the animals, and the whole way of life. It wasn't the done thing for a girl, but I was a tomboy. My mum was quite distraught over it because she really wanted a little girl with frills, but if I could put on a pair of my brother's trousers and work in the fields, that suited me.

'When the summer came, there was haymaking. It all had to be cut with the binder and made into haycocks, then got ready for the wagons. We children used the pitchforks, it was quite difficult but we managed it. We didn't get any money for it. We didn't want any. We did it because the men had all gone to war, we did it to help win the war. It was a terrible time. They were good men and they were killed. We wanted to do our bit to help.'

While the utilisation of child labour was liberating for a small number of children, for many others it was nothing more than simple exploitation. Very often it was their own parents who acted as browbeaters. This was particularly marked in small family businesses where sons and daughters had to help do the work of absent fathers. Maud Cox, though only eight, had to assist with the running of the family's general store in the mining village of Methil in Fifeshire. Her mother had no sons to help with the daily chores, a fact that Maud felt she was constantly blamed for.

'My mother didn't like me. All she wanted in her life was a son. She had one, her first, called Percival Kitchener, and he was three years old when he was killed in a freak accident. After that all she got was five daughters, and I was the fifth. She wouldn't even look at me because the doctor had promised her a son and she got me. She never forgave me for not being a boy. My father explained it to me and I felt sorry for her because sometimes she would beat me up. Once she split my lip. So when the war came and Daddy was away, a lot of the work fell on me to run the shop. I was eight then and I could do more things and my mother made me do so much. I didn't mind really, I felt I was helping Daddy. I'd unpack things, deliver things, I'd arrange all the papers, I'd dust the shelves and put things out. One job I liked doing was cutting up the tobacco with a guillotine into little half-ounce packages. I got to the stage where I could accurately cut half an ounce of tobacco on that guillotine.'

The largest numbers of under-age children were at work in urban areas. Accurate numbers will never be known, partly because it was in the interests of so many involved – employers, inspectors, parents and even some education authorities – to turn a blind eye. As a rule, the younger the child in full-time work, the more desperate the family circumstances tended to be. Among those struggling to keep their families together were war widows, whose allowances were barely enough to live on. Feelings of vulnerability, grief and exhaustion only added to their impoverishment. One survey, conducted after the war, found that 12 per cent of widows died within a year of their husband's death. Many more became seriously ill. In these circumstances their only hope lay in their children, however young.

This family tragedy was probably greatest in Scotland: 26 per cent of all the men in Scottish regiments were killed in action, compared to just under 12 per cent in English regiments. The primary reason for this was the frequent use of Scottish divisions as 'shock troops' – men known for their fighting prowess who would be reliable in battle. Divisions such as the 9th Scottish Division and the 51st Highland Division were renowned for their ability to take objectives. Inevitably, success in battle meant frequently taking heavy casualties. One Scottish boy who lost his father was Dennis Gilfeather. His father had served with the King's Own Scottish Borderers, a battalion in the 9th Scottish Division, and had been killed at the Battle of Loos in September 1915. The family had once enjoyed modest prosperity from a share in a Dundee coal-delivery business, but now they were forced on to the breadline. After battling for two and a half years, Dennis's mother became seriously ill.

'After Dad was killed, Mum received the magnificent sum of £1 2s 6d [£1.12p] that was her pension every week for herself and us four kids. It wasn't enough by any means. Life was very hard and Mum went down with erysipelas and became close to death. I felt my whole world was changing. The sunshine was leaving my life. Your mother's in bed in hospital and they're prophesying her death. I remember saying to her, "Now you canna go, Mum. I love you so much." That's when she said to me, "If anything happens to me, you'll look after the bairn and Annie" – that was the two youngest. I said, "Yes, I'll do that." And that's what I tried to do. Mum really didn't want the family broken up, she dreaded that. I done the things in the house, I began to take authority over the younger ones. Then after about six weeks, Mum started to recover. She was a fighter and, although she was still weak, she managed to come home again.'

Though out of hospital, she still did not have enough food to eat or money to pay the bills. So she suggested that Dennis take a job at the local jute mill.

'My mother started to lean on my shoulder, telling me her troubles, she said, "You could get a job in the mill." I was just a wee boy, I was only nine when I started in the mill. I was in Cox's mill which employed six thousand people. The raw jute was being processed into things like sandbags for the soldiers. Anyway, they badly needed the labour because all the men were gone. At the mill they gave young boys a new name, often the name of someone who'd been killed in the war, that was how they got round the rules. In the books I was down as David Morris, I found out later he'd been killed at the front when only seventeen. They knew you weren't that person, but that's what they did.

'You got tired working on the looms because it was long hours, six in the morning until six at night, five days a week and a half day on Saturday. It was non-stop work, you never got a second to rest. But the women would look after you, they knew you were just a kid. The thing I abhorred most, though, was when the jute got in your eyes, they would start watering, this particular jute was nicknamed salt and sugar; everybody hated it. It made me feel terribly sick and I remember looking out of the window over the beautiful loch and the burial ground and thinking, God, if I could just get a job with a farmer, with the fresh air and greenery.

'I would work at the jute mill for maybe six weeks or three months at a time. I got away with it because there was only one school inspector for Dundee and you'd get a fair run before he came in. He just went round all the mills checking up, because boys were working everywhere. The inspector would say, "Oh, it's you again," and he'd send me back to school. They'd be talking about verbs and nouns and semi-colons and I didn't know what they were speaking about but I could cope with that. I was a proud boy because when I got my pay and took it back home to my mum, I knew it would make her happy. I felt six foot tall.'

Working-class families were helped significantly by the introduction of general food rationing in February 1918. By April, all of Britain was required to have meat rationing. All districts, whether rich or poor, got equal shares of meat, whether of good or poor quality. By July, a comprehensive system had been established throughout the country, developing from initiatives taken in cities such as Birmingham and London. Every household had to register with a retailer who supplied the appropriate rationed goods, in particular sugar, butter, margarine and lard which were all compulsorily rationed, and tea, cheese and jam rationed according to the decisions of local food committees. Shops emptied of all food became a thing of the past, as were the tell-tale queues. Shopping confidence returned to families who knew their allocation of food was safeguarded and did not depend on hours of waiting in line. As a result, feelings of resentment that the better-off were getting more than their fair share quickly receded. The only queues were now purely temporary as shopkeepers tried to master the novelty of ration cards.

The new rationing system was backed up with the full force of the law and thousands who broke it ended up in the courts. The most common offence was shopkeepers selling goods above the prescribed price. One Stepney grocer, charged with selling margarine above the maximum, was reported as saying, 'It is my shop, my margarine and I shall do what I like with it.' The magistrate, replying that traders were now trustees for the public, fined him £50 and sent him to prison for six weeks. Consumers could also find themselves in trouble. New regulations forbade both hoarding and wasting food. Though well intentioned, these regulations could lead to bizarre, bureaucratic and time-wasting prosecutions, as chronicled by Sir William Beveridge, one of the architects of the rationing system, in his book *British Food Control*.

> It became a crime for a workman to leave a loaf behind on the kitchen shelf of the cottage from which he was moving (£2 fine), for a maiden lady at Dover to keep fourteen dogs and give them bread and milk to eat (£5), for another lady in Wales to give meat to a St Bernard (£20), [and] for a furnaceman dissatisfied with his dinner to throw chip potatoes on the fire (£10). A Lincolnshire farmer finding himself able to buy seven stone of rock cakes cheaply from the army canteen used them to feed pigs; as the Food Executive Officer and a police sergeant were able to pick some of the cakes out of a swill-tub and taste them without bad consequences, the farmer was fined £10 for wasting human food.

Even the most patriotic middle-class families bent the rules a little, using their influence and money so they could get just a bit more of their favourite food. But there was often a price to pay. While most avoided prosecution, they lived in fear of the knock on the door from the food inspector or the police officer, as lawyer's daughter Kathleen Leek Roe remembers.

> 'One of my father's clients had asked would he like half a sack of sugar. He could get it for him and Father said,

MINISTRY OF FOOD.   R.R.2.

RATIONING ORDER, 1918.

Instructions for the use of the New Ration Card. (N.86.)

1. During the autumn and winter you will require a Ration Card in place of the present Ration Book.

2. If any member of your household does not receive his Ration Card (by the time when re-registration begins in your district) he should make enquiries at the Food Office.

3. If any Card is sent to your house which you cannot deliver to the owner, send it back at once to your Food Office with a note explaining why it cannot be delivered.

4. See that your name and address and the name of your Local Food Office are correctly entered in the spaces at the top of your Card. If there is any mistake, ask the Food Office to correct it.

5. You will be required to register afresh, by means of the counterfoils on the Ration Card, for Meat, Butter and Sugar, with the retailers you choose. Unless you do this you will not be able to get proper supplies of these foods during the winter.

6. Your Food Office will announce, publicly, the week during which you must register, and any retailer will be able to tell you.

7. To register, write your name and address on the counterfoils A (Meat), B (Butter), and C (Sugar) on the lower part of the Ration Card, and give them to the retailers you choose.

8. See that your retailers stamp or write their names and addresses on the spaces A, B and C on the top of your Card, and also on the right hand side of the counterfoils.

9. The Food Office will require a short interval to ascertain the supplies which retailers will require for the customers who have registered with them by means of this Card. The new registration will, there-fore, not come into force till Monday, October 15th, 1919; until this date you must continue to deal with the retailers with whom you are at present registered. After that date, you will, normally, unless you are the holder of an Emergency Ration Document, be able to obtain supplies of rationed food only from the retailers with whom you have registered by means of the counterfoils from the Ration Card.

10. The spare spaces D, E, and F, at the top of the Card, and the spare counterfoil, D, are for use in case other foods are rationed. Keep these spaces and the spare counterfoil blank until you receive instructions how to use them. Till then do not detach the spare counterfoil.

11. **The top portion of the Card will take the place of the Ration Book. You must keep it carefully. You must produce it to your Retailer if he asks you to do so.**

12. Supplies may be drawn only from the retailers whose names appear at the top of the Card and only so long as the holder of the Card is living in Great Britain, is not drawing Government Rations, is not staying in an hotel or boarding house, or is not living in an Institution (hospital, asylum, workhouse, etc).

13. If you are the person making purchases on behalf of the household you will either at the time when you give your retailers the counterfoils of the household, or at any time before October 15th, receive from each of the retailers with whom the household is registered a "Purchaser's Shopping Card." Each retailer must write or stamp his name and address on the Card and will enter on it the number of persons in the household who are registered with him for the food or foods in question. You must write your name and address on each card and must produce it to the retailer who issued it to you when making purchases from him. The cards will have spaces, one for each week, to be marked by the retailer when you make purchases. There will be two forms of Shopping Cards. One with spaces for meat which you will receive from the butcher, and one with spaces for butter and sugar. If you are registered with different retailers for butter and sugar you will receive a card from each, and each retailer must cross out the set of spaces which do not apply to him.

14. **The "Purchaser's Shopping Card" will be valid only for purchases from the retailer whose name and address is on it. A Card which bears no retailer's name and address is not valid. The card will be valid only in respect of the members in each household registered with the retailer at the time of each purchase, and only for a food for which they are registered with him. When a household removes and changes its retailers it will get new cards from the new retailers.**

15. If any member of a household removes or registers with another retailer since the Shopping Card has been issued to you, you must inform the retailer so that the number of persons stated on the card as being registered with him is altered. It will be an offence to make purchases on the card in respect of such members of the household.

16. PERSONS ENTERING INSTITUTIONS.—If the holder of a Ration Card enters an institution, the Ration Card must be given up to the head of the Institution.

The introduction of a ration card detailing exactly how and where it could be used.

"Oh, thank you, yes I would." He could also have some cheese. Anyway, this man got him half a truckle of cheese which he very happily had and my mother was delighted. Afterwards we heard that inspectors were coming round and anybody who'd been caught food hoarding would be prosecuted. My father was terrified. He said, "I can't be found out like this. It must go back at once." Well, Mother says, "Not likely, I'm the housekeeper here and I'm keeping it." So she put it into the baby's cradle. In the night cradle it was, up in the attic. She covered it over with rugs and pushed it through the door that led on to the roof, and there it stayed. She used tiny little bits from it and of course the inspectors never came round. People used to come in for supper and they'd say, "You've always got a little piece of cheese," and Mother would say, "I've got a very good grocer, he lets me have a bit extra sometimes." Father was in a terrible state over it though.'

The drive to ensure that people had enough to eat was further helped by the opening of National Kitchens. They began in the poorer parts of London and spread rapidly, with a total of 623 by August 1918. They offered cheap and cheerful meals like oxtail soup, Irish stew, potatoes, beans, bread, jam roll and rice pudding, all at a price the working man and woman could afford, with ration coupons being surrendered at the same time. The food was cooked in large quantities, and the economies of scale proved that it was possible to offer cheaper meals than those cooked at home. The centralisation of the cooking process also meant an appreciable saving in much-needed coal.

The introduction of food kitchens went hand in hand with an effort to feed workers in their factories. By 1918, over a thousand works canteens were in operation. The government's new concern with the welfare of workers was motivated not by a new-found benevolence, but rather by the demand for efficiency in the drive to win. Workers had to be fed well so as to be healthy enough to turn up every day and operate their machines.

To this end, the Health of Munitions Workers Committee appointed middle-class ladies as welfare supervisors. Some were well liked, while many others were loathed for their patronising attitudes and intrusive behaviour. One of the jobs of the supervisor was to organise daily exercise and sporting events for women munitions workers.

In the spring of 1918, Frieda Sawden joined the growing band of factory welfare workers. She was one of the more popular ladies involved in maintaining morale by keeping the workers fit. Her regime worked wonders and not just for the staff. When interviewed, Frieda was still going strong at the age of 105.

'I was at the end of teacher training when I applied for the post of physical instructor in a factory producing naval shells in Dudley. I had to go in there and chat to the women workers, get to know them and organise some sort of sports for them. It was very noisy in the factory, you could hardly hear them speak it was so bad, but I did it. There were three shifts a day and I had them for an hour before they went on their shift. I went to the shops to try to buy sports equipment, but they virtually had nothing, just a few cricket balls, so I decided to do athletics. Running and jumping, relay races, that sort of thing: we had a high jump and a long jump and I managed to scrounge some sand from somewhere. We exercised on the beautiful lawns there, and the girls loved it being out in the fresh air. Then they went back to work and production went up, as Lloyd George said it would. Output increased and Mr Millington, the owner, he congratulated me because he was getting more shells. And I said, "Thank you very much." '

For the British army on the Western Front there had been some respite after the battering they had received in the spring. June and July were months of recuperation, retraining and re-equipping. There seemed to be cause for cautious optimism in

France and at home. Then came another blow, from a totally unexpected source: the influenza epidemic.

Flu first struck Britain in June. By July it was becoming a major cause for concern, when 700 Londoners died in a week. Schools all over Britain closed to reduce the risk of infection. Church attendances dropped as congregations feared catching the killer disease. The epidemic abated, but not for long, returning with a vengeance in the autumn and taking the lives of 18,000 Londoners alone. Doctors, already overstretched, were so few in numbers they could only make occasional visits to patients but even then, with no known cure, there was little they could do. Undertakers were so overwhelmed that they did not have sufficient coffins to bury the bodies. One of the lucky survivors was south London girl Margery Porter, who contracted the disease in the summer.

'I was an only child and I lived with my mother and father. When we all got the flu we couldn't do anything else but go to bed, because we just couldn't stand up. Your legs actually gave way, I can't exaggerate that too much. Everybody at our end of the street had it. Next door but one lived my grandparents and my three aunts. They all had it, but my grandfather was the only one who died in our family. The rest of us recovered but it took a long time, because that flu took charge of your whole body. I don't remember having a cold or sneezing. I just remember terrible pains in all my limbs, and I just didn't want to eat anything. I think my bout of flu lasted about two weeks until I started going back to school again. I was so lucky. That was the worst illness I've ever had.'

The scourge of the 'Spanish Lady', as it was called, is thought to have originated far away in army camps in the United States and to have been brought over by soldiers. The flu did not attack the usual victims of an epidemic – the weak, the poor and the old – but, seemingly on the contrary, many of the victims were young, and both affluent and healthy. In London, for example, prosperous Chelsea and Westminster were struck down harder than impoverished Bethnal Green, while outside the capital the incidence of flu was higher in the spa town of Bath than in industrial Birmingham. Total estimates of the number who died in Britain before the epidemic finally abated in the spring of 1919 vary from 150,000 to 230,000. Estimates of those who died around the world fluctuate wildly, although it is thought that upwards of half the world's population eventually caught the illness.

Relief was in sight for, on the Western Front, it was the Allies' turn to break through and advance. The Germans had become exhausted after countless attempts to force a decisive victory in France before the arrival of American troops in numbers. The Germans had failed, leaving the Allies to forge ahead in the late summer and early autumn, as the exhausted German army began, slowly but inexorably, to collapse.

After such a long war, victory was not expected in 1918. However, the national crisis of the spring and early summer had certainly passed, and with it died the spirit of industrial harmony. There was a new outbreak of industrial strikes, as long-standing grievances once again came to the surface. Among those withholding their labour were men of the London police force, so often used in the past as the government's strike breakers. They claimed that during the previous four years their pay had steadily declined compared to other workers, so that now they were on a par with the lowest paid and unskilled. One constable, asked by a superintendent why he was striking, replied, 'We want more pay, sir. I don't get sufficient money to keep my children in food and boots. My second son has just been called up by the army and I have to go caretaking to keep out of debt.' The government agreed to a substantial increase in pay, as well as allowances for the children of policemen. It was a portent of the industrial conflict that would quickly re-emerge as soon as the war was over, and of the government's desire to have the capacity to tackle the problem

---

When the war ended, many people could scarcely believe it. George Louth, the disabled soldier who for two years had been working on the land in Dorset, could think only about his true love, Ella, the daughter of his landlady.

'It was just me and Ella, my first love. I was very lovey dovey then. We had courted for eight months. She worked in a shop in Blandford, and slept there. After she finished work we used to meet and go off in the country and walk miles together. It was so quiet, different altogether to what I'd been through. I was partially deaf after being at the front but Ella got used to speaking louder to me so I could hear what she was saying. We'd decided to get married on November the 11th, 1918. Of course I didn't know the war was going to end, so when the ceremony was over and we came out of the church, and there were flags flying and bunting everywhere, bells ringing, well we thought it was all for us! It was Armistice Day. That's when we started our life in Blandford. We would have a happy life together. A very happy life.'

Young munitions worker Jennie Johnson had turned up for work as usual on 11 November, but she would not stay there a second longer than she needed to. For her, as for so many others, the end of the war meant the end of a nightmare.

'I was on the six o'clock shift. Then at eight o'clock all the bells at St Hilda's Church started to ring. Ships started blowing their hooters. The war was over. So I put my hat and coat on. I went in the cloakroom and the foreman said, "Where are you going?" I said, "Home." He said, "You can't." I said, "I am and I'm not coming back." He came up to see my father and he said how silly I was, I'd lose all my money. Anyhow, I got the money. But I was delighted just to go. It was the best day of my life to be walking out and I never went back again. I thought, thank goodness, I've had enough of this. I just walked out, and that was the first time in my life I'd ever done what I'd wanted. I went to the Queen's Picture Hall as an usherette. Then, after a few months, they put me in the booking office and I enjoyed that, I loved it.'

CHAPTER TEN

Bittersweet Victory

I T WAS NOT ACTUALLY THE END OF THE WAR, BUT THAT DID not seem to matter. At 11 a.m. on Monday 11 November 1918, the country went wild with joy: maroons exploded from the roofs of police and fire stations, church bells pealed, and hooters blasted out from factories and ships. In the capital, the 'All Clear' was sounded from the plinth of Nelson's Column, the base of which would be badly damaged in the evening by celebratory bonfires. No civilian considered the fact that the Armistice was no more and no less than an agreement to call a temporary halt to hostilities. As far as those who thronged the streets in every town and city from London to Glasgow, Cambridge to Swansea, were concerned, nobody else would have to die, the fighting was over, and the terrible cloud of war was lifted from the nation after four years and three months.

It is perhaps fortunate that neither the stipulations of the Armistice, concluded at 5 a.m. on the 11th, nor the Allies' determination to see them imposed, were ever vigorously tested. The strict conditions demanded by the terms were such that, had the Germans failed to comply, the war would have started again in thirty-six days.

The country had reawoken to peacetime living. In London, thousands poured on to the streets, waving Union Jacks and the French tricolor, celebrating at the usual venues: Hyde Park, Trafalgar Square, the Mall, and Buckingham Palace, where the King and Queen were to be seen waving from the balcony. The war had, in a way, come full circle, for the sights and sounds —

while more frenetic – were eerily reminiscent of those seen and heard on 4 August 1914.

As a seventeen-year-old, Vic Cole had been one of those who had joined the crowds pouring up the Mall that fateful day. Now, aged twenty-one, and wise far beyond his years, Vic was back in Britain, but not in London. Shortly before 11 o'clock, he found himself standing in the Quartermaster's store at Fort Pitt near Chatham. He was about to be discharged from the army as medically unfit for further service. After being wounded twice in action, Vic had been left with a chunk of shrapnel, a painful souvenir, permanently lodged between two vertebrae. He had been in hospital for over seven months, for the most part confined to bed, and he had only recently been discharged from hospital – 'perhaps my happiest period of the war', he would sagely acknowledge years later. After leaving hospital, he had used his statutory seven-day leave to visit his grandmother and aunt at their home in Gypsy Hill. Four years earlier, both had shed a tear when he had enlisted, and his grandmother had given him a quick hug. 'At the end of the war, my gran and my aunt seemed very old and tired,' recalled Vic. 'I had never noticed it before, the strain of the war, I guess, and trying to live on a greatly reduced income.'

As he waited for his new civilian suit, Vic heard the sudden peal of bells and the sound of factory whistles.

'It was the Armistice and I was a civilian once again. I had signed on for the duration of the war in Kitchener's Army and had kept the contract to the very hour and the very minute. On my way to the station, I passed through crowds of cheering, boisterous people packed densely in Chatham High Street. I had lots of drinks with men I had never seen before and never saw again, and finally, in my ill-fitting suit, with cloth cap and heavy boots, I arrived home to the quiet, orderly and peaceful atmosphere at Gypsy Hill to rest and relax my tired brain and aching back.'

Like so many soldiers, Vic was exhausted, and in truth had only gone through the motions of celebrating on his way home. There were few ex-soldiers around, and, not being one to turn down a free drink, Vic had had a pleasant time, but nothing in comparison to those around him. For so many soldiers, news of the Armistice was a time for a mixture of emotions, relief, disillusionment, sadness, anger and fear – fear for the future in a world in which the army would no longer guarantee their pay, food, accommodation and a fully filled timetable. Many soldiers hardly raised a cheer at the news that the war was over.

Not so the civilians. 'Oh, when the end of the war came, the village went mad, I don't think there was one person in their home,' recalls Ruth Armstrong.

'Everyone was out in the streets, and we had a lovely band in those days and they were playing, and everyone was dancing, whether they knew each other or not, and the streets were covered in decorations and Union Jacks hanging out of everybody's windows. Oh, it was a wonderful time, then we had another do to celebrate and I was dressed up as a little Red Cross nurse, and a little boy next to me was Charlie Chaplin.'

Maud Cox's memory of events hardly differs.

'When the war ended, everybody celebrated, we marched through the streets till we were exhausted, waving our little Union Jacks and singing "When the Boys Come Marching Home", "Pack Up Your Troubles in Your Old Kit Bag", and "Keep the Home Fires Burning", we sang until we were hoarse. When I got home at night, I could hardly speak. My mother had to send one of my big sisters out to drag me off the street because we marched round and round and round and then one of the bands came out, the colliery band, and it started to lead us, and everybody was exhausted, they were dropping off, especially the younger ones who were getting dragged indoors. People were bringing bottles of wine on to the streets, anything they could get hold of, and drinking each other's health.'

Singing and dancing were popular expressions of frenetic exuberance, particularly dancing, which allowed a publicly acceptable expenditure of raw emotion. At times during the war, dancing had been frowned upon as an inappropriate display of happiness and joy at a time of national crisis and death at the front. Now the war was over, there was no holding back; dancing became a public mania, and in time would become one expression of a general desire to expel all the pain and anxiety of the war years, helping people forget; the dancing did not stop for years.

For Letitia, the mother of Joyce Crow, there was relief that the war was over, but there had also been an overwhelming sense of resignation. Writing of her feelings thirty years later in her memoir, she noted:

> The Armistice was signed. The world went mad with relief. For myself there was just a feeling of relief that the slaughter was over. Then the months of agonised waiting in the hope that among the prisoners of war, among the men in hospital who had lost their memory, Arthur might even yet come home . . . It would have been a merciful blow if we had heard that he was killed – but he was missing – and even after this lapse of time, those years of hopes that were deferred don't bear thinking of.'

The joy that so many had expressed at the end of the war quickly turned to anger and bitterness vented on the Germans, who were universally blamed for starting it all. German war guilt was taken for granted, and the evidence of atrocities allegedly committed by the enemy was broadly accepted as unimpeachable. There was an insistent demand for swift retribution and the punishment of the German nation and its criminals, starting at the top with the

Kaiser. Within weeks, a commission had been set up to report violations of the Laws and the Customs of War to the Peace Conference sitting in Paris, and a suggestion was made in February 1919 that any extension to the Armistice was dependent on Germany handing over war criminals, 3,000 of whom were eventually accused.

At home, there were rash comments made in the House of Commons and in the newspapers about making the Germans pay. Such crude statements were hardly likely to be toned down when a general election was called for 14 December. Taunts and accusations against the enemy were popular appeals to public sentiment and were often inflated to win votes. Recent changes in electoral law had enfranchised millions more people, effectively doubling the number of voters. For the first time the electorate included women, or rather married women over thirty, of whom there were six million. It was more important than ever to appear in tune with general public opinion, which had been swayed by years of wartime propaganda. After the Armistice, this opinion was honed to hatred by a vitriolic press, led in particular by the *Daily Mail* and *The Times*, both of which belonged to the uncompromising Lord Northcliffe.

As a result, Lloyd George, who had briefly appeared conciliatory towards the Germans, now became belligerent. By the start of December, he was calling for the prosecution of the Kaiser, the punishment of many in the German military leadership and the expulsion of all German citizens from the country, including all internees. It was politics at its most ugly and pragmatic. Within weeks, Lloyd George and the coalition had been returned to government with a majority of 262 seats. The public sentiment had made itself clear at the ballot box and it was not an edifying sight.

The decision to repatriate German citizens had serious repercussions for Elfie Druhm, the British-born daughter of a German father and English mother. In 1914, her parents' hairdressing salon had been smashed up and her father interned.

'When the war was over, my father was sent back to Germany, directly. Now the wives could easily have divorced their husbands and stayed in England. Some did and some didn't. My mother wouldn't, so she was sent to Germany, and of course I went with her. I was very close to my mother, and very trusting, and what she did was right.

'It was February 1919, and it was really cold, making it a terrible journey. Miss Elsie Hope, my mother's one dear friend, came and saw us off from the station. She loved me as if I was her daughter and she brought me an eiderdown, a coat and a pair of boots because she knew it would be cold. But my grandmother and my mother's sisters didn't come to the station to wave goodbye. There was bad feeling about that for many years; they knew we were being sent to Germany.

'When we were in Germany in 1919 we kept contact with some of the families Father had met in the internment camp. Stalenbrusher was one family we met up with, another family was the Stemlers. They used to live nearby and they had a daughter whom I used to meet. But she went back to England. Germany was terrible in those days with the riots and skirmishes and the food situation being so awful, that Frau Stemler left her husband and went back home taking their daughter with her. She couldn't stand it any longer.'

The repatriation programme helped cut the German population in Britain by over 60 per cent between 1914 and 1919, leaving just over 22,000, where once there had been 53,000. How many British subjects, born to a German parent, also left is unknown. Elfie describes their journey:

'I do not recall the crossing but the trains we went in on the other side were war-damaged, with their windows all

broken and no heating; it was pretty bleak and freezing.
We went through Holland and each evening we got out of
the train where the Quakers or the Dutch Red Cross
helped us until we got into Germany. It took nearly a
week to get there, waiting in Germany for trains to take
us on towards Berlin and the little town of Lugenwaldt,
about 50 kilometres south of the city.

'We went to the place where my father's parents were,
and they welcomed me. My grandfather sat me on his lap
and tried to teach me a few words of German. They said
the best way for me to learn the German language was to
go to school, so the week after, they took me to school.
The first lesson we had was French, imagine, out of
German into French, and I only knew English. Yet the
children were so nice they rivalled each other to take me
around, there was no anti-English feeling whatsoever. They
really couldn't do enough for us.'

As Elfie was making her way to Germany, thousands of British
soldiers were going west to the French or Belgian coast and on to
Britain, many to be demobilised from twenty-six points of
dispersal made ready at such camps as Canterbury and Ripon.
They were finally free to go home to their families. Ruth
Armstrong remembers her father's homecoming.

'We didn't know my father was coming home. He just
walked in and the screams of delight – we hung all round
him, you know, we wouldn't let him go and he had a
beard – very soon shaved it off, he looked really rough. I
was a proper daddy's girl and I remember him bringing
my mother a great big bottle of eau de Cologne. I
remember him pulling it out of his pocket. She was
thrilled with it.'

Kathleen Barron's brother Dick had served at Gallipoli and then
later at a base camp in France before finally coming home.

'I was delighted to see him again and have him back with
us but he looked ill and very thin – as though he'd suffered
a lot. He wasn't quite the happy-go-lucky, fun-loving
person he was. He'd altered, I mean he'd suffered a lot,
nearly died, and then there's the fear there too. The first
time I saw him again, I could see this great big helmet with
Dick underneath, I couldn't help feeling he looked funny.
He'd shrunk, he'd gone to a thin little man from a fine
physical figure, and it was very noticeable. But I've never
seen my mother look so beautiful as she did when she saw
her son – it was the elation, the feeling of seeing him. She
was a good-looking woman but she looked extra special
that day, she radiated the feeling of happiness.'

It was only natural that the celebrations should catch all the
attention at first; the parties and banners eclipsed the inevitable
grief felt by so many who preferred to shut their doors and not
participate. The civilians could never know what it had been like
to fight on the Western Front. Equally, the bulk of soldiers could
never understand the feelings of a father or mother who might
have lost one, two or more sons to war. Len Whitehead recalls
the perennial sadness.

'We used to sing:

> Keep the home fires burning,
> While your hearts are yearning,
> Though the lads are far away,
> They dream of home.
> There's a silver lining,
> Through the dark clouds shining,
> Turn the dark cloud inside out
> Till the boys come home.

'And my mother always at the end of it said, "Ah, but
some of 'em will never come home, you see." It was

always there, the fact that he would not come home
again.'

The memory of George strutting about his mother's bedroom,
cane under his arm, was a memory all the family would hold
dear.

'George was never forgotten. My mother was very sad. We
didn't hear that the Armistice had been signed until late in
the afternoon, we were isolated on the farm. My sister
had cycled into Braintree and saw all the people coming
out of the factories to celebrate, you see, waving flags. But
my mother didn't take part in any celebrations. One of her
precious family wasn't coming home.'

The men who did come home from France fell into many
different camps: some felt 'made' by the war, others equally felt
'destroyed'. In one regard, though, there was almost total unison,
and that was dissatisfaction with the slow rate of demobilisation,
and the inequality of its application. Vic Cole had been excep-
tionally lucky – perhaps the first man discharged from the British
army, post-war. He was the first of 3 million men who were to
follow him back into civilian life. By January 1919, Vic was back
in employment, but the majority would be kept hanging around
in khaki, uncomprehending as to why, with the fighting over,
they could not just go home.

To make matters worse, orders were given for each command,
home and abroad, to give details of the composition of their
forces by 'industrial groups'. In effect, men were to be demobilised according to the strategic importance of their civilian
occupation, not length of service. A coal miner deemed a 'pivotal
man' was, therefore, likely to be released before a carpenter, even
if the carpenter had already served for four years in the ranks and
the miner six months. The natural sense of inequality was at first
ignored by the government, giving extra fuel to already smoul-
dering resentment. To further complicate the issue, different

groups of men had enlisted under different terms. According to the conditions of the Derby scheme, for example, men could not be retained for longer than six months after the cessation of hostilities. In theory, men could simply walk out of their camps after 11 May 1919. There were calls to do so, although there is no evidence that the threat was actually carried out.

In the winter of 1918/19, soldiers chanted 'lies, damned lies and demobi-lies', a refrain heard at camps across the United Kingdom and France. It was heard too among the occupying forces in Germany, and as far away as Kantara Camp in Egypt. Soldiers who had signed to serve for the duration of the war hankered after freedom. But only slowly did the government, which had become too absorbed in the general election, start to take notice. It was almost a month before the policy of even partial demobilisation was begun, and soldiers were getting restless. In January there were widespread manifestations of disobedience when as many as 10,000 soldiers at Folkestone refused to board ships to return to France. In Dover town centre, 2,000 soldiers began a demonstration; elsewhere, others refused orders to parade or clean equipment. It was not long before there were riots and even deaths recorded among soldiers straining at the leash to go home and find a job.

Harry Patch took part in one rebellion on the Isle of Wight. He had been at Golden Hill Fort, near Freshwater, undergoing final training before he was due to return to France.

'On the day of the Armistice we were on the rifle range and we were told to fire our remaining ammunition out to sea. Then the sergeant got us together and we marched back to camp and to a church service, after which we were told we would not be allowed out of camp. The men didn't like this and later they chased this sergeant along the pier at Freshwater, and when he got to the end they chucked him in the sea, and that night we had hell's delight, a real party.'

Such a dunking could be passed off as boisterousness, of soldiers getting carried away, but it hid an impatience with authority that would boil over in time. The next incident, a few weeks later, was to have potentially far more serious repercussions.

'We had an officer, a captain, a peacetime officer, risen from the ranks, and he took E Company out, they were all ex-servicemen who'd seen active service, and he took them for a route march. He started them at the double, well, half the company went at the double but four Birmingham boys said they weren't going to double for him, they stayed marching, and the rest of the company followed suit. The officer didn't know what to do, so anyway, they got back to camp and the men decided that they'd had enough of him and wouldn't parade again. The sergeant major came into the huts and the first door he opened, he shouted, "On parade, E Company!" Somebody threw a boot at him and he reported it to the officer.

'We'd had enough. We were absolutely fed up with this officer giving us right turn, left turn, about turn and bayonet practice. The men had gone over the top and they'd used the bayonet, damn it, they didn't want bayonet practice! A group of men went up to the officers' mess and asked for this officer and after they'd spoken their mind the officer pulled his revolver out and you could hear the click, click, as the hammer went back, whether it was loaded or not, I don't know. Nobody said anything, they simply went back to their huts, rounded up what ammunition they could find, and went back and asked for him again. He came out, click, click, went the hammer, and back went thirty rifle bolts, someone shouting, "Now, you shoot, you bugger, if you dare." Had he not backed down he would have been shot, there's no doubt about it. Anyway, down went the revolver and he scarpered.

'We had mutinied, and so a brigadier was sent for from the mainland. He heard the officer's side of it and then he interviewed about thirty men from E Company, and his verdict was that E Company was only for fatigues and the officer was to be taken right away from the fort. By this time most of us were down for immediate demobilisation and we had decided we were more or less civilians, and that army rules no longer applied to us.'

Demobilisation was speeded up, on an initiative overseen by the new Secretary of State for War, Winston Churchill. He agreed that men belonging to vital industries should still be rapidly demobilised but he added that, 'Military needs must be considered as well as industrial needs.' His plan was that the army, while retaining large numbers of soldiers for the time being, must nevertheless let go 'those who are the oldest . . . those who came in the earliest . . . those who have suffered the most'. The idea of releasing these men quickly was more equitable, although the actual details of the plan could still keep a married man in his mid-thirties, with three years' service, in His Majesty's ranks, at least for the time being.

Whichever way the new policy was applied, it is notable that ten months after the Armistice, one million men remained in uniform, while in February 1920 there were still 125,000 awaiting their return to civilian life. Many soldiers were in no mood to be retained for any length of time, let alone a year, and inevitably there had been trouble.

Freda Philip was fifteen years old, the daughter of a police inspector in Epsom, in Surrey. In 1919 she was present at a particularly violent demonstration at the police station, which was directly below her parents' flat.

'The soldiers were more or less killing time. They used to come down from the camp at Woodcote Park and spend their money in the town, in the pubs. It usually ended in a fight. It was the mood they were in, I suppose, frustrated

that they were being kept waiting so long before they
came home.

'On this particular night, two of the soldiers were
causing a lot of disturbance in one of the pubs,
quarrelling, fighting. The publican called the police and
the two men were arrested, taken to the station and put in
the cells. Word got back to the camp and all the others
got together and came down to try to free their friends.

'They all came down in hordes, about four or five
hundred of them. On the way, they pulled down fences,
gathered up stones and bricks and, of course, they threw
these through our windows. They trampled all over our
front garden, pulling the railing down. They ripped the
iron bars out of the windows and they tried to get into
the cells. Eventually the Military Police arrived and the
rioters were rounded up and sent back to camp. Dad had
a big gash on the back of his head, which had to have
stitches. There were several of them who had head
injuries, you see. Sergeant Green was taken to hospital but
very sadly he died the next morning of his injuries.'

The reality of being a civilian again did not always match up to
expectations. Many soldiers came back home hoping to pick up
their lives where they left off, taking the jobs back that had been
promised to them when they left. Some were lucky and walked
into employment, others took years to find a job and were
forever scarred by the memory of searching for work of any kind.
One veteran, Bert Fearns, was not untypical. He worked in a
gentlemen's outfitters in Southport but had enlisted in the army,
much to his employer's ire. In March 1918, he was badly
wounded and taken prisoner, being repatriated to Britain the
following year. When Bert returned to his employer, he found
his job at the outfitters no longer existed and was told in no
uncertain terms that he had let his boss down when he had
joined up. Two women were now doing his job for the same
money. Bert spent many months fruitlessly searching for any

work until he finally secured a job as a school caretaker. He grasped the position, never letting go for the rest of his working life, 'too terrified', as he said himself, that he might not get another one. In the end he had been 'lucky'. In 1922, the British Legion estimated that one million ex-servicemen were unemployed, and many had never had a job lasting more than a few days or weeks since the end of hostilities.

There seemed to be a simple route to re-employing most men and that was to sack all the women who had taken the jobs. Just under five million women were in work before the war, well over six million by 1919. Some 750,000 had already left work by the end of 1918, many voluntarily like Jennie Johnson, who had simply picked up her coat and walked out. Munitions work had attracted large numbers of women, not because they all burned with ambition to begin careers outside the home, but because war work paid far better than the traditional jobs open to women, such as domestic service. It was quite possible for a girl in munitions to earn £2 a week, while those employed on piecework in the most dangerous jobs, working with TNT, could earn as much as £5 a week. Yet working in munitions was hard, dirty work and many women like Jennie, who were not reliant on the money, were quite happy to leave. For those women who needed the money, the decision to leave was not one they necessarily wished to take, but the pressure was put on them. It had once been their patriotic role to fill the gap, whether in an office or on the factory floor; now it was their duty to leave and return to the home.

Those who remained, especially married women, were increasingly criticised in the press, and derided for spending their money on mere fripperies. As early as 6 December, the Reverend Andrew Clark was noting in his diary that in London, 'The women who have been discharged from various government offices are receiving, temporarily, weekly pay. A friend this week saw a crowd of them outside a pay-office, waiting for their pay. They were very showily dressed (fur coats; jewellery), and looked for all the world like flash barmaids.' Working women, once among the heroines of the war, were now being widely talked down.

There were easy but simplistic assumptions made. Those women who were titled 'Miss' rather than 'Mrs' were given greater dispensation to work, as it was assumed, often incorrectly, that anyone who was married had a husband who would provide for the family; there was little excuse to take work from another family man. But 160,000 women had lost husbands in the war, and the pensions rarely made up for the financial hardship. Working was not just about the money either; a job gave many widows a release from thinking too much about their predicament. Joyce Crow's mother Letitia lost her son Arthur in the Somme fighting of 1916. Then, in 1917, Letitia's husband died after a prolonged and chronic illness. 'The money problem was now really acute,' she acknowledged in the memoir she wrote. Letitia found work at the local coal office. She wrote candidly:

I am certain that going there saved my reason. The subject was sufficiently exacting for me to have to give it my whole attention. I had to stop pacing about. I had to meet dozens of strangers and try to help with their difficulties. For months I had lived with a weight on top of my head and a tight string round my forehead. I used to feel sometimes that it would be a relief when the knot snapped and I could give up.

For Letitia, work safeguarded her sanity and kept her family financially viable.

As Letitia had not been involved in war work, she had not taken a share in the booming salaries that such vital work had produced. Salaries connected with war production had doubled during the conflict. Although inflation eroded the value of money, many who participated in war work earned wages that left the pay of even skilled workers in non-war-related work far behind. These salaries, coupled with the brief financial clout of soldiers receiving and spending their war gratuities (typically £25 to £40 a man), brought a short-lived post-war boom to industry and the economy as a whole. By late 1918, wage disputes were spreading, led by workers keen to arrest the inequalities and restore wage parity. In 1919, there were serious strikes among cotton workers, railwaymen and even the police. When the police came out on strike in Liverpool, there was a riot as a hungry mob ran amok in the city centre, smashing shop windows and looting over a mile of premises of every variety.

Eight-year-old Nellie Wallace witnessed the carnage.

'Every shop was smashed in, everyone breaking the windows and picking stuff up, tins of corned beef, tins of everything. The meat shop, that got done, all the legs of lamb, then the bread shop, with boxes of cakes thrown through the window. Everyone was running with the stuff in their hands, running to plant it, hide it. When the soldiers came, oh, we had to run and get in our houses, quick.'

The riot was eventually quelled, but only after the army had fired shots over the crowd and tanks drove down the main street. Even a battleship, HMS *Valiant*, was sent up the River Mersey, as a precaution. Some 370 people were arrested, testifying to the size and potency of the mob.

Such civil disturbances were not isolated incidents. There was widespread trouble in 1919 in towns as diverse as Wolverhampton, Swindon, Luton, east London, Cardiff and even Salisbury, during the spring and early summer. The rapid growth of trade union membership to almost half the working population, coupled with the electoral muscle of the wider public enfranchisement, caused the government to buckle and give in to wage demands. The authorities were nervous about growing union militancy, and the link between unions and revolutionary ideas arriving from the Continent. Shrewd management of these competing demands was seen as the key to ensuring that militancy did not grow out of control.

The boom turned to economic slowdown and then bust, just as the remaining soldiers were demobilised in late 1919 and early 1920. Unemployment rose dramatically and with it the criticism of working women. It was not just in munitions work that women were made redundant. In jobs not traditionally associated with females – bus conductors, railway guards or tram drivers – men were allowed to reassert their predominance. Only in clerical, secretarial and shop work, where large numbers of women had been employed before the war, were women allowed to hold on to their modest gains in the labour market.

Adjusting to civilian life was not easy for anyone. Things had changed, even the most mundane aspects of life. 'My dad didn't like to come back and see us altered and growing up,' recalls Ruth Armstrong. 'He still thought he was going to come back and see two children.' In the same vein, the wives and children of returning soldiers had to adjust to having a man about the house again, one who might be prone to short temper, restlessness or sleepless nights. Young children, born just before the war, hardly knew their fathers except through letters and the odd leave from the front. Without a father figure, some children had been able to run wild and now resented having their freedoms curtailed. Wives, too, had to tread carefully. The men who returned were not always the husbands who went away. Ruth Armstrong was delighted to see her father, and initially he had appeared to reintegrate himself back into family life with few problems.

'He very soon got back into his routine of chopping up the wood and bringing in the coal and seeing that the windows were shut at night, and he used to walk around with me on his shoulder, and he told me nice stories. The nasty stories, he told my mother. I was outside the door one day and I heard him telling her about the things that he saw, and what the Germans had done. They had no idea I was listening.

'After my father had been home some little time, things
seemed to go funny between them. He was accusing
Mother of carrying on with a soldier while he was away, a
New Zealander, he reckoned. He'd found a letter written
to my mother: "Dear Kitty, I'm sorry I haven't seen you
for a long time but I've still got the children's comics for
you, which I will keep for them until I see you again,
hope to see you soon, lots of love, Con." Of course
Mother got in an awful temper about it because she told
Father straight, you know, that it was a lot of lies, but he
wouldn't listen, he got it in his head and he was a changed
man.'

During the war, soldiers at the front had commonly feared for
the fidelity of their wives. Many relationships broke down when
couples were unable to see each other from one year to the next.
Suspicions on both sides grew and multiplied for illogical
reasons, letters arriving late or becoming irregular, the tone of
words appearing distant or uncaring. For women at home, there
was the terrible burden of not knowing if their husbands would
return. Then, should the worst happen and a loved one be posted
'missing believed killed', there was a fearful wait. Often there was
no proper confirmation of what had actually happened, and in
the end death was presumed. Most were indeed dead, but a few
survived, kept as prisoners but neither registered as POWs with
the International Red Cross, nor able to send a message home. It
was perfectly possible for men to go missing in 1914 only to turn
up alive in 1919, by which time their wives had remarried in the
certain belief there was no hope.

Mary Morton Hardie, from Wishaw in Scotland, was only four
when her mother received a telegram to say that her husband was
'missing believed killed' in 1916.

'Of course, everyone was very upset, but after two years
had gone by, my mother took up with another man who
was a tailor and the two of them worked in our house. We

were all very happy. Then, right at the end of the war, another telegram came to say that Father had been released from a prisoner-of-war camp, was on his way home and would be arriving the next Saturday. Well, my mother fainted. My Uncle Hugh, as we called him, he was really upset, Mother was eight months pregnant to him at the time. So, on the Saturday morning when Father was due to arrive, Mother disappeared with Hugh.

'We all went, my sister and I, with my father's family to meet him coming off the boat train, and we brought him home. The first thing he did was to look at us and then he said, "Where's Mary?" That was my mother's name. My granny told him what had happened. He was very angry, his face was scarlet, and he said, "I've heard about this happening to others, but I never thought it would happen to me." Next morning when we woke, we were told we were going into a home and that he was going to sell the little house. Granny couldn't possibly look after the three of us, she was too old.

'Dad was furious and applied for a divorce. Our mamma was a very sweet and happy lady, always singing, cuddling us. She asked for custody of us children in court, but Father said, "The slut will have none of my children." He was so angry about her being pregnant. I think that was the worst bit for him to swallow.'

The children were inevitably the victims in the break-up of marriages and for Mary and her sister, things were about to get even worse.

'It was suddenly announced that Father was coming to take us away. He had bought a house in Rothsay and had remarried. Father took us to the boat which would take us to the island. It was crowded and we dashed up on board to the top deck. I was looking forward very much to having a home with Father and, I suppose, his new wife too.'

Mary was sent with her sister to live with her new stepmother. The arrangement was a disaster. The stepmother refused to have anything to do with the girls, while the father, in an effort to expunge any memory of his former wife, decided to change his daughter's name.

> 'Father said I was to be called Minnie. And I said, "Why? I don't like the name." "Because your mother's name is Mary and I don't want to hear that name ever again. This is your new mother, call her mother." I said, "I will not call her mother, that's not my mother," and he gave me a resounding slap. Beatrice, his new wife, looked at me and I always remember the awful look she gave me as though she hated me from that moment.'

At first Ruth Armstrong's father was equally adamant that he would leave his wife. 'All he wanted to do was clear out and take me with him,' remembers Ruth. In the end the situation was resolved, but not quite as her father intended.

> 'I was sitting by the fire and the door flew open and my father came in. During the day, we'd moved from one house to another and left the old house we were in. He was shocked and said, "What the hell's going on here?" So Mother said, "Well, it's all over, George, I've had enough of being blamed for what I haven't done." Mother was a very stubborn lady and she wouldn't change her mind once it was set, she had left him. At this point Father broke down and he promised this and promised that and he got down on one knee and begged her to come back, trying to catch hold of her hand. She wouldn't, she wouldn't forgive him because he wouldn't listen to what she had told him. "I've had my say, get out." I was sitting on the stool by the fire and I fell off the stool crying, nearly into the fire.
> 'Mother got to work because if you left your husband

in those days you could not claim a penny off him. She got a job for 28 shillings a week in the next village, Shrewton, at the laundry. Oh, the war broke up lots of homes. I cried every night over the parting because I loved my father so much, it broke my heart.'

Bald figures on casualties, dead, wounded, even the shell shocked, hide a mostly untold story of massive individual dislocation from family, friends, even society at large. One former serviceman, Harold Clegg of the Liverpool Rifles, wrote that he belonged to a generation of men 'who, even if they had escaped its shells, were destroyed by the War. Youths of 18–20 were thrown back into civilisation whose only training had been that of musketry, bombing, killing and bloodshed; those who regarded carnage with complacency.'

Many former soldiers were less than enamoured with the government's response to their plight. Too many men found that their freedom was in fact abandonment: they were left alone to fight again, this time for a living. Less than two years later, ex-servicemen marched to Downing Street with a banner that read:

REMEMBER!
1914 YOUR COUNTRY NEEDS YOU.
1918 WELL DONE.
1920 FORGOTTEN!

This sentiment lasted.

The emphasis, or so it seemed in 1919 and 1920, was more on the dead, those who had made the ultimate sacrifice. In time, the government organised ways of remembering the fallen which would prove a comfort to many, helping them to come to terms with their own loss. The wearing of the poppy and the black armband, as well as the two minutes' silence, were all part of the subsuming of the individual's grief in that of the whole. The Cenotaph, built in Whitehall, was the greatest symbol of this collectivisation, and many millions rightly paid their respects. But equally, many others stayed away to remember the dead in private.

For the first time, the commemoration of death was egalitarian. At every level, from the former Prime Minister's son downwards, men had been killed, from the most promising to the repeatedly criminal, and, if their bodies were found, they were buried next to each other. No one took precedence. The Unknown Warrior, as likely as not a man of lowly rank, was borne with all the reverence given to a monarch and buried among the great and the good at Westminster Abbey.

Grief was managed, and without doubt this was greatly appreciated by many who took comfort from the communal moment of reverence. It was resented by others. Charles Carrington, an officer in the Royal Warwickshire Regiment whose brother was killed on the Somme in 1916, felt that 'to march to the Cenotaph was too much like attending one's own funeral' and that the whole occasion had been 'captured' by 'do-gooders'. Carrington and other fellow officers had 'no end of a party' each Armistice Day to celebrate missing friends, 'until we began to find ourselves out of key with the new age'. Similarly, there were civilians who were inevitably constrained by the unrequited desire to bury their loved ones, or to mourn their loss as they saw fit. They saw no reason to take any active part in the nation's honouring of their own dead. 'She would never accept any invitation for any civic function of any kind to remember the fallen,' recalls Joyce Crow of her mother Letitia. 'She was even invited to Westminster Abbey to attend the burial of the Unknown Warrior, but she wrote back politely refusing the offer. Her grief was a private matter.'

There was one further problem. The vast majority of dead were civilians in military uniforms, not regular soldiers. The army had taken these men into its ranks, volunteers and conscripts alike, and had kept them. Their names were inscribed on classical memorials to the missing – each man's name together with his rank and number included – or buried in parade-like rows in military cemeteries. For many, perhaps the vast majority, this did not present a problem, but there could be no choice.

One other person whose body would return home, with almost as much pomp and ceremony as that of the Unknown Warrior, was Edith Cavell. Her execution in 1915 by the Germans in Belgium had become nothing less than a national, indeed an international, cause célèbre. At the war's end, there had been extensive negotiations over her funeral conducted by members of the aptly named 'Public Funeral of Miss Edith Cavell Executive Committee' as well as other interested parties, such as the police and the Admiralty. In May 1919, her body was brought to Dover on a torpedo boat and then taken to London by train. The next day her coffin was followed by a large military escort as it was taken to Westminster Abbey for a service at noon. The cortège passed through London amid enormous crowds. She was by no means the only nurse to have been killed in the war. It was the manner of her death, cold-bloodedly shot by soldiers, that was deemed such a terrible violation both of her womanhood and the sanctity of her profession.

One witness to the cortège was twenty-four-year-old Alice Mckinnon from Bourne in Lincolnshire. For the last two years she had been nursing in France, but at the end of the war had returned home. In May 1919, she found herself in the capital.

'I was walking along the street with my suitcase when I heard that Edith Cavell's funeral procession was to pass through that part of town in the morning. So I decided to stay where I was on the spot and pay my respects. I put the suitcase down and sat on it and waited. The traffic was going past, you know how noisy traffic can be, when suddenly it all went quiet, very quiet. There wasn't a sound and then they came along, and I put my head down and I cried and cried. Somebody asked me afterwards did she have a horse-drawn hearse and I said I didn't really see; I was so upset.'

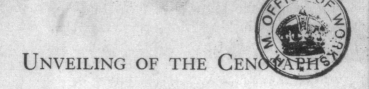

UNVEILING OF THE CENOTAPHS

Admit Bearer

to the Reserved Standing accommodation on
the footpath between Derby Street and
Richmond Terrace, Whitehall.

[P.T.O.

A ticket inviting the recipient to attend the unveiling of the Cenotaph in Whitehall in 1920. The stone plinth replaced an earlier wooden and plaster structure used for the commemorations a year earlier.

The public trauma witnessed at her funeral seemed to express everybody's feeling that nothing was sacred any more in the land of the living.

The dead were sacred, though, as was their memory. Ironically, perhaps, they were also portrayed as contented, happy in their duty done, and no longer growing old. Their service to King and Country was honoured every year in churches up and down the country, and millions attended without fail. Many took comfort in the words spoken, others less so. One woman for whom words and rituals could never have been enough was Julia Souls from Gloucestershire. She had lost all her six sons in the war, five in action and the sixth from meningitis, and never again felt inclined to stand up during the playing of the National Anthem.

Harry Patch, one of the very last surviving veterans, was, and remains, deeply thoughtful about his contribution, and the manner by which his dead comrades were remembered.

'I left the army with my faith in the Church of England shattered. I could never understand why my country could call me from a peacetime job and train me to go out to France and try and kill a man I never knew. When I came out of the army I joined a church choir to try and get the faith back – it didn't come. Armistice Day parade – no. Cassock and surplice – no. I felt shattered, absolutely, and I didn't discuss the war with anyone from then on and nobody brought it up if they could help it.'

Harry's friends had been blown to pieces, but ultimately, in the grimmest possible way, he at least knew what had happened. For almost half of those who lost loved ones, there was no clear idea; conjecture and speculation were, too frequently, the main sources to draw on. There were 'miracles'. Mary Hardie's father had returned from the POW camp when all hope had appeared lost. His survival was the exception: so many others were hoped for but were never seen. Not knowing for sure what had happened to a loved one led to endless enquiries through the War Office, Red Cross and other charities as to the possible whereabouts of missing men. In all, five million servicemen were interviewed and over a third of a million reports compiled in response to requests. Correspondence continued until the early 1920s before the files were finally closed. Unwilling to rely on official organs alone, families wrote to wounded soldiers and former comrades, hopeful that someone might have seen something. Advertisements were placed in newspapers, while, as one prisoner of war returning in December 1918 recalled, he was forced to witness the piteous sight of women walking along the train carriage in which he stood, holding up pictures of the missing, in the hope, however tiny, that someone might have information. Hope lingered on for years, and in many cases was never entirely extinguished.

It might take years, even decades, but sometimes the truth emerged, as Emily Galbraith discovered. Her brother Peter had been reported missing presumed killed in 1916, while serving with the 2nd Royal Sussex Regiment. No body was ever found and the exact circumstances of his death remained a mystery.

'My father wrote every week to the War Office to know what had happened and all we heard was that he had been at a place called High Wood, but what happened we never knew.

'After the war, a memorial at Hornchurch was dedicated to local men who'd died, including Peter's name. And we discovered a young man used to go on every anniversary of my brother's death and lay flowers on the memorial. We never knew the reason. Anyway, in the 1930s, after my parents were dead, this boy's mother and sister asked me to their house at Manor Park in London. While I was there I decided to visit the memorial at Hornchurch, which was some twelve miles away. I had my dog with me and thought I would take him for a walk, and the man insisted that he walked with me all twelve miles – he said we would go by bus on the way back but we never did.

'We walked twelve miles to put flowers on the memorial and then walked eleven and a half miles back before he said anything about my brother. My brother had been killed helping someone else – him. A machine-gun had started firing and Peter and three friends were in a bunch together. They all got into shell holes, and this man in the shell hole on Peter's right went into a panic. He screamed for my brother to come and my brother got out of his safe shell hole to help but as he did so a sniper shot my brother and he fell, dead.

'How could I react to this revelation? I just took it calmly, you couldn't alter anything.'

As Peter's body was never found, his name was later inscribed on the Thiepval Memorial, along with those of the other missing soldiers of the Somme battles. Approximately half of those killed on the Western Front have no known grave, the other half lie in hundreds of cemeteries scattered across the old battlefields. Inevitably, a demand grew for families to see the graves of those buried there, and very quickly pilgrimages began to take thousands of visitors across the Channel. The YMCA was one of the first to organise tours, followed by the British Legion, the Red Cross and the Church Army, at a reasonable price in order to include as many people from as wide a range of backgrounds as possible.

One of those who visited her father's grave after the war was Irene Smith. Her father, Sergeant William Rhodes, had been a Territorial before the war, and had served abroad for three years before he was killed in the Ypres Salient in July 1917.

'When he died they didn't find him for a long time, he was missing, and they had a memorial service at church when they knew he wouldn't be coming back. Then they found his body, and mother was given what was on him, a muddy little ribbon for his DCM, a photograph a German soldier gave him at the 1914 Christmas Truce, and a service prayer book.'

Irene was a war baby, conceived during her father's only leave in early 1917. She was born three months after his death.

'We always talked about him and we knew about what had happened to him. He was never put to one side. We talked about how he had sandy red hair, how he'd worked in the cotton mill; that he had a great singing voice, and that he was a wonderful gardener who grew orchids, so he was always round about us, he was always living to me.

'The first time that I, with my elder brother and sister Harold and Mary, visited Father's grave was in 1927. The authorities had brought bodies in from different smaller cemeteries to the huge Tyne Cot Cemetery and that's where he was re-interred. I was ten years old, and grown up for my years, and I sat on the grass next to his grave and I remember looking at it thinking this was my dad's grave, but I wasn't thinking of him as dead, I was thinking of him as a great singer, as alive. We brought a bunch of red roses which we laid at the stone, and there we were as a family. It seemed as though then I wasn't without my daddy.

'There was a full service in Tyne Cot. We came especially for that, with a train full of people, and then we visited the whole battlefield. The Cloth Hall in Ypres was still in ruins and we saw famous sites like Hill 60 and St Julien. There were things lying about, bits of wood, weapons, tin helmets, bones – probably animal – and we were looking around at all these craters with water in, near shattered trees: it was an education.

'It was another ten years before we could go again and then we went again for the fiftieth anniversary. The second war came, I had a family, so time got in the way but eventually we started to come regularly together.'

In August 2002, Irene went to visit her father once again, but now she visits alone, for both her brother and sister died in recent years.

'I was upset because we always came together, we were all fit and well and then suddenly both my brother and sister died within ten weeks of one another. I'm the last, and as long as I am capable I will come, even if I have to struggle. None of my family are there with me any more, and that was the first time I felt that. It is a sadness that they aren't there to do this.'

Irene's pilgrimages will continue for as long as she can travel to Belgium. To follow on from the stories of our other interviewees: Elfie Druhm remained in Germany; neither she, nor her mother, was ever interned. After the Second World War, Elfie worked as a translator, and met and married an Englishman serving with the Army of Occupation. Then in 1948 Elfie, with her parents, returned to Britain. 'My parents decided to come back to England again as my father loved England – after thirty years away, he still felt it was more or less his home.'

Mary Morton Hardie eventually found her mother. She had moved to Belfast, and remarried.

'I saw a very stout lady dressed all in black and I went up to her and it was something about her eyes that I remembered. She said, "Hello, Mary, how are you or do we call you Minnie now?" Sadly, the reunion was not a success. "I've something to ask you. Call me your aunt. I have a young family and they don't know about you." I was so disappointed, I felt life wasn't worth living. It was my uncle who comforted me. He told me to look at the glowing cinders in a fire. "Now, if you blow on a cinder it'll fan into flame. You'll find something that'll make your life worth living, and the cinder will glow for you." It wasn't long after that that I met James, my future husband.'

Emily Galbraith will, with luck, be 108 this year. She still lives in her own house, encircled by home-helps and nursing staff devoted to her welfare; it is hardly 'work' to care for Emily. She is gently cosseted by the family effects of a bygone world of mid-Victorian furniture and ornate photograph albums. Emily greeted us with a century-worth of civility and etiquette, inviting us into the living room for tea. She truly has charm, if it is possible, beyond her years. We talked about her life, how she rejected the stuffy world of her Victorian mother to embrace the new world of Edwardian Britain, how she recalled seeing Queen Victoria, and remembered the conflict in South Africa. And then, of course, there was the First World War and the loss of her brother, Peter.

Her memory of him is still vivid and very fond, and on her

bedroom wall there is his photo, holding the family dog. Peter's body remains, possibly undiscovered but more likely unidentified, in a cemetery near to High Wood on the Somme, where he fell. This year he will have been dead eighty-seven years – he was twenty when he was killed, and he was Emily's younger brother. She is the last tangible link with Peter, and when Emily dies, a small part of the First World War itself will pass into history.

Select Bibliography

Asquith, The Earl of Oxford and Asquith, *Memories and Reflections 1852–1927 Vol 2*, (Cassell and Company Limited, 1928).

Beckett, Ian F. W., *The First World War, The Essential Guide to Sources in the UK National Archives*, (Public Record Office, 2002).

Bell, Ernest W., *Soldiers Killed on the First Day of The Somme*, (Privately Published, 1977).

Barnett, L. M., *British Food Policy during the First World War*, (HarperCollins, 1985).

Beveridge, William, *British Food Control*, (Oxford University Press, 1928).

Blake, Robert (ed.), *The Private Papers of Douglas Haig 1914– 1919*, (Eyre & Spottiswoode, 1952).

Braybon, Gail, *Women Workers in the First World War*, (Croom Helm, 1981).

Brown, Malcolm, *The Imperial War Museum Book of the First World War*, (Pan Books, 2002).

Bryden, Linda, *The First World War: Healthy or Hungry?*, (History Workshop Journal 24, 1987).

Cameron, James, *Yesterday's Witness*, (British Broadcasting Corporation, 1979).

Carrington, Charles, *Soldier from the Wars Returning*, (Hutchinson & Co Ltd, 1965).

Dakers, Caroline, *The Countryside at War 1914–18*, (Constable, 1987).

DeGroot, Gerard J., *Blighty: British Society in the Era of the Great War*, (Longman, 1996).

Englander, David, *Landlord and Tenant in Urban Britain 1838–1911,* (Clarendon Press, 1983).

Ferguson, Niall, *The Pity of War,* (Penguin, 1999).

Ferris, Paul, *Sex and the British: A Twentieth Century History,* (Michael Joseph, 1993).

Gillam, Geoffrey, *Enfield at War 1914–1918,* (Enfield Archaeological Society, 1982).

Goodall, Felicity, *A Question of Conscience: Conscientious Objection in the Two World Wars,* (Sutton, 1997).

Haldane, Viscount, *Before the War,* (Cassell and Company Ltd, 1920).

Harvey, Brian W. and Fitzgerald, Carol (eds), Heron-Allen, Edward, *Journal of the Great War, From Sussex Shore to Flanders Fields,* (Sussex Record Society, 2002).

Haste, Cate, *Keep the Home Fires Burning: Propaganda in the First World War,* (Allen Lane/Penguin Books Ltd, 1977).

Haste, Cate, *Rules of Desire: Sex in Britain: World War 1 to the Present,* (Chatto and Windus, 1992).

Haydon, Peter, *The English Pub, A History,* (Robert Hale Ltd, 1995).

Hinton, James, *The First Shop Stewards Movement,* (Allen & Unwin, 1973).

Humphries, Steve and Gordon, Pamela, *A Labour of Love: The Experience of Parenthood in Britain 1900–1950,* (Sidgwick and Jackson, 1993).

Humphries, Steve, *Hooligans or Rebels: An Oral History of Working Class Childhood and Youth 1889–1939,* (Blackwell, 1981).

Hyde, Andrew P., *The First Blitz: The German Air Campaign Against Britain 1917–1918*, (Pen and Sword/Leo Cooper, 2002).

Liddle, Peter, Bourne, John and Whitehead, Ian (eds), *The Great World War 1914–45 Vol. 1 Lightning Strikes Twice; Vol 2 Who won? Who lost?,* (Collins, 2000).

Liddle, Peter, *The Worst Ordeal: Britons at Home and Abroad 1914–1918,* (Pen and Sword/Leo Cooper, 1994).

MacDougall, Ian, *Voices from War: Personal Recollections of War in our Century by Scottish Men and Women,* (Mercat Press Edinburgh, 1995).

MacLean, Ian, *The Legend of Red Clydeside,* (John Macdonald, 1983).

Markham, John (ed.), *Keep the Home Fires Burning,* (Highgate Publications (Beverley) Limited, 1988).

Marlow, Joyce (ed.), *The Virago Book of Women and the Great War 1914–1918,* (Virago, 1998).

Marsay, Mark, *Bombardment! The Day the East Coast Bled,* (Great Northern Publishing, 1999).

Marwick, Arthur, *The Deluge,* (The Bodley Head, 1965).

Morris, Joseph, *German Air Raids on Britain 1914–1918,* (Sampson Low, Marston & Co Ltd, 1925; reprinted The Naval and Military Press, 1993).

Munson, James (ed.), Clark, Reverend Andrew, *Echoes of the Great War, The Diary of the Reverend Andrew Clark 1914–1919,* (Oxford University Press, 1985).

Panayi, Panikos (ed.), *Racial Violence in Britain 1840–1950,* (Leicester University Press, 1993).

Pankhurst, Sylvia, *The Home Front, a Mirror to life in England during the World War,* (Hutchinson & Co Ltd, 1932).

Peel, Mrs C. S., *How We Lived Then,* (The Bodley Head, 1929).

Shephard, Ben, *A War of Nerves: Soldiers and Psychiatrists 1914–1994,* (Jonathan Cape, 2000).

Slater, Guy (ed.), *My Warrior Sons, The Borton Family Diary 1914–1918,* (Peter Davies, 1973).

Statistics of the Military Effort of the British Empire During the Great War, 1914–1920, (HMSO, 1922).

Steel, Nigel and Hart, Peter, *Tumult in the Skies: The British Experience of the War in the Air 1914–1918,* (Hodder and Stoughton, 1987).

van Emden, Richard (ed.), *Last Man Standing, The Memoirs of a Seaforth Highlander during the Great War,* (Pen & Sword, 2002).

van Emden, Richard (ed.), *Tickled to Death to Go, Memoirs of a Cavalryman in the First World War,* (Spellmount Ltd, 1996).

Waites, Bernard, *A Class Society at War,* (Berg Publishers, 1987).

Wilson, Trevor, *The Myriad Faces of War: Britain and the Great War 1914–1918,* (Polity Press, 1986).

Winter, Jay M., *The Great War and the British People,* (Macmillan, 1986).

Index